Organizational Marketing

For Ellie – whenever

Organizational
Marketing

Dominic Wilson

INTERNATIONAL THOMSON BUSINESS PRESS
I ⓣ P An International Thomson Publishing Company

London • Bonn • Johannesburg • Madrid • Melbourne • Mexico City • New York • Paris
Singapore • Tokyo • Toronto • Albany, NY • Belmont, CA • Cincinnati, OH • Detroit, MI

Organizational Marketing

 A division of International Thomson Publishing
The ITP logo is a trademark under licence

British Library Cataloguing-in-Publication Data
A catalogue record for this book is available from the British Library

First edition 1999

Typeset by J&L Composition Ltd, Filey, North Yorkshire
Printed in the UK by TJ International, Padstow, Cornwall

ISBN 1–86152–480–3

International Thomson Business Press
Berkshire House
168–173 High Holborn
London WCIV 7AA
UK

http://www.itbp.com

—*Contents*

—List of figures

—List of tables

—List of exhibits

—PART I
Discussion

Introduction

THE OBJECTIVES OF THE BOOK

This book is written both for advanced students of marketing (on post-graduate programmes, MBA courses, and specialist final year under-graduate options) and for practitioners wishing to refresh their previous studies at this level, or to understand their professional experiences with the benefit of some theoretical insight.

The principal aim of the book is to open up the field of organizational marketing in a reasonably structured but realistic way to readers seek-ing to understand organizational marketing as it is practised rather than as it might be conceived in some over-rationalized 'ideal'. This is espe-cially appropriate at a time when there is increasing dissatisfaction with mechanistic approaches to understanding organizational markets (and indeed marketing more broadly) and yet when there is still no clear consensus over what alternative approach is appropriate.

Discussion embraces not only the traditional models and theoretical concepts developed over the past 30 years but also the emerging theory of interorganizational collaboration and relationship marketing which many regard as the preferred basis for managing the increasingly com-plex marketing relationships between organizations surrounded by the fast-moving and uncertain environments of the emerging new millen-nium (Gummesson, 1987; Christopher et al., 1991; Grönroos, 1994; Buttle, 1996). The discussion seeks to remain constructively critical, especially where theory seems not yet to have fully meshed with prac-ticality – the intention is to explore with an open mind rather than to ele-vate any one perspective by trampling on others. To assist this process there are many references to the very considerable body of research in and around organizational marketing which, hopefully, will encourage readers to pursue their own lines of enquiry.

THE SCOPE OF THE BOOK

Organizational marketing is a diverse, complex and fascinating field embracing all forms of exchange relationships between organizations, as opposed to marketing between organizations and consumers. Obviously, there are many differences between organizational and consumer markets, with important implications for the theory and practice of marketing. However, it will also become evident in the course of this discussion that many of the concerns of organizational marketing overlap increasingly not only with issues in consumer marketing but also with the concerns of other management functions, such as production management. It is no longer clear in the late 1990s where the boundaries of *organizational marketing* are and so this is a field ripe for sensible and critical reassessment. Therefore this book aims not only to inform but also to stimulate such reassessment in the minds and actions of its readers.

As with so many fields of marketing, artificial divisions into convenient 'topics' such as organizational marketing reflect relative differences, rather than absolute distinctions. While these divisions are useful, even necessary, for teaching purposes, it would be a mistake to expect marketing management problems in the real world to present themselves in such reassuring and familiar uniforms. So while the book starts by accepting the traditional categorization of organizational marketing (Chapter 1) and its attendant sub-divisions of buying behaviour (Chapter 2) and the marketing mix (Chapter 3), the discussion then proceeds by considering more realistic, complex and multi-dimensional aspects such as interorganizational relationships (Chapter 4) and concludes with a look at some of the many emerging challenges facing practitioners and theorists of organizational marketing today.

A BIAS TOWARDS IT?

Many of the examples in the discussion and in the cases are taken from the author's research and personal experience in organizational markets over the past twenty years. This means that there is a definite illustrative 'bias' in the book, especially towards the IT sector and its organizational customers (and, less so, towards automobile manufacturing), though that does *not* mean that readers need any technical knowledge to benefit from the material. This bias certainly can be a weakness in that it does not reflect the infinite variety of organizational examples available, but it also offers the following advantages:

- The bias gives rich insights which would not be available with a less focused and 'shallower' approach.
- The bias illuminates a very large, varied and strategically important sector which has customers (potentially) in all other sectors.
- IT issues are a major dynamic in the development of organizational marketing at the moment and this bias helps to put this dynamic into perspective.
- Having cases and illustrations from related backgrounds enables a fuller

appreciation of the case issues and a more extensive and sophisticated discussion.

■ Many readers will at some point have been involved in the purchase or management or use of IT systems and so this bias will benefit from the personal experience that they will bring to bear in reading and in collective discussion.

THE STRUCTURE OF THE BOOK

The book has three parts: Discussion, Readings and Cases.

Part I is a critical discussion in four chapters of the current theory and practice of organizational marketing with particular attention to the emerging alternative theoretical bases and their implications for management practice. Because this discussion is limited to just part of this book, there are inevitably imbalances in what is addressed and what is not (for example, the lack of specific attention to customer service, environmental and societal issues). The balance is a reflection of what seems most relevant, important and interesting, based on the author's experience as a teacher, researcher and student. For those who do feel the need for further discussion of particular aspects, there are numerous references throughout which should lead them in helpful directions.

Chapter 1 introduces *organizational marketing* with a discussion of what is meant by the term, how this term has developed, and why organizational markets are important.

In Chapter 2 the central topic of buyer behaviour in organizational markets is considered, followed by a discussion of the findings of research into various aspects of the buying process. Buying behaviour is historically the foundation of organizational marketing theory and remains the most developed area of theory (Ford, 1980a). Then some of the key practical issues of organizational purchasing are considered in the light of the previous discussion of theory and research in organizational buying behaviour.

Next, Chapter 3 builds on this understanding of organizational buyer behaviour by exploring the implications for marketing management and the marketing mix of organizations seeking to engage in organizational marketing. The chapter takes a broad view of the traditional marketing mix, extending the discussion to the overall strategic management of the marketing effort in what is now, by common consent for most organizations, an increasingly uncertain and competitive environment and one where the potential of IT is a vitally important and still largely undeveloped competitive factor for marketing.

Chapter 4 discusses the theme of interorganizational relationships and the management of such relationships which many theorists now regard as more promising than the traditional marketing mix as a basis for structuring our understanding of organizational marketing in complex environments.

Finally, a brief conclusion rounds up the discussion and anticipates the remaining two parts of the book – the readings and the cases. This is followed by a note on current research directions in organizational marketing which may be of interest to those considering dissertations and theses in this field.

The readings in Part II have been chosen for their relevance specifically to the intended audience of this book. So these readings are not necessarily seminal articles which have had great impact on theory development, or critical studies which have offered impressive empirical research. The readings have been selected because they provide critical insights to the issues addressed in Part I, they include discussion of the relevant literature or memorable and practical examples, and they are clearly structured and easily readable. The result is, inevitably, a personal and severely restricted selection which not all would endorse but which should give readers familiarity with some of the more important theoretical and practical foundations of much of the discussion in Part I.

The case studies in Part III are of two types: longer cases illustrating complex issues in context, and shorter mini-cases sketching more recognizable issues with less need for contextual detail.

It may help readers to study the readings and cases if they bear in mind the six key themes which emerge from the discussion in Part I and which reflect some of the more important dynamics currently changing our understanding of organizational marketing. The themes are:

- the increasing significance of marketing strategy for the overall competitiveness of organizations;
- the emerging 'spanning' role of the marketing function integrating with other functional areas . . .
- . . . and with different organizations through relationship marketing, partnership, collaboration and other forms of strategic alliancing;
- organizational marketing as the continual management of interorganizational relationships (rather than as preparing and negotiating individual purchasing 'deals');
- the increasing complexity of organizational marketing responsibilities and the significance of information technology (IT) in managing this complexity;
- the convergence of marketing theory with respect to organizational and consumer markets (important differences of emphasis notwithstanding).

As with all marketing programmes, whether organizational or consumer in orientation, it is important to establish channels of communication whereby customers can question or comment on aspects of the programme. This book is no exception and readers are invited to contact the author through his e-mail address (dom.wilson@umist.ac.uk) if they have any questions, or points they would like to discuss, or critical suggestions for improvement of the book, or research ideas they wish to pursue.

1 *Organizational markets and organizational marketing*

This chapter focuses on three questions:

- What is meant by the term *organizational marketing* and how has this field of marketing evolved over time?
- What are the features of organizational marketing that distinguish this field from others within marketing?
- What is the significance of organizational marketing?

1.1 THE MEANING OF ORGANIZATIONAL MARKETING

Organizational marketing is *marketing between organizations* but first it is necessary to clarify what we mean by 'marketing' and 'organizations'.

Marketing is a term surrounded with many definitions and rich controversy (Parkinson, 1991). Most conventional dictionaries still associate the term 'marketing' with selling and advertising and this narrow perception probably also holds true for many individuals who are not themselves engaged in the professional activity of marketing – even, as Doyle (1998) suggests, for some who are. The association with selling and advertising is particularly unfortunate in the UK because of the lingering cultural distaste for such activities which still seems to pervade the way much of the British public relate to the broad fields of business and commerce.

In short, marketing still has something of an image problem, especially perhaps in the UK. It is difficult to correct this public misperception of marketing as 'selling' (often 'over-selling') as there is little agreement even amongst marketing experts over how best to define marketing. McDonald's useful definition provides a good illustration of the problem of definition:

> *Marketing is a management process whereby the resources of the whole organization are utilized to satisfy the needs of selected customer groups in order to achieve the objectives of both parties. Marketing then is first and foremost an attitude of mind rather than a series of functional activities.*
>
> (McDonald, 1989, p. 8)

This definition seems to prioritize marketing over other organizational functions and so can expect to be challenged by proponents of these other functions. McDonald's definition also fails to specify the functional activities of marketing and so dissatisfies many marketers who prefer a more precise charting of the marketing territory. Other definitions of marketing have tended to list the activities of marketing (e.g. pricing, communications, product development), an approach which nevertheless fails to identify the core concepts binding these particular listed items, and only these items, as 'marketing'. Critics might also point out that 'satisfaction' and 'customer needs' are potentially elusive and divisive terms; that organizations have a wide range of 'objectives' and rarely focus only on profit; that in organizational marketing it is often the case that the resources of not one but several organizations are needed to meet customer objectives; and that the marketing challenge is often not so much the management of the resources involved as the management of the relationships involved between organizational suppliers and customers. In line with these criticisms, and the developments in the understanding of the role of marketing that lie behind them, organizational marketing can be seen not only as *the marketing of products and services between organizations* but more widely as *the management and development of exchange relationships between organizations.*

A view is emerging here of marketing as an integrated activity involving the entire organization in managing a portfolio of interdependent and developing relationships but for the moment it is convenient to accept a more atomistic approach to marketing as specific aspects of the marketing mix between organizations are considered.

Meanwhile, it is also important to clarify what we mean by the term 'organization'. This can be defined simply as 'a group of people pursuing a common aim [or aims] through coordinated activities' (Turnbull, 1994, p. 217) yet the organizations referred to in 'organizational marketing' can be very diverse and include many groups which may not be primarily concerned with generating profit and which may not be engaged in commerce at all (see Exhibit 1.1). Furthermore, the 'group of people' in an organization may be small or very large, culturally homogenous or varied, located together or scattered, professionally managed or anarchic, with a clear and positive shared vision or held together more by a vague negativity towards some dimly perceived external threat. So in practice the organization's 'common aim' is more likely to be a mix of overlapping and opaque aims, some relatively explicit and commonly held but with other aims held only by some members of the organization, and not easily definable or explicable. Thus an organization may be defined in terms of its publicly stated aims while in reality this merely provides a 'flag of convenience' for a variety of not necessarily consistent or compatible sub-groups continually at odds with each other. Numerous examples of such organizations spring

---

EXHIBIT 1.1

The diversity of organizational activities

- Raw material extractors and refiners (e.g. bauxite mining, electricity generation, petroleum refining, water supply)
- Agricultural and marine producers (e.g. farming, forestry, flower growing, fishing, abattoirs, fish processing)
- Manufacturers of products, processes and components (e.g. cars, furniture, paint shops, assemblers, engines, electronics, clothes)
- Commercial and professional service providers (e.g. banks, accountants, architects, consultants, cleaners, trainers, gardeners)
- Resellers and distributors (e.g. retailers, wholesalers, hauliers, merchant shipping, import/export agencies)
- Hiring and leasing agencies (e.g. commercial plant and machinery hire, property leasing, car hire, staff bureaux)
- Government departments, agencies and authorities (e.g. customs, income tax, social security, foreign affairs, legislation, justice)
- Armed forces and paramilitary organizations (e.g. armies, navies, air forces, police, prisons, enforcement agencies, guards)
- Not-necessarily-for-profit organizations (e.g. schools, hospitals, charities, social clubs, professional societies)

---

to mind, from political parties to families to large commercial organizations, though it would be invidious to name specific instances.

With such a vast variety of organizations – from, say, IBM, the Roman Catholic church and the People's Republican Army of China on the one hand to a local tobacconist, a rural primary school and a student protest group on the other – it is difficult to make claims and observations which apply comprehensively to all organizations, or to all instances of organizational marketing.

1.2 THE ORIGINS OF ORGANIZATIONAL MARKETING

The origins of organizational marketing as a field of scholarly research lie in the study of marketing in industrial (as opposed to consumer) contexts in the mid-1990s when this subject was typically referred to as *industrial marketing*. Later it was recognized that not all organizations were engaged in manufacturing and that the term 'industrial' did not readily convey the scope of marketing between organizations engaged in business – so during the 1980s the term *business-to-business marketing* or *business marketing* emerged. More recently it has become accepted that the principles of marketing are appropriate to any organization from charities to opera houses and from armies to government departments, not just to industrial, commercial or business organizations, and so the term *organizational marketing* is becoming more widely used. Nevertheless, the earlier terms are still widely used because of their familiarity and perhaps because of the persistent paradigm that associates marketing with commercial activities.

This confusion is reflected in the titles of three of the most prominent academic journals focusing on this area (and also in successive editions of some popular textbooks):

- *Industrial Marketing Management*, established in 1971 and now also using the sub-title of *The International Journal of Organizational Marketing*;
- the *Journal of Business and Industrial Marketing* founded in 1986;
- the *Journal of Business to Business Marketing* founded in 1993.

Despite being widely recognized by marketing scholars and practitioners as a coherent field of marketing activity – like service marketing or not-for-profit marketing – it remains the case that many marketing writers do not recognize organizational marketing as a distinct and separable field of marketing *theory*. This can be seen as part of the broader debate over the theoretical credentials and status of marketing itself, and more broadly of management, as independent disciplines – as opposed to fields of theoretical and practical study concerning the application of generic disciplines such as sociology, psychology and economics.

These are important issues but for the moment it is worth noting that the uncertainty surrounding the academic status of marketing remains, together with the implied critique (even ridicule) of those scholars seeking a comprehensive theory of marketing. The popularity of management and business studies with students, and the consequent rapid development of new faculties in universities, have also not endeared proponents of this 'new' discipline, already sullied in academic eyes by its commercial focus and jargon, to those well-established disciplines (many of which were actually 'established' only within the past century) which resent what they see as 'poaching' of their academic territory and associated resources.

This uncertainty and peer-critique has played its part in encouraging a compartmentalization of management research, largely into functional components, and a piecemeal empirical approach to theory development at all levels within management studies. In organizational marketing studies this pattern is reflected in the priority given to the central themes of purchasing and organizational buyer behaviour. The pattern is changing somewhat now with the growing interest in reconceptualizing marketing in terms of evolving networks of exchange relationships but the long preoccupation with buyer behaviour is proving resilient. Indeed, even in some of the most recent marketing textbooks organizational marketing is seen as either little more than organizational buying behaviour (e.g. Davies, 1998) or not worth differentiating from the default consumer context so often assumed for introductory marketing discussions (e.g. Doyle, 1998).

1.3 THE DISTINGUISHING FEATURES OF ORGANIZATIONAL MARKETS

If organizational marketing is not to be seen simply as organizational buyer behaviour then we must consider what are, or seem to be, its distinguishing features.

Much of marketing theory was initially developed in the context of consumer markets and it was only with the study of organizational purchasing in the 1950s that it became recognized that organizational markets were significantly different to consumer markets and so required a separate, though related, theoretical explanation. It is important to clarify these differentiating features since they demarcate not only the separateness of organizational markets but also the areas of similarity with consumer markets.

The distinguishing features discussed below are broad generalizations and – inevitable exceptions notwithstanding – their validity seems to be supported by common sense and routine observation. Perhaps because of this, there has been little serious research to test the validity of these features and in most cases there would seem to be little point in empirical verification because of the eminent reasonableness of the features and the methodological problems in verification. However, a variety of emerging changes, especially perhaps in IT, have generated questions over the continued validity of these features in distinguishing between organizational and consumer markets, and of the usefulness of such a distinction. The features discussed below should be considered with this in mind.

1.3.1 The complexity and size of organizational markets

As a rule, organizational markets are thought to be larger and more complex than consumer markets, in terms of total transaction value, the number of people involved in any one purchase, the scale and variety of customers' operational activities, the number and duration of production stages, and so on. Gross *et al.* (1993) estimate that organizational markets are as much as four times larger (in value-added) than consumer markets. This can easily be demonstrated by considering that for every consumer market there are usually several upstream organizational markets manufacturing, supplying and assembling the products which are then marketed to consumers. It may be that the price of the eventual consumer offering reflects the cumulation of all upstream costs, rents and profit margins, and so the consumer market is logically larger in monetary terms than its attendant organizational markets, but many organizational markets do not generate conventional consumer products (e.g. government agencies, armed forces, charities) so in most respects it is the organizational markets that are larger.

An example from vehicle manufacturing is given in Figure 1.1 which shows something of the complexity and interdependence of the organizational markets feeding into the consumer car market. The example shows not only some of the raw materials, components, sub-assemblies, goods and services involved; it also lists other requirements involved (the separate box in the top right-hand corner of Figure 1.1) such as finance, labour, energy, premises, data, and security services which may have no physical manifestation in the final product marketed to consumers. The example also emphasizes the downstream activities following manufacture such as distribution, maintenance and marketing services which are also organizational markets. Finally, there may well be organizational customers even for the final product, such as ambulance services, public utilities or police forces which require vehicles specially adapted for their own needs.

Furthermore, the number of organizational markets is not constrained by the number of downstream commercial consumer markets, large though this is. There are also organizations (with associated organizational markets) which have little or no involvement in conventional consumer markets at any stage. For example, some organizations provide services to 'consumers' without direct payment (e.g. churches, charities, schools, hospitals) and in other organizations it is often difficult to see the role of consumers at any stage (e.g. military forces).

1.3.2 The nature of demand in organizational markets

In organizational markets, as in consumer markets, demand is difficult to forecast and depends on a combination of many factors. However, because organizational markets generally feed through to consumer markets in a sequence of added value stages, it is the demand for the eventual consumer product or service that draws down supply from the preceding organizational markets. Thus demand in organizational markets is said to be *derived* from the successive demands of the various added value stages between the organizational market and the eventual consumer market. For example, in the newsprint market, demand is derived primarily from the demand for newspapers on the street and for advertising space, moderated by the willingness of newspaper publishers to store newsprint (which might reflect the demand on their storage space, on their purchasing budget, and the differential demand for the currencies involved), coupled with an allowance for

Figure 1.1 An illustration of organizational markets: motor vehicle manufacturing

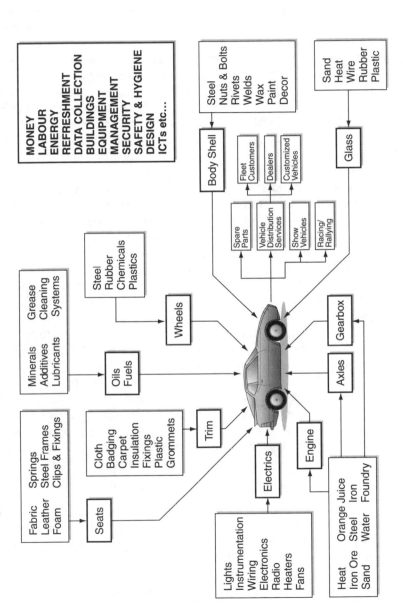

[Source: author]

inefficiency, inaccurate forecasting and experimentation in production and distribution processes.

In markets which do not have clear consumer involvement through direct payment at point of consumption, demand is derived from the succession of purchasing decision points between the organizational supplier and the eventual point of consumption. In government markets, for example, demand may be a function of political and legislative commitments, economic circumstances, political priorities and lobbying. Thus the demand for hospital theatre operating tables in the UK is not only a reflection of the demand for surgery (which is potentially unlimited) but also of the willingness of political parties to vote the funding priority for the National Health Service, and of the NHS (and non-NHS hospitals) to prioritize hospital capital budgets over other spending alternatives, and of individual hospitals to invest in theatre facilities as opposed to other treatment scenarios.

Forecasting this derived demand can be very awkward even with the collaboration of key customers. Many organizations can do little more than estimate demand on the basis of historical trends adjusted in the light of discussions with key customers about the dynamics of consumer markets and environmental developments. Some other organizations, especially small ones, do not even attempt this modest degree of analysis, perhaps because of management complacency, or inadequate familiarity with marketing, or because they lack the necessary relationships with key customers – or because an intuitive adjustment to the previous year's figures has always worked before so why not do the same again? Where markets are particularly exposed to volatile change and uncertainty, for example in corporate computer markets, an inability to forecast demand at least as well as rivals can be competitively disastrous – as IBM and others discovered in the early 1990s (Wilson, 1994). But where the competitive environment is relatively placid, an intuitive approach can work adequately and this certainly avoids the problems of a more analytical approach to forecasting.

1.3.3 The nature of purchasing in organizational markets

Two further distinguishing features of organizational markets are important not only in their own right but also because of their implications for the nature of purchasing in organizational markets. These features are *the small number of buyers* compared to consumer markets and the typically far *larger order sizes* in scale and value. It therefore follows, given the variety of customer requirements and contingent circumstances:

- that it will often be important to adjust the specification of the purchased goods and services according to customer requirements;
- that this will involve negotiation and so selling will often be direct and personal;

- that purchase decisions will often have strategic implications both for customers and for suppliers;
- that the degree of risk associated for both parties can be significant, so risk perception, risk tolerance and risk management will be involved;
- that to reduce the scope for misjudgement and for abuse there are likely to be a number of people involved in significant purchase decisions;
- that the processes involved will often be complex;
- and that it will be important to be able to manage these processes carefully and professionally.

All of these purchasing features seem, at first glance, to distinguish organizational markets from consumer markets and this is certainly the stance adopted in most textbooks for many years. However, closer examination suggests that it can be useful to explore the relevance of consumer purchasing research to the context of organizational purchasing, and vice versa – more on this in the Conclusion of the book.

1.4   MANAGING MARKETING IN ORGANIZATIONAL MARKETS

Textbook discussions of marketing management used to assume (and many still do) that marketing between organizations is best understood in terms of a series of semi-independent decisions by managers who are rational, professional, well-motivated individuals. More recently, expanded explanations have been offered and it is appropriate that readers be aware of what the assumptions of this book are with respect to such fundamental issues.

Here organizational marketing is understood in terms of evolving relationships between organizations, that is, in terms of continuing interactions, rather than as a sequence of encounters where 'manipulative suppliers' engage with 'suspicious customers' (Han *et al.*, 1993). Understanding interorganizational relationships as continuing interactions is important not only to understanding organizations but also to understanding the competitive and strategic dynamics of markets (Turnbull and Valla, 1986; Håkansson and Snehota, 1989). While the idea of a collaborative interactive relationship is implicit in the idea of marketing as a *mutually advantageous exchange*, as Chisnall (1995) points out, marketing (more accurately 'selling') in industrial markets has long been presented as an antagonistic zero-sum game where the customer's gain is the supplier's loss.

This raises many conceptual and practical questions, not least of which is the difficulty of reconciling traditional views of organizational relationships as necessarily competitive with the increasing representation of these relationships as fundamentally mutually dependent and collaborative. Some of these questions are defused, to some extent, by the intuitively compelling suggestion that presentation of organizational selling as antagonistic has been exaggerated and owes more to the ease of analyzing and explaining organizational selling situations as 'zero-sum games' than it does to the underlying realities of how individuals relate in selling situations. Continuity is usually easier to manage than change and it would seem likely that supplier–customer relationships in organizational markets were characterized more by a degree of mutual tolerance than of mutual antagonism. So the 'new' emphasis on inter-organizational collaboration may be less of a revolution than some of its advocates seem to imply.

Underpinning this image of marketing as relationship management is that of the manager as an individual with personal objectives, a full in-tray of competing demands on his or her attention, and discretionary power rather than, as seems to have been assumed in much of the earlier marketing literature, as a strictly rational and inexhaustible servant of the executive routinely enacting corporate policies. There are many implications arising from this rather obvious view of the manager as a person and not an automaton, and these implications are crucial in appreciating the difference between 'recommended best practice' (i.e. academic theory) and optimal practice (i.e. what can reasonably be expected from hard-pressed managers). However, as Ames observed in his seminal article of 1970, there are many senior managers who simply pay lip service to organizational marketing and fail to benefit from the competitive advantages that it can offer. Many years later, competitive dynamics have eroded the number of organizations unable to develop effective and realistic marketing strategies but there are still many managers who seem to understand little of organizational marketing beyond the basics (Parkinson, 1991).

1.5   THE SIGNIFICANCE OF ORGANIZATIONAL MARKETS

The significance of organizational markets to the supplier and customer organizations involved will be evident from much of the above discussion. What should also be clear from the discussion of the variety of these organizations is the overall significance of organizational markets to national economies. This importance is so obvious that it hardly needs to be stated, yet organizational marketing still seems to be treated as a peripheral variation of marketing in most marketing textbooks, perhaps meriting a chapter or two once the more important issues of consumer marketing have been covered. Nevertheless, while awareness of organizational marketing issues is certainly growing, there are still far fewer organizational marketing courses within marketing programmes than there are courses on consumer marketing or service marketing or international marketing (Lichtenthal and Butaney, 1991). It seems to come as a surprise to most students that their careers in marketing are more likely to involve organizational marketing than consumer marketing. And despite the frequent finding that purchasing costs far exceed labour costs for most organizations, it is labour costs rather than purchasing budgets that often seem to be the focus of cost-reduction strategies (New and Myers, 1986; Heinritz, 1991; Baily *et al.*, 1994).

2 *Organizational buyer behaviour and the purchasing process*

The exchange of goods and services between organizations is, of course, the lifeblood of organizational markets, and the processes involved, especially the buying process, have tended to dominate research and teaching in this field. Nevertheless, the full significance of organizational buying (also referred to as purchasing or, less often perhaps, as procurement) as a whole to overall economic success and operating efficiency seems not to have been fully appreciated by many organizations (Ellram and Carr, 1994), while the complexity of the detailed processes involved has resulted in ever more esoteric attempts by researchers to model the multiple factors involved. It is difficult to see how some of these models could help practitioners to make specific decisions, except at a generalized and conceptual level, and many of the more experienced industrial sales professionals might question the value of attempts to generalize about such intuitive, intricate and personal processes. Yet without an understanding of how and why organizations purchase goods and services, little progress can be made in improving the marketing of these goods and services to organizations.

These models are discussed in more detail later in this chapter but first it will be helpful to establish the significance, objectives and contribution of organizational purchasing from the practical perspective of the organization itself.

2.1 THE SIGNIFICANCE OF ORGANIZATIONAL PURCHASING

Heinritz *et al.* (1991) shows how important organizational purchasing is by pointing out that the combined purchasing of the largest 100 US corporations amounts to about 10 per cent of the entire US economy. At the microeconomic level in the UK, the British Institute of Management reported that in a manufacturing operation, there was typically three times as much investment in materials as there was in labour (New and Myers, 1986). This means that equal percentage reductions in the costs of purchasing and labour would return much greater economies in purchasing. And yet, as the BIM report argued, much greater attention is generally paid to the management of the labour process and its costs than to the material side of the business. Obviously, labour management presents additional human issues and imperatives which are not usually as dominant in the purchasing of goods (though purchasing services can be another matter, Jackson and Cooper, 1988) but this does not explain the historical relative lack of organizational investment in the management of purchasing. However, since perhaps the 1980s there clearly has been very much greater pressure on most organizations to reduce costs, in response to increasing competitive pressures, and this has generated much closer managerial attention to effective and professional purchasing.

Some insight to the reasons for this increased attention to purchasing professionalism is provided by Baily and Farmer (1990) who suggest that the importance of purchasing in an organization will significantly increase when the product life cycle of the organization's output becomes shorter (e.g. computer suppliers), or when the organization's markets become particularly volatile (e.g. TV production companies), or when the cost of the organization's purchases form a particularly large proportion of its income (e.g. armed forces). All three factors are clearly associated with increased competitive pressure. Other factors likely to increase the significance of purchasing could also be suggested, all of which have featured in the last years of the twentieth century: economic recession; the introduction of new technology (reduction of labour costs through automation leaves a higher priority on managing purchasing costs); deregulation and open tendering; and the adoption of collaborative customer–supplier strategies.

While the costs of professional purchasing are considerable because of the training and processes involved, the costs of poor purchasing are very much greater, potentially comprising not just the cost of the goods/services involved, and of the administrative and management effort involved, but extending also to the cost of the corrosive effect on relationships with suppliers and customers (loss of goodwill and reputation), the costs of scrap and wastage, the costs of blame allocation and problem resolution (possibly including litigation), and even possible strategic costs to branding and public relations.

So there seems little doubt that organizational purchasing has recently gone through something of a renaissance in terms of its strategic priority. To understand how effective organizational purchasing – and its reciprocal, organizational marketing – might be managed, the focus now turns to the practitioner's perspective of what purchasing aims to achieve and how research suggests this might best be achieved.

2.2 THE OBJECTIVES AND CONTRIBUTION OF PURCHASING

The objectives of purchasing for an organization can vary considerably according to the sort of goods and services typically purchased, the exposure of the organization to increases in costs, how the managers involved rate purchasing amongst the competing priorities of an organization, and according also to how professionally purchasing is managed (Parkinson and Baker, 1986).

In some organizations, such as consultancies or professional service providers, most purchasing will probably be seen as routine and fairly insignificant (office stationery, utility services, professional insurance, furnishings) with only occasional and infrequent large-scale purchasing tasks such as computing facilities and premises demanding careful attention. At the other extreme, the competitive pressures on profit margins for most manufacturing organizations generate careful scrutiny of all aspects of purchasing and a much greater emphasis on professionalism in purchasing management.

Two examples of professionalism in purchasing are given in the first mini-case in Part III. These examples help to illustrate the difference professionalism can make to the process and the effectiveness of purchasing. The examples also show how professionalism in purchasing can be encouraged by competitive pressures.

Clearly then, efficient and effective purchasing can have a major impact on a business' cost structure, on its production efficiency, on the overall quality of its products and services, on its flexibility of design, on its ability to develop products in line with market requirements, and on cost management. Mini-case 13 shows how some of these benefits were achieved in a public sector hospital. This adds up to an important impact on the overall competitive strategy of a business when competitive advantages can be derived and sustained on the basis of cost structure, of perceived quality, of vertical integration, and of responsiveness in design (Walsh et al., 1992). Effective organizational marketing should aim to provide a service (in addition to the actual items purchased) which will support the effectiveness of the customer's purchasing operations and thereby enhance the competitiveness of customer organizations.

A good working relationship with suppliers can also provide the purchasing function with valuable competitive information and insight (Monczka, Nichols and Callahan, 1992). Similarly, suppliers with an intimate awareness of their customers' products will be well placed to recognize developments in their own technological environment which could be potentially beneficial to customers, for example suppliers of car seat covers recognizing the potential of developments in glue technology and computerized fabric cutting to produce intricate cloth inserts in interior trims for high-specification cars. Also, any new products of existing competitors might be more easily assessed with the cooperation of expert suppliers (e.g. in reverse engineering, costing and profitability assessment). And new entrants might be detected at an early stage through their preliminary tentative discussions with appropriate suppliers.

To illustrate the potential scope and importance of purchasing to an organization's broader strategic and tactical operations, Exhibit 2.1 records some of the specific purchasing objectives cited by leading UK motor manufacturing organizations.

Given the perceived significance of buying in organizational markets,

---

EXHIBIT 2.1

Typical organizational purchasing objectives (derived from internal corporate documents and textbooks)

- To ensure suitable quality in purchased goods or services
- To avoid excessive expenditure throughout purchasing
- To avoid disruption to the supply of goods and services
- To avoid unneeded inventory, WIP, excess stock, waste, or scrap
- To identify and develop excellent and appropriate sources
- To monitor and warn of problems in sensitive purchases
- To research new purchase ideas, opportunities and sources
- To contribute to the strategic marketing planning process
- To manage and support purchasing relationships
- To play a part in developing the organization's competitive position
- To develop purchasing staff and systems in line with objectives

An example

One leading UK manufacturer stated its purchasing objectives in an internal document as:

To buy specified components and services at:

- the right price
- the right quality
- the right quantity
- the right time
- the right source

to enable efficient product manufacture.

Obviously, other organizations with different operations would change the last line to reflect their own organizational objectives and competitive priorities (e.g. . . . 'to enable efficient service provision', or . . . 'to achieve customer satisfaction') though the rest of the specification might well remain broadly appropriate.

---

it is not surprising that buying is often characterized as a complex and highly professional activity, especially compared to consumer markets. We now turn to attempts to understand this behaviour and the processes involved more fully.

Over the past 30 years, research into the management and processes of organizational buying has been extensive and is summarized below in terms of its three principal areas of concern: the classification of buying occasions; the composition of the buying centre or decision-making unit; and the analysis of the buying process as a sequence of 'buy-phases'. These studies have encouraged recognition of the importance of organizational buying both internally, with respect for example to efficiency, quality and cost management, and externally with respect to competitive advantage and customer responsiveness. In line with this academic interest, organizational buying has become increasingly recognized as a professional field of management for a variety of practical, operational and strategic reasons (Browning and Zabriskie, 1980; Parkinson and Baker, 1986).

2.3 BUYING CLASSIFICATIONS

Perhaps the most obvious way to categorize buying occasions would be in terms of the technical formats used since these do, to some extent, correspond to different needs. Exhibit 2.2 shows four frequently used categories of organizational buying plus the usually ignored but still significant category of 'miscellaneous expenditure', which may also help to illustrate the discussion for those unfamiliar with the technicalities involved.

In the 1960s Robinson, Faris and Wind argued that organizational buying could more usefully be classified into three broad categories or *buy-classes* based on the novelty of the purchase: **new task**, **modified rebuy**, **straight rebuy** (Robinson, Faris and Wind, 1967). These are useful categories which are still widely recognized. Each is explained in turn below.

2.3.1 New task

This is the most complex form of organizational buying and refers to the first time a particular product or service is purchased by an organization. Extensive preparation is assumed to take place for 'new task' buying though, in practice, this is likely to depend, *inter alia*, on the cost and significance of the purchase, the similarity with previous purchases, the experience of the staff involved, and the efficiency of the purchasing process overall. In principle, 'new task' buying involves all the early phases of the buying process (see 2.4 below) and may involve careful trial arrangements to establish the ability of prospective suppliers and their products to perform to agreed specifications and terms. For example,

---

EXHIBIT 2.2

Five typical categories of organizational buying

Approved purchase orders – for routine and frequent purchases in pre-determined order units and delivery arrangements (e.g. chemicals, stationery, consumable tools and materials, bulk raw materials). Delivery can be triggered by various means such as reorder levels, agreed schedules or just-in-time (JIT) procedures.

Special purchase orders – for occasional extra needs of items on approved purchase lists over and above the routine delivery (e.g. after unscheduled overtime or adverse consumption variance) or not normally required (e.g. drains clearance services, special project requirements).

Periodic contracts (often annual) – for commodity items where the order unit may be open ended or continuous (e.g. energy, security and cleaning services, rentals of premises or vehicles, fleet maintenance).

Capital expenditure – one-off purchase of assets though often with implications for other purchasing alternatives for service, support and associated consumables (e.g. computer systems, vehicles, buildings, land, machinery, major equipment items, mining rights, furniture).

Miscellaneous expenditure – occasionally any organization will need to buy things without going through elaborate procedures which may exceed in administrative costs the value of the items purchased or where the urgency of need demands procedural short-cuts (e.g. to fill unexpected shortages of low-value items, or for regular trivial payments which it would be inefficient or inappropriate to enmesh in procedure). Managers often have discretion to approve miscellaneous expenditure of this sort up to stipulated levels reflecting their seniority and responsibilities; similarly, many offices have 'petty cash' funds. Abuse of such discretionary arrangements can lead to ethical and accounting difficulties.

---

before Sainsbury introduced electronic point of sale (EPOS) checkout systems in all its supermarkets, pilot schemes lasting several months were conducted in selected stores to establish the capability of rival EPOS systems to cope with varying trading conditions and levels of staff expertise. An example of a new-task purchasing decision is given in Mini-case 2 to illustrate something of the intricacy and complexity of these buying decisions.

2.3.2 Modified rebuy

Where non-trivial changes are proposed with respect to the product or service purchased, the negotiated terms or the supplier, a degree of renegotiation will be involved (though not to the extent of a 'new task'). This is referred to as a 'modified rebuy'. This level of renegotiation is generally prompted by one or more of the following three stimuli:

1 unplanned developments such as problems (e.g. in quality, supply, terms, supplier status) or environmental changes (e.g. in competitive situation, legislation, end-user needs, technology, macro-economic situation);
2 changes in the customer's needs (e.g. volume, delivery terms, service levels) or in the supplier's offering (e.g. price, product developments);
3 periodic review of purchase arrangements either by the supplier or by the customer.

2.3.3 Straight rebuy

This is routine renewal of established purchasing arrangements where there is no significant change in the suppliers, products, services or terms involved. For example, when a customer is content with its purchases of paper from a wholesale stationer, and any proposed changes in pricing and technical specification are within the agreed contracted arrangements for inflation and product improvement, there is little need for significant renegotiation and this would generally be approved routinely as a 'straight rebuy'.

These buying classifications help to prioritize different categories of purchasing decisions and have implications for the management of purchasing (e.g. in delegation and in establishing standard purchasing procedures). Nevertheless, it may not always be easy to allocate specific buying occasions to a particular 'buy-class' and it seems unlikely that the novelty of the purchasing situation will be the only useful approach to purchasing categorization worth pursuing.

While Robinson, Faris and Wind's classification does offer valuable insights to the purchasing process, it fails to reflect the broader context and strategic significance of a purchase which can raise crucial problems for the organization. Anticipation of such problems can make considerable differences to the purchasing process involved. For example, some *new task* purchases may be trivial, perhaps because they are easily specified commodities and widely available (e.g. furnishings, fixings, office computers), or because they are low-cost low-volume items (e.g. stationery, paint, light bulbs), or because they are simply seen as relatively unimportant to the organization at the time. Equally, some *straight rebuy* purchases may be highly sensitive and meticulously managed owing to a shift in strategic circumstances. For example, the McDonald's chain of restaurants in the UK was used to continual purchasing of bulk frozen beefburgers from several familiar UK suppliers but the reaction of the British public to announcements about possible health risks in British beef during the mid-1990s made this straight rebuy a highly sensitive purchase with major strategic and competitive implications. It is also obvious that pressure of work can result in modified rebuys being treated as straight rebuys or urgent new-task purchases being accelerated through abbreviated procedures.

So there are many strategic and contingent factors that distinguish one type of buying process from another, even if one accepts the simple threefold classification of Robinson, Faris and Wind. Figure 2.1 attempts to represent this with three vectors representing customer requirement, supplier offering and purchase significance. The degree of change in any one (or more) of these vectors outwards from the centre position of negligible change can explain why a purchase is treated as a straight rebuy, a modified rebuy or an initial buy. In the McDonald's example above, what was normally a straight rebuy of frozen beefburgers became, in effect, an initial buy owing to the dramatic shift in purchase significance involved (and in customer requirement). Readers may wish to consider other examples from their own experience.

A glimpse into some of the pressures of purchasing and the managerial aspects of the profession is provided by Exhibit 2.3 which shows an abbreviated job description for a junior purchasing officer specializing in buying glass products for a car manufacturer.

Figure 2.1 What distinguishes buying classifications?

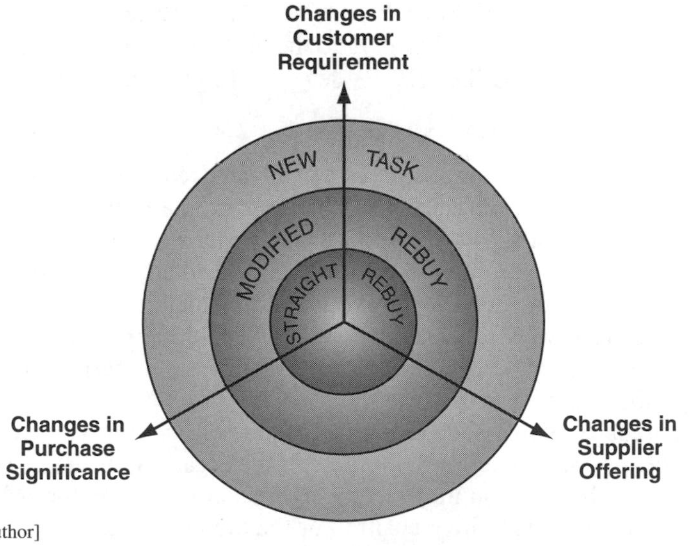

[Source: author]

EXHIBIT 2.3

Job description of an automotive glass buyer

- Make enquiries concerning purchase of glass products/services
- Undertake negotiations as appropriate with potential suppliers
- Place orders and monitor progress of ordered goods/services
- Monitor progress of supplier's manufacturing
- Monitor progress of delivery to buyer
- Confirm delivery and invoicing
- Maintain records and filing
- Create and maintain good supplier relationships
- Nominate development sources
- Suggest new products or methods of manufacture to suppliers
- Ensure production programmes are supported
- Dispose of scrap and obsolete material
- Support planning and control as required
- Establish adequate supplier manufacturing capacity
- Ensure timing programmes are supported
- Initiate measures for cost-savings and inflation fighting
- Undertake additional tasks as assigned by senior managers

[Source: edited from internal company documents]

2.3.4 Classification by purchasing problems

Recognizing the limitations of the Robinson, Faris and Wind classification, Lehmann and O'Shaughnessy (1974) suggested a reclassification of industrial purchases according to the problems inherent in their adoption and Hill and Hillier (1977) developed this idea into the following four categories:

1 *routine* and familiar purchases (which are frequently ordered and are not expected to raise problems in usage or in associated procedures);
2 purchases with associated *procedural problems* (e.g. where the product itself is unproblematic but its users need additional training or it needs adjustment to the environment in which it will be used);
3 purchases with associated *performance problems* (e.g. where the product itself is unfamiliar and will involve a learning process in terms of how it is best used);
4 purchases with associated strategic and *political problems* (e.g. high-cost items, or where several parts of the organization are involved, or where the decision may have a significant impact on the public perception or competitive position of the organization).

It is also worth noting that whereas Robinson, Faris and Wind's categories are mutually exclusive, the more flexible and realistic categories suggested by Hill and Hillier can overlap and the same purchase task can fall into different categories on different occasions.

2.4 PHASES IN THE PURCHASING PROCESS AND THE BUYGRID MODEL

Like many marketing activities, the purchasing process has also been analyzed as a logical succession of phases or stages. Robinson, Faris and Wind (1967) not only distinguished the three buy-classes discussed above (new task, modified rebuy, straight rebuy) but also correlated these with eight 'buy-phases' in a *Buygrid model* derived from their empirical research (see Table 2.1).

This representation of the buying process as a sequence of buy-phases is useful for descriptive purposes but it should not be taken literally as a managerial model since it lacks any predictive power or causative explanation of buying decisions (Webster and Wind, 1972). Nor would it be sensible to take the implied sequential logic of the eight buy-phases too literally as it will always be possible to identify further 'phases', to skip some and revisit others in revised sequence, or even in parallel, and to shift seamlessly through phase divisions which may be more apparent (and useful) to researchers than to practitioners.

Table 2.1 The Buygrid model

	Buy-classes		
Buy-phases	*New Task*	*Modified Rebuy*	*Straight Rebuy*
1 Anticipation and recognition of need and general solution			
2 Determination of features and quantity of needed item			
3 Description of features and quantity of needed item			
4 Search for and qualification of potential sources			
5 Acquisition and analysis of proposals from suppliers			
6 Evaluation of proposals and selection of supplier(s)			
7 Selection of an order routine			
8 Performance feedback and evaluation			

[Source: from Robinson, Faris and Wind, *Industrial Buying and Creative Marketing*. Copyright © 1967 by Allyn & Bacon. Reprinted/adapted by permission. Cited in Webster and Wind, 1972, p. 24.]

Nevertheless, the Buygrid model is not without value. It supports various observations and conclusions, such as what Robinson *et al.* refer to as 'creeping commitment' (the increasing reluctance of customers to consider new suppliers as the process unfolds), and the different significance of the buy-phases in different buy-class situations.

Using the Buygrid model as a basis, an annotated and elaborated description of purchasing as a process with approximately discernible phases (which may overlap or be omitted depending on circumstances) is presented in Exhibit 2.4 as an illustration in general terms of how the process might be observed for more complex new-task purchases. Obviously, practice can be very different, especially for minor or routine purchases, or in sectors with especially elaborate procedures (e.g. defence, pharmaceuticals, ethical finance). Some of the phases may seem relatively trivial or pedantic but it is easy to forget the scope for mismanagement – generating irritation and cost – from phases ignored in more simplified versions of this process. For example, payment delays are notorious as a major problem for smaller organizations; and it may not be until deliveries arrive in the rain that shortcomings in packaging become apparent (e.g. barcoded labels which cannot be read by computer if the label is damaged, or because the ink runs when wet – causing sudden bottlenecks as vehicles cannot be admitted to factories, nor pallets to automated storage/retrieval systems); and goods

---

EXHIBIT 2.4

An extended description of 'phases' in the purchasing process

1 **Perception of requirement** – implicit demand reflecting ultimate customers, explicit demand from process of adding value.
2 **Analysis and assessment** – gathering and assessment of information as to demand and supply, including establishment of provisional specifications, probable size and frequency of order, possible costs, make-or-buy decision, profiles of potential suppliers.
3 **Criteria setting** – identification and ranking of the most important purchasing factors which will vary on each occasion.
4 **Identification of possible sources** – including request for quotations, prototype submission, pilot studies, trials, visits to suppliers' premises and reference sites, pursuit of references, capacity and liquidity assessment, leading to a short-list of one or more possible suppliers.
5 **Value engineering** – systematic evaluation of the functions of the short-listed offerings to assess which of the offerings is

best able to provide the customer's needs at the lowest net cost taking into consideration all the offering-related aspects (this may be a technical matter which purchasing staff may not be competent to address).

6 **Negotiation and decision** – the outcome of the previous phases is considered in the context of broader aspects where appropriate and final negotiations may be conducted at senior levels to adjust any residual uncertainties until agreement is struck with one favoured supplier.

7 **Delivery and receipt** – delivery procedures will have been agreed but receiving procedures are often overlooked, will vary considerably and can often lead to administrative confusion, frustrating delays, deterioration of goods and problems of payment. This includes sub-phases of **Inspection** – usually on arrival and before receipt but this may not be practicable because of weather, nature of packaging, type of good/service or congestion in receiving area; and **Storage** – preferably for as short a time as possible but this will vary according to *terms* (it is often cheaper to purchase, transport and store in bulk), *storage-life* (extending shelf-life may be excessively costly but can be offset by bulk discounting), *cost of storage* (spare space, interest rate, scarcity of supply, minimum economic quantity of transport), *safety stocks* (in terms of production continuity, cost of storing WIP, access to supply, predictability of cost), and so on.

8 **Payment** – through regular periodic bills (e.g. energy, labour, rates); or on a partial basis to establish conformity to agreed performance levels; or, more usually, following processing of delivery and receipt documentation; through computerized debiting arrangements where the cycle of order, despatch, receipt, storage, issue and reorder are managed by EDI.

9 **Review** – after an agreed period, or as part of the customer's normal purchasing practices, all purchasing arrangements should be subject to review which should take close account of the judgement of production management and workers as well as consulting finance (for scrap and obsolescence rates), goods receiving (for delivery performance), quality control, and product engineering (for compatibility with any proposed changes to product design or production systems).

10 **Reassessment of requirement** in anticipation of major changes (e.g. in product design, in suppliers, in technology) and linking cyclically back to the start of this process.

[Source: author]

may deteriorate in storage unexpectedly if not prepared and packaged appropriately. Marketing managers are well advised by Shapiro to follow all the phases of ordering closely in order to ensure that customers' interests are foremost throughout (Shapiro *et al.*, 1992).

Using this extended set of buy-phases, an adapted version of the Buygrid model (for original version see Table 2.1) is presented in Table 2.2 to indicate the varying relevance of different buy-phases to the three buy-classes. A similar grid could also be developed based on the Hill and Hillier problem-oriented buy-classes.

It is important to recognize that this indication of the 'relevance' of phases in the purchasing process to different buy-classes will depend also on a number of other factors, most importantly the perceived significance of the purchase in question. Thus 'straight rebuys' of vital products or services (e.g. energy, machinery) can still involve considerable complexity and negotiation, and 'new buys' of relatively trivial purchases (e.g. stationery) can be very straightforward.

This way of depicting the changing nature of the purchasing process is unsatisfactory in a number of ways; for example, the last phase (reassessment of requirement) is similar to the first phase (perception of requirement), especially in well-managed organizations where such perception is routinely prompted and questioned by scheduled reassessment

Table 2.2 An adapted version of the Buygrid model

Purchasing Process Phases	New Buy	Modified Rebuy	Straight Rebuy
Perception of requirement	–	–	–
Analysis and Assessment	–	–	
Criteria Setting	–	–	
Identification of Sources	–	–	
Value Engineering	–		
Negotiation and Decision	–	–	–
Delivery and Receipt	–	–	–
Payment	–	–	–
Review	–		
Reassessment of Requirement	–	–	–

– = usually relevant where shaded and possibly relevant where unshaded processes. More important, the purchasing process is, obviously, deeply affected by the marketing activities of would-be suppliers yet the conventional model of the purchasing process seems to be divorced from any reference to marketing or sales activities. The purchasing process is better thought of in terms of a cyclical 'model' such as that in Figure 2.2 where the various process phases are indicated by numbers and are shadowed by a concentric cycle of marketing activities.

This cyclical model starts with the square numbered 1, and moves through the numbered phases of the new-task purchasing process with inputs at various appropriate stages from the marketing and sales activities of potential suppliers (those listed in the model include sales force, technical support, environmental scanning analysis – and there will be others according to the particular circumstances of any specific purchase). The losing suppliers depart when the purchase decision is taken at square 6 but they will generally hold some sort of review to learn from their experience and perhaps to plan for the later occasions when they may be able to re-enter the process. The new-task process continues through its final phases and, after some time, there are likely to be various straight rebuy situations for restocking, followed eventually by a modified rebuy process to take account of accumulated adjustments and developments in requirements and supply. Then there are further straight and modified rebuys before, at some point, the successive adjustments and developments are rationalized in a complete reassessment, triggering a full new-task process again. Naturally, the number of straight and modified rebuys, their timing and sequence will

Figure 2.2 The purchasing process

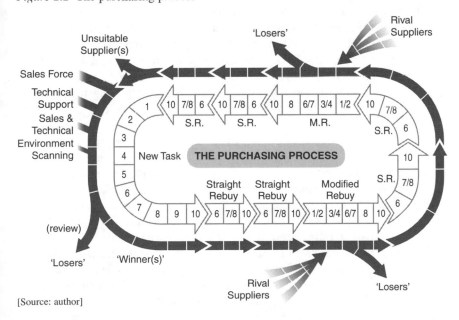

[Source: author]

vary according to many factors – this is simply a descriptive generalized model. The model also helps to show how rival suppliers can challenge the established supplier(s) at various stages and may provide a useful input to suppliers planning their marketing strategies for key contracts and accounts.

2.5 THE BUYING CENTRE

In the 1960s and 1970s several surveys of industry purchasing practices in the UK and USA (Kennedy, 1983) established, *inter alia*, that industrial purchasing decisions usually involved many individuals from different functions within an organization in what is now generally referred to as a *buying centre* or decision-making unit (DMU). Since then some doubts have been raised about how typical joint decision making is in such circumstances (Patton, 1997) and it seems likely that collective decisions will be more typical of complex, expensive or controversial purchasing decisions in larger organizations whereas routine decisions and those in smaller organizations may be more typically made by individuals than by groups. However, even in cases of decisions apparently made by individuals, there will still be many other roles influentially involved in the phases of the purchasing process before and after the actual decision itself.

Webster and Wind (1972) identified five buying 'roles' within the context of the buying centre: *users, influencers, buyers, deciders* and *gatekeepers* and a further category of *initiator* was added later by Bonoma (1982). This classification is now widely accepted as a general model though additional roles may be identifiable on closer examination of specific instances. In particular, the increasing professionalism of purchasing has led to some further specialization of purchasing roles in large purchasing departments and independent purchasing consultancies where purchasing *analysts* seem to constitute a valuable new category in the buying centre.

In many cases the important factors affecting the purchasing decision will not necessarily be confined to the buying centre or its membership. In these cases it makes sense to think in terms of an 'expanded' or 'contextualized' buying centre which could also comprise significant buying-centre influencers – as opposed to members – such as *sources* and *observers*, though research has yet to demonstrate the significance of these influence roles empirically. *Sources*, in this context, are external individuals or agencies which provide information concerning the purchase. This information can be highly influential, especially where the purchase requires complex and unfamiliar information. The most obvious of such sources is the supplier itself, or rather the sales staff and technical experts employed by the supplier to prosecute the sale. *Observers* are external individuals or agencies which can be highly influential when those more directly involved in the purchasing decision attempt to anticipate external reactions (e.g. politically sensitive decisions; children's reaction to packaging). Observers do not need to be aware of their influence and so can be active or passive. Research has yet to establish the effect of these roles and what might be appropriate management responses but, once again, the parallels with consumer buying behaviour will be apparent.

The complexity of the situation is further heightened when one recalls that the roles adopted within the buying centre may also be allocated to different individuals, departments and levels of seniority according to the circumstances of each purchase, and some roles may even be duplicated or subsumed on occasion.

An expanded version of Webster and Wind's buying centre, showing the eight basic roles mentioned above, is shown in Exhibit 2.5.

With the development of more collaborative approaches to interorganizational marketing such as *partnership sourcing* (see Section 4.2 below), which can involve long-term mutual commitments between

---

EXHIBIT 2.5

Who is the buyer in organizational buying?

There are many buying roles involved in the purchasing process, not all of them represented in all meetings of the buying centre or DMU. The following are fairly typical for major purchases; less significant purchases would not generally involve all these roles, at least in a formal sense:

Initiators who identify the need for the purchase (e.g. purchasing staff, production workers, customer liaison staff) – the way in which initiators identify the need (e.g. complaint, demand, cost-saving suggestion, problem solution, investment opportunity) can influence much of the ensuing process and the specification of the requirement.

Sources who provide information (internal and external sources, formal and informal, specialist and generalist) – the information provided (especially word of mouth) can be very influential but may also be partial and often requires processing and analysis before it can be used.

Gatekeepers who can control the flow of, and access to, much incoming information (e.g. telephonists and receptionists denying sales reps instant access to managers, PAs screening mail and calls to protect their bosses, nominated referees and inspection sites refusing to cooperate, administrative staff stalling paperwork, punctilious managers who insist on 'due process').

Analysts who assess information and alternatives (e.g. purchasing staff, referral points, external consultancies and agencies, quality inspectors, sample testers) – most formal information is processed and analyzed in some way before it reaches the members of the buying centre so the analysts can be very influential (especially in highly technical and complex purchases).

Influencers who tend to set the parameters within which the purchase requirement is determined (e.g. production engineers, R&D technicians, designers, service staff – experts and authorities of all sorts).

Buyers who manage relationships with suppliers and conduct most routine negotiations (e.g. buying agents, purchase officers, quality managers) – buyers may also advise on relationship issues such as a reliability, reputation, solvency and competitive prospects of potential suppliers.

Deciders who make or approve the final decisions on specifications, terms and successful suppliers (e.g. chief engineers, chief purchasing officers, directors of finance or production, general managers, CEOs, major stockholders) – deciders may also be middle or even junior-level managers according to their sign-off authority.

Users who actually use (or decline to use) the product or service (e.g. production workers, foremen, maintenance engineers, secretaries, end-use customers) – they may have a formal role (e.g. as advisers) in the buying centre but they will always have a crucial role as the ultimate authority on whether a purchase proves practicable or not.

[Source: author]

customers and suppliers, incremental purchasing decisions become much more a matter of 'supply management'. In these situations the role of the buying centre is ambiguous as the fundamental purchase decision has been made and subsequent issues relate to adjusting and developing the supply of goods and services between the two organizations. Logically, one would expect that the membership, expertise and responsibilities of a 'supply management centre' would differ significantly from that of a 'buying centre'; for example, suppliers would routinely be represented in the former but never in the latter.

Although organizational buying is usually coordinated and managed by the marketing or purchasing departments, the buying centre can comprise representatives from almost any other part of the organization as well (Katrichis, 1998), including:

- Engineering and R&D for technical specifications, performance evaluation, and to ensure consistency and compatibility with related product lines;
- Personnel for issues concerning health and safety, and industrial relations;
- Production and Materials Handling for issues involving reliability, delivery, storage, quality, and 'user-friendliness';
- Finance for cost aspects, payment terms and cash flow issues;
- Corporate Executive for discussion and approval of major items and strategic issues.

Further studies suggested that the composition of the buying centre and the influence of these departments and functions on any particular purchase occasion may vary according to such variables as: buy-class (new tasks require more extended buying-centre composition than rebuys); the specific purchase criteria and their relative importance (e.g. an emphasis on price may require additional finance representation); phase of the purchasing process; the complexity of the product/ service under consideration; the competitive and strategic significance of the purchase; the cost of the purchase over its useful life; the relevance of the purchase to different departments within the organization; the involvement of individuals from outside the organization making the purchase; and the cultural attitude of the organization and buying-centre participants to perceived risk (Wind, 1978; Johnston and Bonoma, 1981; Choffray and Lilien, 1978; Greatorex, Mitchell and Cunliffe, 1992; Venkatesh, Kohli and Zaltman, 1995). It has also been recognized for some time that the political and cultural 'pecking order' of departments and individuals within an organization can be an important variable (Strauss, 1964).

The next section looks at attempts to model the buyer behaviour of organizations but first it may help to try to pull together the various aspects of purchasing addressed so far. The diagram in Figure 2.3 tries to do this and should be considered in association with Figure 2.2 (The purchasing process) above.

To understand this integrated illustration of the purchasing process in context, consider that an organization has a stream of purchases (the centre right box of the diagram) from which there are all sorts of strategic and operational implications both for the organization (customer) and for its supplier(s).

The implications for the customer include, for example, links with other aspects of their portfolio of offerings, the possible effect on their corporate reputation, any risk involved (and the need to insure against unacceptable risk), the implications for enhancement of organizational capabilities, and the effect on the cost structure and cash flow of the organization. Implications for the supplier include the effect of the sale on their reputation (especially if the customer is either notorious in

Figure 2.3 The purchasing process in context

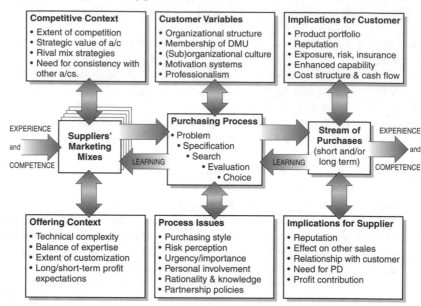

[Source: author]

some respect, e.g. for ethical reasons, or highly respected, e.g. for quality), the possible impact on other sales (e.g. in terms of production capacity), the relationship implications with the customer and others (e.g. for additional sales of the same or other offerings), the possible need to adjust product development plans, and the profit contribution of the sales stream both in the short and long term.

This purchase stream is initiated and controlled largely by the buying process of the organization and also by the organization's anticipation of what the implications are likely to be (and also by the supplier's assessment of the implications for itself). This buying process is affected by a range of issues to do with the process of buying (such as the rationality and risk attitude of the process, the degree of perceived urgency, and the organization's purchasing style and policies) and also by a series of customer variables (such as the cultures and structures involved, and the motivation and professionalism of the organization's purchasing staff). It may be difficult at times to distinguish clearly between these two sets of *variables* and *issues*.

Finally the buying process is also crucially affected by the supplier's marketing mix or, rather, the mixes of several potential suppliers. The marketing mix itself can be regarded as a function both of the offering in question (e.g. its technical complexity, the expertise required, the degree of customization, and expectations of profitability) and also of the supplier's competitive context (e.g. the intensity of rivalry, the perceived strategic value of the account, the need to compete with individual elements of rival mix offerings and the need for consistency with comparable accounts).

All of these various iterative processes, implications and influences are facilitated and accelerated by the learning processes involved – and by the different capacities of the organizations in question to benefit from these learning opportunities.

With this greatly simplified representation of a complex socio-rational phenomenon in mind, we now turn to a more detailed examination of the behavioural aspects of organizational purchasing.

2.6 MODELLING ORGANIZATIONAL BUYER BEHAVIOUR

Thus far, a number of contributions to understanding organizational buyer behaviour have been discussed, but while these have focused on specific aspects of the process they have not shed much light on buying behaviour *per se*, nor on the purchase decision itself. So now we look at attempts to model the behavioural aspects of the buying decision and the complex combination of variables acting on those involved as they progress through the process described above. For a brief review of the research behind these developments and the models see Parkinson and Baker (1986, especially Chapters 4, 5 and 7), while Turnbull provides a convenient and lucid discussion of the Sheth, Webster and Wind, and interaction models (Turnbull, 1994). It should be noted that none of these 'models' claims to be predictive; all three are attempts to describe a complex process as a necessary preliminary to further analysis. Consequently it is difficult, and probably inappropriate, to 'test' the theoretical status of these models.

Exchange behaviour between buyers and sellers has long been studied in the context of consumer markets and is now recognized as fundamental to an understanding of organizational markets also, though with significant differences. The subject has developed from an analysis of individual purchases in consumer and organizational markets to one of the broader strategic implications of buyer–seller relationships and of the environmental and personal influences permeating the purchasing context.

Much of the early research was concerned with attempts to develop normative models of industrial buying behaviour based on implicit assumptions of managerial rationality. These models also tended to present the process as a series of compartmentalized phases, influences or variables, managed sequentially and cumulating in a mutually satisfactory transaction. In practice such neat descriptions can be suborned and distorted in all sorts of ways. This approach to modelling reflected the research involved (in the 1960s) which tended either to examine major capital equipment purchases (where careful analysis and discussion were to the fore), or to observe closely a very limited number of organizations (risking unsupportable generalization), or to survey members of the National Association of Purchasing Management in the USA or of the Institute of Purchasing and Supply in the UK (a convenient and tempting methodology but one which seems likely to generate an atypically professional and conscientious sample).

The early model builders clearly recognized that managerial rationality (assuming this dominates the process) is mediated through a range of cultural, psychological, social and political dynamics, though awareness of the full extent and influence of these additional dynamics has become far more developed since the 1970s. These dynamics can include, for example, the influence of personal paradigms and perceptual distortion, risk tolerance, organizational and sub-group cultures, socio-political power relations, career aspirations, and a variety of cultural and intellectual prejudices (relating especially to gender, age and ethnicity). Nor are these dynamics necessarily limited to the individuals and functional groups most directly involved since the political and strategic implications of purchasing can attract the attention and influence of a wide range of interest groups within and beyond the organizations in question (Drumwright, 1994, provides an example).

It is also self-evident that while professionalism and rationality (however the terms are understood) may characterize more important and high-profile purchasing decisions, especially in large and publicly accountable organizations, a more casual and habitual approach may be more typical in less exposed decisions. Yet, as Chisnall argues, the more important and high-profile purchase decisions may be particularly vulnerable to the blinkering effects of what he refers to as 'post-decisional dissonance' (Chisnall, 1995, pp. 89–90) and anticipation of this can also lead to pre-decisional dissonance-avoiding behaviour such as marginalizing and discrediting particular purchase options and sources of information (Brockner, 1992).

Finally, all three of the models discussed below tend to assume that there is sufficient commonality in organizational purchasing to justify a single model though, as argued above, the differences in process and professionalism between major and minor examples of purchasing and between more and less competent individuals seem too extensive – in realistic terms – to be accommodated within a single model. So none of the models are able to accommodate the distorting effect of excessive workloads, personal preoccupations, limited competence, and fatigue. Whereas all the models have some insight to contribute at a theoretical level, for practical insights there is no substitute for experience of the real thing.

2.6.1 The 1970s models

The next two models (especially the Webster and Wind model) are still widely cited in current textbooks. The models were developed in the early 1970s and though research has moved on since then, some US scholars claim that these models are still compatible with more recent research (Johnston, 1994). While the 1970s models provide a sensible basis for understanding much of what is involved in an idealized purchasing process, they do not fully capture much of the rich and hugely influential interpersonal dynamics of the process in reality which more recent research has emphasized (see the following discussion of the Interaction model).

Webster and Wind modelled the organizational purchasing process (see Figure 2.4) as a set of four contextual influences (environment, organization, group, individuals) with particular emphasis on the role of organizational culture and individuals as the ultimate decision makers in the buying process (Webster and Wind, 1972). *Environment* is derived from the idea of the marketing macro-environment and refers to the context of national and sectoral conditions together with the broader information sources relevant to specific instances of organizational buying. *Organization* refers to similar issues (technological, cultural, economic, physical) relevant to purchasing within the context of the organization itself. *Group* refers to the individuals involved in a specific purchasing occasion and includes acknowledgement of the 'interactions' and 'sentiments' generated amongst the group. *Individuals* refers to the potential variation amongst individuals in terms of motivation, personality, perception and capability. Finally, the model recognizes that some purchasing decisions are individual processes rather than group processes but without indicating how the previous categories are affected in each case.

The major weakness of this model in terms of enlightening our understanding of organizational buyer behaviour is that it provides a compartmentalized list of influences without indicating which are more or less effective on any particular occasion, nor how the influences affect what is going on. Even within its own terms, the presentation of the model also tends to underestimate the influence, say, of the *environment* on the *individual*, or of the *individual* on the *group*. In other words, the design of the model should indicate iterative and multiple influence rather than sequential uni-directional influence. As a check-list of 'things to be aware of' it has some interest, especially in its emphasis on the role of the individual, but as a descriptive model of a dynamic process it is weak.

Sheth's (1973) model (see Figure 2.5) was adapted from a model of consumer buyer behaviour (Howard and Sheth, 1969) and perhaps this provenance explains its greater emphasis on the role of individuals and the need for conflict resolution in group decision making, compared to the Webster and Wind model. Similarly, there is less attention in the Sheth model to organizational variables, greater focus on multiple participation, and more explicit recognition of the effect of information sources from both the macro- and the micro-environment. The Sheth model also attempts to represent some of the more important vectors of

Figure 2.4 Webster and Wind model

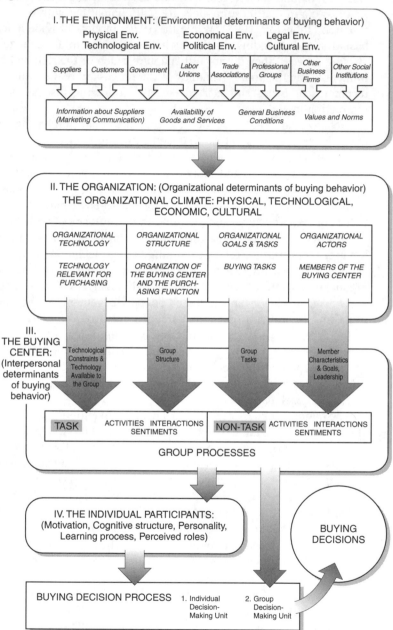

[Source: Webster, F.E. Jr and Wind, Y. (1972), 'A General Model of Organizational Buying Behavior', *Journal of Marketing*, 36(2), April, pp. 12–19. The material protected by this copyright has been translated for the express purpose of this publication. The American Marketing Association cannot be held responsible for any misinterpretations caused by the translation. Reprinted with permission from *Journal of Marketing*, published by the American Marketing Association, Webster, F.E. Jr and Wind, Y., 1972/36(2), pp. 12–19.]

Figure 2.5 The Sheth model

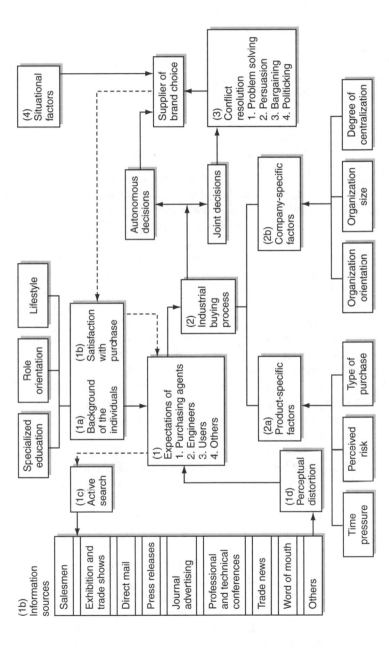

[Source: Sheth, J.N. (1973), 'A Model of Industrial Buyer Behavior', *Journal of Marketing*, 37(4), October, pp. 50–56; the model is on page 51. The material protected by this copyright has been translated for the express purpose of this publication. The American Marketing Association cannot be held responsible for any misinterpretations caused by the translation. Reprinted with permission from *Journal of Marketing*, published by the American Marketing Association, Sheth, J.N., 1973/37(4), pp. 50–56.]

influence between the factors charted in the model though without any indication of the relative scale or rationale of such influence. Attempts, however subtle or tentative, to indicate causation – or vectorial influence – between variables always invite criticism not only because of the fundamental problems of unequivocally isolating causal logic in complex social phenomena, but more immediately because the logic of such attempts implies that other possible vectors not shown in such models are necessarily less significant or invalid. One should not forget that these models are intended as conceptual simplifications, analytical tools or complexity reduction aids, not as prescriptive models in a scientific sense.

2.6.2 The Interaction model

Both the Sheth and the Webster and Wind models take the buying decision itself as the unit of analysis yet much of the research undertaken by the IMP (Industrial Marketing and Purchasing) Group over the past 25 years (see Ford, 1997, and the fourth reading in Part II) suggests that greater insights to the buying process may be available from taking the relationship between organizations as the focus of attention. The advantage of this approach is twofold. Firstly, the active role of the supplier is recognized (often overlooked in studies which focus on buying decisions) in a balanced perspective which avoids implying that the buyer is somehow a passive processor of marketing inputs (a weakness of many studies focusing on organizational marketing strategies). Secondly, with the relationship as the focus of attention, each purchase decision is necessarily seen in the context of the previous and continuing interactions between those within and between the organizations involved. As an illustration of the importance of the interaction approach to understanding organizational buyer behaviour, it will be obvious to those with experience of purchasing that some decisions are made at least as much to maintain relationships with valued suppliers (a strategic asset in itself) as they are for conventional purchasing reasons. This sort of decision could not easily be captured in the Webster and Wind or Sheth models.

Based on the IMP research, a model of buying behaviour in organizational markets has been developed (see Figure 2.6) which presents the process as an *interaction* between individuals within supplier and customer organizations. These relationships are conducted over time and are built up through cumulative 'exchange episodes' involving mutual exchange of purchases, remuneration, information and socialization. New participants entering such exchange relationships do so both as inheritors of the established pattern of behaviours, commitments and trust developed over time, and as developers of this pattern bringing novel perspectives and contributions to the process. From this perspective it is clear that long-established and habitual relationships can be hugely

Figure 2.6 The Interaction model

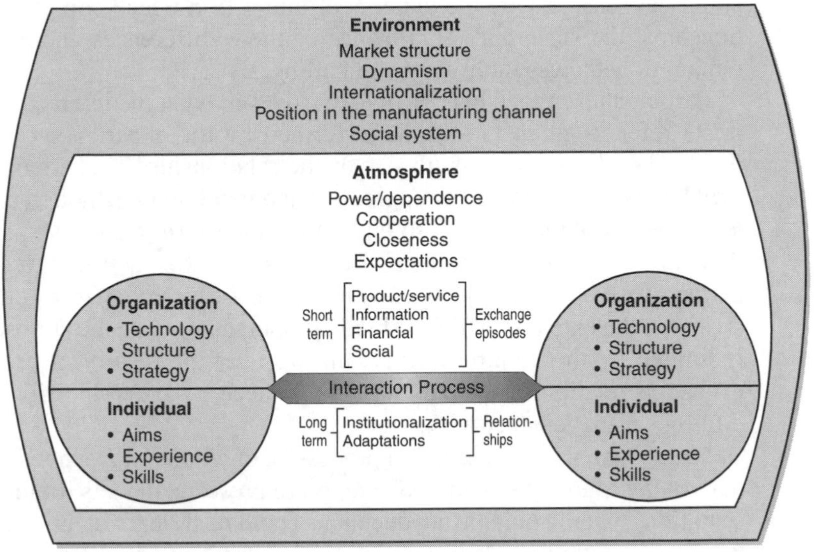

[Source: slightly adapted from Håkansson, H. (ed.) (1982), *International Marketing and Purchasing of Industrial Goods: an Interaction Approach*, John Wiley & Sons, Chichester, UK; the model is on page 24.]

important to the efficiency and effectiveness of purchasing. Indeed, the perceived costs of mutual familiarization and relationship-building in switching to an alternative supplier may be so great as to lead both parties to tolerate a surprisingly high level of dissatisfaction. These switching costs can explain something of the conservatism and routinization characteristic of purchasing relationships in many sectors and help to explain the entry barriers facing more competitive suppliers.

The participants in these exchanges are both organizations and individuals. The IMP research cites major organizational variables as being technology, size, structure, experience and strategy; while the key individual variables cited are motivation, aims, experience, skills, attitudes and perceptions. The scope for variation with so many variables is constrained by the tendency for continuity in organizational evolution, and convergence in human behaviour through socialization and work-related interdependence. What emerges are patterns and paradigms of behaviour which can become characteristic not only of organizational sub-groups and organizations themselves ('organizational cultures') but even, more loosely, of entire sectors ('sector cultures'). For example, there are obvious difference in the cultures and paradigms associated with, say, IBM and Apple, just as there are differences at an even less aggregated level in cultures and paradigms between hardware and software sectors in the electronics industry, and between the electronics industry and, say, the pharmaceutical industry. While these cultural and paradigm differences are, of course, very difficult to specify in any empirical sense, as are the patterns of interaction which comprise relationships, the scale and significance of these differences and patterns remain nonetheless intuitively compelling.

Participants engage in exchange episodes in what the interaction theorists refer to as an 'atmosphere' formed by the experience of those involved and the previous history of the relationship. This atmosphere may be open and friendly or aggressive and manipulative though the latter extreme obviously tends to undermine long-term relationships. Participants may wish to 'manage' the atmosphere for their own reasons, perhaps to avoid ethical criticism or to facilitate a particular negotiating style, but the extent to which individuals can manipulate the atmosphere is limited by the cultural norms built up over the history of previous exchange relationships, and by the tolerance of other individuals to different management styles.

Finally, the whole interaction process is, of course, surrounded by the macro-environmental features common to previous models. In this presentation, specific purchasing decisions could be thought of as 'punctuation' in a continuing stream of interaction, and best understood in the long-term context of the relationship. Therefore, individual decisions cannot be adequately understood unless one also takes account of the ongoing relationships in which these decisions are embedded and from which they emerge. This approach is fundamentally different to that of previous models which tended to see purchasing decisions as atomistic events to be explained and modelled in terms of the dynamics and issues prevailing at the time, rather than as part of a historic and continuing process.

There are also obvious parallels between the IMP research and research into strategic decisions more broadly which assumes that strategy is formed through interactive relationships and longitudinal processes rather than as a sequence of atomistic planned decisions.

The Interaction model of the exchange relationship between suppliers and customers is illustrated above and also in the fourth reading in Part II.

The Interaction model represents a bilateral relationship, largely for the purposes of simplification, but it will be obvious from the discussion above that any one organization is likely to have a wide range of relationships with many other organizations, both as customer and as supplier. To a greater or lesser extent, each individual relationship will be influenced by (and will influence) each other relationship. The result is a network of mutually influential interactions which it would be impossible to depict in the model above but which has important implications for many aspects of organizational marketing, not just purchasing. These implications are discussed further in Chapter 4.

2.6.3 Further attempts at modelling

There have been some further attempts at modelling organizational buying behaviour which are worth noting, though the results have supplemented rather than supplanted the models described above:

- Hill and Hillier (1977) analyzed purchase decisions in terms of intended usage, reasons for the purchase and complexity of the purchase – aspects which also apply to consumer buyer behaviour.
- Choffray and Lilien (1978) looked at the decision-making process with respect to the purchase of new products (a particularly complex instance of organizational purchasing). They concluded that interpersonal factors such as shared preferences (or personal paradigms), the exercise of power and the need for consensus were vital aspects of the process which were inadequately represented in the available models.
- Baker (1996) has attempted to develop a composite model of buyer behaviour applicable both to individual consumers and to organizations. He offers a formulaic model which suggests that purchasing behaviour is a function of the following sequence of ordered variables: selective perception, precipitating circumstances, enabling conditions, information search, expected performance factors, anticipated cost–benefit, and behavioural response (a catch-all variable covering subjective and judgemental factors such as prior experience and attitudes). Baker acknowledges that it will never be possible to determine the relative influence of each variable in this formula, and by placing selective perception at the start of the sequence he implies that all subsequent variables can vary considerably (actually from domination to absence) according to differences in the way different individuals perceive the variables. The result does not take us much further than a check-list of potential factors affecting buyer behaviour. But his approach does point out some of the similarities between individual and collective buying decisions.

It is also interesting to look at organizational buyer behaviour in terms of a typology, an approach which is more established in the context of consumer buyer behaviour. In consumer contexts these typologies are based on psychometric and 'life-style' analysis, generating categories such as 'empty nesters', 'young sophisticates' and 'quiet family men' (for a basic review of this approach in consumer markets see Lunn, 1986). However, in organizational contexts a more useful approach would be to develop categories based on emporographic data and relationship management style. Research into segmentation and purchasing behaviour in the oil lubricant market has produced one such analysis which is summarized in Table 2.3. Whether such purchasing characteristics can be extrapolated to more general typologies has yet to be established.

Table 2.3 Four buying groups for a 'commodity' (lubricants)

1. Conservatives	4. Professionals
■ Not innovative and largely unaware of rivals ■ Think (assume) that they have the best supplier ■ Think (assume) that they have the best deal ■ Don't really know their own requirements ■ Stress service aspects of the relationship ■ Price not that important ■ Long-term mutually cosy relationship ■ 90% of lubes come from the long-term source ■ 10% of lubes come from speciality suppliers	■ Mostly large firms (e.g. Ford, British Steel) ■ Go to tender every 1–2 years ■ Tight product/price specifications ■ Expect service also from their suppliers ■ Expect 'mutual back-scratching' ■ Will lever price-cuts by threats of switching ■ Prepared to switch at once for lower price ■ Don't care which supplier is used ■ Juggle 8+ suppliers at a time
2. Hard Bargainers	3. Tenderers
■ More proactive than the conservatives ■ Don't really know their own requirements ■ Generally not oriented towards tendering ■ Culture of bargaining 'machismo' ■ See negotiations as a zero-sum 'game'	■ Generally not oriented towards price issues ■ Establish the technical detail in the tender process ■ Know broadly what they require ■ Interested in service issues also ■ Expect regular contacts with their supplier

[Source: field research by postgraduate marketing students at Manchester School of Management, UMIST, 1994, building on research into the Eire lubricants market by Yip, 1993.]

What emerges from these additional studies is a general recognition that, in line with interaction theory, a greater emphasis should be placed on the personal and social aspects of buying processes, and on the effect of pre-existing influences such as experience, personal paradigms, cultural preferences and habituation. Successful marketing then becomes much more a matter of developing and managing the appropriate relationship with the appropriate people. It is worth noting that this also highlights some of the similarities between organizational and consumer buying behaviour.

2.7 SOURCING ISSUES IN ORGANIZATIONAL PURCHASING

In addition to the extensive discussion above into aspects of buying behaviour and the purchasing process, there are some additional decisions concerning sourcing which can have major implications for organizational marketing strategies and so require attention.

Three aspects in particular have important implications for organizational marketing: first, the decision over whether to buy goods and services or to provide them from internal resources – the make-or-buy decision; second, the choice between multiple sourcing and single sourcing, an issue which is more extensively discussed later under the heading of partnership sourcing; and third, issues involved in the choice between international and domestic sources, an increasingly significant aspect of purchasing with the spread of deregulation and globalization.

2.7.1 Make-or-buy decisions

An important alternative to purchasing is to supply the goods or services in question from internal sources. Equally, of course, before undertaking internal production of goods or services it is important to consider whether external purchasing might provide a more efficient or preferable alternative. This issue has many strategic and operational implications (Ford and Farmer, 1986; Venkatesan, 1992; Ford et al., 1993) beyond the relatively simple aspect of cost control (Dale and Cunningham, 1984; Welch and Nayak, 1992) and underlines the importance of links between purchasing and production issues (Dale and Cunningham, 1983).

Make-or-buy decisions can also apply to internal services such as marketing, research, planning, accounting and design, which may be better undertaken by external specialists with economies of scale and specialized investments (Anderson and Weitz, 1986). For example, during the 1980s considerable pressure was placed on local government authorities and the National Health Service in the UK to tender many internal services to open competition. It was alleged, with some justification, that purchasing services such as refuse collection and cleaning from external specialist suppliers could result in significant cost reductions compared to internal sources. The political furore which was stimulated by some of these decisions to tender services is a vivid reminder of the significance, complexity and functional diversity of purchasing decisions, and many organizations found it virtually impossible to decide uncontroversially between internal and external supply.

Arguably, in-house supplier arrangements appear to offer potential advantages of political control, of cost manipulation (e.g. in transfer pricing to minimize tax liability), of acquitting national content requirements, and of flexible response (see Exhibit 2.6). But there can also be significant problems of cost control, quality, delivery and service where the commercial pressures of market forces are (or are perceived to have been) suspended. It can also be very difficult to estimate the full costs involved in internal sourcing (Ellram, 1993) including, for example, the costs of any residual disposal and rectification (Johnson and Leenders,

EXHIBIT 2.6

The benefits of making rather than buying

- Control over sensitive processes (e.g. in-house customized software; seat manufacture to satisfy the quality standards of a key customer; on-site ambulance stations to ease employee relations and respond better to legal requirements)
- Costing advantages based on marginal pricing through utilizing slack assets (e.g. spare parts manufacture between production runs and in periods of low demand; in-house training using obsolete equipment and semi-retired supervisors)
- Responding to political pressures (e.g. special plants to employ disabled staff; favouring of group subsidiaries over more attractive external sources)
- Strategic flexibility to vary operations (e.g. seat manufacture enabling more integrated styling and rapid variation of specification and trim levels)
- Reduced risk where the availability of a vital component may be subject to uncertainty in terms of supply (e.g. where demand exceeds supply, or where demand can be volatile compared to supply) and price (due to fluctuations in demand and in currency exchange rates) (e.g. IBM's in-house production of microprocessors and electronic memory units)
- Need to demonstrate added value (e.g. manufacturing operations in Europe by Far Eastern competitors with high-quality established sources outside of Europe but who have to demonstrate some level of operations beyond 'screwdriver assembly' in order to win the right to produce within the EU)
- Fundamental strategy and corporate image (e.g. a car manufacturer might decide to make its own engines partly because this is where it sees its R&D most effectively focused and partly because it would be reluctant to be perceived as 'merely' assembling vehicles from parts supplied by rivals)
- Convenience of production flow (e.g. if the paint shop processes in vehicle manufacturing were to be subcontracted there would be considerable bottlenecks in the manufacture of body shells and of finished vehicles)

[Source: author]

1997). Decisions in this area are frequently concerned with political, cultural, personal, historic and strategic issues rather than with more technical purchasing concerns. Some of the more important benefits of internal supply are listed in Exhibit 2.6.

An example may help to illustrate the complexity of many make-or-buy decisions. A large UK manufacturing company decided that, rather than pension off experienced employees injured at work, it would establish a factory exclusively for disabled workers wishing to continue their work. The factory was successfully established in South Wales, producing labour-intensive simple castings and semi-machined parts such as clutch and brake pedals for the motor industry. The factory workforce was highly productive despite a generally low level of investment in capital equipment or new technology. When competitive pressures forced the parent company to consider rationalizations in its production operations it was concluded that the Welsh factory was uneconomic compared to alternative less labour-intensive external sources. Nevertheless, the political, social and cultural costs of closure, both in the workforce and beyond, were thought to far outweigh any considerations of purchasing efficiency. The factory remains open, under-capitalized and productive. It also has a better health record than most of the factories it supplies.

The term 'outsourcing' seems to have replaced other terms, such as subcontracting and tendering-out, to refer to the decision to source an organization's internal services (e.g. security, cleaning), functions (e.g. distribution, training) and facilities (e.g. IT systems, catering) from external suppliers. Outsourcing is often recommended as a means of increasing efficiency, reducing costs and refocusing on strategic 'core' competencies (Bettis, Bradley and Hamel, 1992), though some of its early popularity as an apparently easy means of devolving complex administrative tasks while saving money has dissipated (Brown, 1997). In a sense this represents a swing away from earlier strategies of vertical integration and is a further illustration of the widespread recognition that organizations are seamlessly linked into each other so that it may not even be apparent that these services are supplied by an 'external' agency. For example, the security staff from *SafeCo* and the cleaning staff from *Kwikleen* may be indistinguishable from the other members of the client organization and may even (through management buyouts and re-hiring agreements) be the same staff who previously fulfilled these tasks before the outsourcing decision was taken.

An illustration of many of these sourcing issues is given in Mini-case 3 which describes how a national chain of building society branches decided to source its energy by rationalizing from 14 sources to just two, and to outsource its future energy purchasing through a consultant.

2.7.2 Single and multiple sources

Traditionally, the ideal in purchasing has been to use multiple sources for goods and services where the strategic consequences of source failure (e.g. halting production, safety-critical) outweighed the scale economies and convenience of single sourcing. The use of multiple sourcing to increase the customer's negotiating power and provide strategic alternative supply sources in the event of failure was also seen as an important benefit, maintaining a healthy downward pressure on purchasing costs and supplier complacency.

In practice, even where alternative suppliers were approved, they were not always used, perhaps because of inertia, pressure of work, the strength of established relationships or perceived switching costs. It is important to recognize that, in practical terms, changing suppliers can be disruptive, time consuming, resource intensive, costly and even career threatening for purchasing staff who make mistakes. To justify change, clear cost benefits or other advantages have to be identified to overcome systemic inertia, accumulated personal commitment, alternative work priorities, and switching costs. Most of these factors operate to the advantage of existing suppliers. With a satisfactory source in place it will not be easy to maintain the necessary monitoring and updating processes to ensure that current alternative sources continue to be identified. Even where multiple sources are used alternately or concurrently, the possibility of price collusion can be difficult to eliminate. In some situations there may be only one feasible supplier – referred to as a *sole supplier* – and in other cases the use of multiple sources can involve inconvenient compromises.

The advantages of single and multiple sourcing are summarized in Table 2.4 (see also Segal, 1989; Heinritz *et al.*, 1991) and an example of some of the issues involved is given in Mini-case 13.

Table 2.4 Single vs. multiple sourcing

Single sourcing advantages	Multiple sourcing advantages
One relationship to manage	Insurance (against disrupted supply)
Scheduling simplicity	Avoids supplier dependence
Easier supplier training	Optimizes any spare capacity amongst suppliers
Clearer responsibilities	Bargaining leverage (to maintain low prices)
More leverage over supplier	Not limited by capacity of a single supplier
Simpler monitoring arrangements	Greater prompt to innovation
Scale economies	Access to more supplier data
Possible transportation economies	Greater access to indirect competitive insights
Frequent deliveries more practicable	Stimulus to competition
Cheaper tooling costs	Easier to engage a fresh supplier
Greater sense of commitment	Limits potential for monopoly abuse

2.7.3 International sourcing

Full consideration of supplier alternatives should extend to international suppliers rather than limiting choice to the restricted pool of national suppliers. This is increasingly necessary as deregulation encourages competitive search and globalization increases the expectation of international sourcing. International sourcing raises a number of issues for organizational marketing which are briefly listed in Exhibit 2.7. Further discussion of these issues is more appropriately located in a broader analysis of international marketing issues, but readers might look at Birou and Fawcett (1993) for a short introduction.

Recognition of the practical limitations of multiple sourcing may have encouraged organizations to consider single and sole source arrangements less cynically, especially given the important benefits available in collaborative customer–supplier relationships. There are also many benefits associated with collaboration between suppliers and customers (Littler and Wilson, 1991) which have encouraged organizations to think in terms of *partnership sourcing* (Han *et al.*, 1993). Some

---

EXHIBIT 2.7

International sourcing – benefits and costs

The **benefits** of international sourcing may include:

- cost savings from suppliers with less expensive factors of production (labour, raw materials, energy, finance costs) benefiting from government subsidics;
- improved access to local overseas markets through increased local knowledge, increased ability to respond to local requirements for minimum national content, and demonstrable local commitment and investment;
- improved cost control by reducing commitment to one currency and economic scenario.

The **costs** of international sourcing may include:

- reduced control (e.g. geographical and 'psychic' distance; foreign restriction on external control);
- management complexity, administrative inconvenience and difficulty of communication over extended distances and across unfamiliar cultures;
- risk (political, economic, fiscal, legal, social, financial, cultural);
- increased costs (transport, currency conversion or hedging, insurance, intermediaries);
- lagged time response which can be significant in the event of sudden shortfall of supply or increase in demand.

> In deciding whether to engage in international sourcing a customer is likely to consider such aspects as:
> - level of commoditization of the contracted goods (commoditization emphasizes cost factors in the purchase decision since this reduces technical product differences);
> - phase of the product life cycle of the customer's end-product (mature products are generally more sensitive to cost factors);
> - the customer's competitive situation (intense competition is more likely to focus on cost factors);
> - consumer perception and reaction to foreign sources (e.g. compare consumer reactions to Cape fruit, Israeli oranges, Taiwanese electronics, East European cars, US soap operas, etc. – and how these reactions change over time).

of the many issues for organizational marketing which surround collaboration are discussed further in Chapter 4.

2.8   MANAGERIAL IMPLICATIONS OF ORGANIZATIONAL BUYING BEHAVIOUR

The discussion above raises some additional implications both for organizational customers and for their suppliers. Organizational marketing managers can benefit from greater insight to the implications of buyer behaviour for customers, and in some cases supplier–customer relationships can be strengthened (and switching costs raised) to mutual competitive advantage through shared involvement in the management of these implications. So, given the interdependence of organizational purchasing and organizational marketing, it is difficult and probably unrealistic to separate the implications of organizational buyer behaviour for customers and for suppliers, though a difference in emphasis is clear in most cases.

2.8.1 Implications for organizational customers

In organizational marketing it is not always clear what issues are the responsibility of marketing as opposed to related functional areas such as production – nor is it generally sensible to demarcate issues in this way given the interdependence of functional contributions to most organizational tasks. Evidently, purchasing decisions can have significant implications for the operations of functions overlapping with marketing responsibilities and the responsibilities of marketing for representing the organization as a whole to external agencies such as customers and suppliers seems to require brief mention of some of the issues involved.

Collaborative approaches to purchasing may enable a broader and more integrated approach to **quality control** (Morgan and Piercy,

1992). For example, quality might be controlled further up the supply chain which may be less costly and more efficient than addressing quality problems at later stages. Addressing quality earlier also allows more time to redress quality problems before impacting production systems. Delivery schedules, quantities and lead times are important issues for **inventory management** and **materials handling**, especially with international sourcing where the cost of transport and insurance may require some local repacking to meet the needs of **production** flows. Other important aspects in distribution are the format, frequency, unit size and even physical orientation of deliveries which may be crucial especially for JIT systems (O'Neal, 1989; Harrison, 1992; Dion *et al.*, 1992).

It will be crucial for **management accounting** purposes to maintain detailed audit systems with respect to stocks of goods, work-in-progress and assets whether in the factory, in the distribution chain, or at the premises of contracted suppliers; this is partly why electronic monitoring systems such as barcoding and EDI (electronic data interchange) are becoming increasingly important in organizational marketing. Account must also be taken of rectification costs, scrap and obsolescence including attribution of responsibility between supplier and customer. In sophisticated management accounting systems, variance analysis and accounting trails may extend to distant suppliers, as may pursuit of unaccountable invoices and payments.

Key issues with respect to **production** include level of safety stocks, timeliness and predictability of deliveries, quality and durability of received goods and services, continuity of supply, and flexibility of suppliers to respond to unplanned fluctuations in production schedules.

Finally, to achieve the potential benefits of integrated **information systems** between suppliers and customers (e.g. speed and flexibility of response, tracking orders and invoices), it is likely to be important that information and communication technology (ICT) systems are compatible both externally between suppliers and customers, and internally between functional departments. Examples of areas in which the potential benefits of integrated ICT systems can be significant include: statistical process control, computer tracking of materials and tools consumption, automated warehousing, automatic reordering, computerized goods receiving, purchasing authorization, invoicing, accounting, product design, production engineering, service and support systems. All of these areas have implications for more effective and efficient relationships between organizational suppliers and their customers, and they also emphasize the role of other functional departments beyond marketing in the development of these supplier–customer relationships.

By now it should be apparent that suppliers with competent organizational marketing strategies have much to contribute to the competitiveness of their customers. The logical extension of this is that customers – more specifically, purchasing managers – should proactively seek out suppliers that fit their requirements, not only in terms of the goods and services offered but also in terms of the marketing skills and relationship management skills they demonstrate. This proactive approach to purchasing has been labelled 'reverse marketing' and has emerged as an important constituent of contemporary competitive marketing through such central issues as partnership sourcing, total quality management, supply chain management and relationship marketing (Leenders and Blenkhorn, 1988; Blenkhorn and Banting, 1991; Biemans and Brand, 1995).

2.8.2 Implications for organizational suppliers

Obviously, it is important for marketing managers to be aware of the implications of buyer behaviour and different purchasing strategies for their customers and in this sense all the above implications for customers are also implications for suppliers, especially, perhaps, the issue of reverse marketing (Biemans and Brand, 1995). In addition there are a number of more direct implications for suppliers which for convenience are summarized in Exhibit 2.8.

EXHIBIT 2.8

Implications of organizational buying behaviour – for suppliers

- Manage the product development process proactively (not through ad hoc response to powerful customers)
- Involve all relevant departments in marketing issues
- Monitor markets developments and competitors carefully (not just customer developments)
- Use a wide range of internal and external information sources
- Be willing to negotiate non-standard arrangements for customers
- Manage sales accounts as collaborative relationships wherever possible
- Structure business more closely around customers (as opposed, for example, to regions or product groups)
- Involve key customers in product development processes
- Develop customers' perception of *supplier quality* (especially through consultation)
- Develop a more integrated (team approach) to selling which may involve more than just your marketing and sales personnel
- Appoint *relationship managers* for key customer accounts and nominate single points of contact for most relationships

- Sell on a portfolio of issues (especially technology, service, quality, flexibility – not just on price)
- Reduce dependence on independent third-party distributors or develop closer relations (i.e. increase their dependence)
- Improve awareness of foreign firms and markets where these may constitute competitive opportunities or threats
- Reduce costs (e.g. in high stocks, obsolescence, scrap, returns, rectification, administration, untargeted promotions)
- Build switching costs through customer satisfaction (Tanner, 1996; Mohr, 1998)
- Ensure your own organizational purchasing involves all relevant functional departments
- *Above all else – focus on customer requirements*

Once they have recognized the full significance of purchasing, most organizations begin to establish norms of behaviour and standard procedures for purchasing, often in a written set of guidelines and pro forma documentation which, for example, ensure that the appropriate number of estimates and quotations are secured and that the necessary approvals are obtained. While this is a necessary step it can also result in complacency because it bureaucratizes the criteria of assessment and may allow impatient, determined or unethical individuals to attempt to 'manage the system'. For example, managers might seek to guarantee the success of their preferred supplier by ensuring that rival bids are excessively costly or over-specified. There is also, inevitably, a temptation for prospective suppliers to collude in such practices and so close scrutiny and frequent review of purchasing procedures are essential to their effective operation (Turner, Taylor and Hartley, 1994).

2.9 CONCLUSION

Organizational buying behaviour and the purchasing process dominated the early research into marketing between organizations and for good reason since it is the exchange itself that should be the starting point for studies of marketing. While this research has produced many insights there is still no unified model of organizational buyer behaviour and the complexities and diversity of the dynamics involved suggest that no such model is possible, or perhaps even desirable. The most comprehensive models and explanations are, inevitably, the most generalized and conceptual while the more specific models are rarely applicable beyond the industries from which they were derived. Astute marketing managers will take what they find appropriate from a variety of studies (including some studies of consumer buyer behaviour) and will ensure they have some awareness also of the many additional issues faced by purchasing managers, including alternative sourcing strategies. It is also important to remain critical and independent when seeking practical input from these studies as few, if any, would claim to be prescriptive. Finally, do not forget (not that a real marketing manager ever could) the satisficing effect of importunate superiors, overloaded in-trays and personal fatigue on the rationality of decision making. Many of the problems faced by purchasing managers in the real world can be seen as providing incipient opportunities for enterprising marketing managers.

3 *Marketing management in organizational markets*

A good understanding of how and why customers buy is, of course, the fundamental starting point for effective marketing whether in consumer or organizational markets. The previous chapter argued that organizational buying behaviour can vary considerably according to many variables but that some common threads could be identified. The chapter also showed that the identification of who actually is the customer can be surprisingly problematic but it is crucial to appreciate that organizational goods and services are marketed not to anonymous homogenous organizations but by individuals, to individuals, often many individuals, within those organizations.

Building on these fundamentals we now turn to marketing management – the marketing plans, policies and practices which are developed to encourage organizational buyer behaviour. The discussion is structured in line with the traditional elements of the marketing mix, extended to include several more contemporary preoccupations such as branding and societal marketing, and concluding with a closer look at the implications of recent developments in IT for marketing management in organizational markets. It is assumed that readers will be broadly familiar with the basics of the marketing mix as there is insufficient space here to revisit the fundamentals. Readers should also bear in mind that their initial introduction to the marketing mix was very probably conducted in the implicit context of consumer markets and the focus adopted here on organizational marketing may require some readjustment of perspective.

First we consider issues surrounding products and services for organizational markets.

3.1 PRODUCT/SERVICE ISSUES

It is frequently argued that the technical specification of organizational products and services is not only complex but also crucial to the operations of the customer, much more so than would generally be the case for most consumer products. For many examples of organizational products this is a reasonable assertion. Achievement of products and services which match the requirements of the organizational customer may involve extensive consultation between technical and marketing staff on both sides, and seems likely to depend, at least to some extent, on a spirit of collaborative partnership – where both sides gain from 'getting it right'. The same argument supports a partnership approach to issues of quality, reliability, design, delivery, packaging, maintenance and product development.

This pattern is not as obvious in consumer markets though there is an increasing number of exceptions on closer inspection. For example, many service-based consumer offerings (educational, legal, medical, financial, travel services) are tailored to specific customer circumstances while there is increasing opportunity to specify major consumer product purchases such as cars and homes. Similarly, while it makes obvious sense to involve the purchasing functions of key organizational customers in product development processes (Williams and Smith, 1990), in consumer markets the role of 'key' customers tends to be taken by carefully selected representative samples (e.g. in focus groups, surveys, test marketing) in what amounts, nevertheless, to a broadly similar process of iterative product development.

However, it would be a mistake to assume that all, or even most, organizational goods and services have to be so precisely specified, especially given the economic cost of uniquely configured orders. In many cases, close alternatives will suffice or the customer finds that their initial requirements can be adjusted fairly readily to conform to existing market offerings. It is generally only with very large orders, or where the purchase has vital implications for other major processes, that customization becomes economic and even then there may be significant knock-on adaptation costs for the customer. An example of adaptation and compromise over technical specification is given in Mini-case 4 which also illustrates the benefits of collaboration between customer and supplier over product development, and the difficulty sometimes of distinguishing unambiguously between organizational and consumer markets.

While the specification of products and services is an important issue, it is the processual aspect of the issue – product development – that has attracted most scholarly attention. It might even be argued that product development falls largely within the penumbra of organizational marketing, rather than of consumer marketing, since there are few examples of consumer products that could be developed and marketed without the prior involvement of other organizations, especially suppliers and channel agencies. Certainly, the vast majority of product development studies have findings or implications of relevance for organizational marketing though space prevents more than a selective and superficial discussion here.

Most discussions of product or service development in the specific context of organizational markets tend to focus on the large-scale or exceptional situations which offer rich insights to the processes involved by illustrating them in their fullest form. However, by definition such examples are not typical of product development more broadly. Most development is incremental (e.g. product improvements and line extensions) rather than concerned with the generation of *new* products. Indeed, many developments seen as 'new' by those involved, from a customer's perspective may seem only marginally different from previous or rival offerings. This is perhaps not surprising, given the risks of genuinely innovative products and the need for rapid progress through the development phases and into commercialization (Beard and Easingwood, 1996), customer acceptance and profit contribution (McKenna, 1995). It is also worth bearing in mind that important developments can be achieved in production processes, logistics aspects and associated management systems which can have crucial implications for products and services – for example in reducing costs (with implications for price and/or profit contribution) or augmenting quality. Product development is, of course, about developing and improving both the product/service itself and the systems through which it is generated and delivered. So it is important to bear in mind that many – though certainly not all – of the recommendations of product development studies (e.g. the need for wide and early participation, the need for rigorous examination of commercial prospects, the need for extensive market research, the importance of consultation with key customers, the need for senior management support) apply more to the context of 'major' product development processes than to the far more common context of relatively minor incremental and processual developments (Olson, Walker and Ruekert, 1995).

Nevertheless, while product development in organizational markets can be hazardous and costly (Mansfield and Rapoport, 1975), it is widely accepted as crucial to organizational competitiveness even if there remains considerable difficulty in deciding how to measure the 'success' of such products (financial measures are not enough – Cooper and Kleinschmidt, 1995) and what distinguishes the management of successful new products from those that fail (Hart, 1993; Cooper, 1996).

Extensive research into the factors apparently affecting successful new product development in organizational markets suggests that this may depend crucially on matching product development with customer requirements rather than responding primarily to technological possibilities (Cooper, 1975, 1980, 1984). Further criteria highlighted in this research include the role of entrepreneurs, team leaders and product 'champions' (Barczak and Wilemon, 1992), the importance of using information from outside the organization, efficient management of the product development process (i.e. with rigorous monitoring procedures in a parallel rather than serial progression of iterative stages and decision 'gates'), clear and frequent communication between technical and marketing departments (Cooper, 1975), and the availability of adequate funding (Cooper and Kleinschmidt, 1988).

The IMP research (Ford, 1997) has shown that long-term stability in relationships between suppliers and customers can encourage product innovation because of the enlarged pool of expertise and experience available to the product development process. The research suggests that innovative development and diffusion are a seamless process of iterative stimulus which continues throughout the life of a product. This process is particularly dependent on the closeness of relationships between suppliers and pioneering customers in the early stages of the product's development when information concerning actual and potential use is fed back into the supplier's design and production systems (Håkansson, 1987; Parkinson, 1982). Naturally, one also has to take measures to maintain the stimulus of new perspectives and fresh insight which can otherwise become smothered by comfortable long-established relationships.

3.2 LOGISTICS ISSUES

Logistics embraces both the outgoing flow of goods and services generated by an organization, and the incoming flow – even including, some would argue logically, the flow within the organization itself. Figure 3.1 gives a highly simplified illustration of these multiple logistics flows to show what this can mean.

It is not surprising then that 'logistics', like purchasing, is a territory claimed by several branches of management study. In the late 1980s and 1990s, logistics, often under the title of *supply chain management*, has become a field of extensive research focusing on the benefits of total quality management (Oakland, 1995; Carter and Narasimhan, 1994), lean supply (where inventory of all sorts is minimized) (Jones and Ridley, 1987; Womack *et al.*, 1990), collaboration with suppliers and customers (Matthyssens and Van den Bulte, 1994), just-in-time (JIT) production methods (Frazier, Spekman and O'Neal, 1988), the increasing trend towards globalized flows of goods and services (Monczka and Trent, 1992), and the effect on all these of contemporary developments in IT (Bondra and Davis, 1996; Fletcher, 1995).

Given the widespread discussion of the merits of lean supply and low inventory strategies (for example in the popularity of JIT strategies) it is easy to overlook the benefits offered by holding inventory. Exhibit 3.1 provides a convenient summary of the main benefits and helps to correct any mistaken impression readers may have developed that inventory is somehow a thing of the past. For the vast majority of manufacturing and retailing organizations, inventory (at whatever level) is a vital aspect of their operations and suppliers cannot afford to ignore the inventory management strategies of their customers.

Some of these aspects are discussed further in later chapters. At this

Figure 3.1 Purchasing, production, sales and distribution flows in the motor vehicle industry

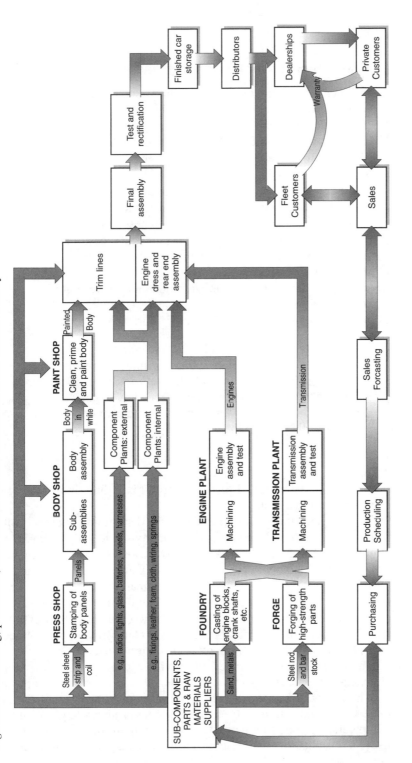

[Source: author]

EXHIBIT 3.1

Fifteen reasons for holding high levels of inventory

- To ensure continuous (and credible) customer service
- To allow for sudden promotions or price cuts
- To respond promptly to sudden large orders
- To cope with (and enable) production variations
- To manufacture according to EBQs (economic batch quantities)
- To enable flexible procurement scheduling
- To delay investment in further production capacity
- To develop scale economies in distribution
- To maintain storage facilities (e.g. pipes, tanks)
- To reduce dependence on forecasting and measurement
- To protect against labour disruption
- To protect against 'acts of God'
- To protect against variance in production factor costs
- To maintain control over pricing and supply
- To speculate against prospects of future gain

[Source: Gross, A.C. *et al.*, (1993), *Business Marketing*, Houghton Mifflin, Boston, p. 508. Reprinted by permission of *Harvard Business Review*. An Exhibit. From 'Questions for solving the inventory problem' by James I. Morgan, July/August 1968, p. 98. Copyright ©1963 by the President and Fellows of Harvard College; all rights reserved.]

point attention is restricted to a few issues more directly impacting on organizational marketing.

Some organizations undertake their own distribution but this is often a specialist function. Managers are often advised to keep operations as simple as possible, to focus only on those aspects where the organization can add significant value (Porter, 1985), and to recognize the limitations of their expertise (Peters and Waterman, 1982). Even vertically integrated retailer/manufacturers, such as Laura Ashley was in the 1980s, may subcontract many aspects of distribution management to specialists, for example in transport or warehouse management, possibly even extending to franchising of the retail operation as Benetton does.

The potential benefits of using specialist intermediary distribution channels are extensive – including reduced administrative complexity, less inventory, lower transaction costs and operational simplicity. Yet there can be exceptions. For example, some products (e.g. mainframe computers, air conditioning systems) may require manufacturer expertise for installation, while some customers may prefer an exclusive relationship with the manufacturer, especially where quality control is a key issue.

Clearly then, intermediaries are a necessary part of distribution for many organizations and ignoring them risks undermining the effectiveness of marketing strategies. While this is stating the obvious, it is easy to forget intermediaries in the pressure of more immediate internal priorities (Magrath, 1990) or to blame them for marketing failures. A cooperative and integrated approach to channel management and development is generally sensible (Gentry, 1993; Kistner *et al.*, 1994).

Where intermediary channels are used there may be a need for investment by the supplier in the distributor – or vice versa – (e.g. in ICT systems, training, shared marketing costs, specialized assets, dedicated tooling, loan facilities to ease cash flow fluctuations) though this can become a sensitive area (e.g. in disputed ownership of assets) (Watts and Hahn, 1993; Krause, 1997). Equally there may be opportunities for the distributor to feed information – perhaps on competitors, technologies, market trends and customer requirements – to the supplier. In short, distribution relationships can be managed collaboratively to the mutual advantage of both parties. For example, ICL recognizes this potential distribution synergy in a vendor accreditation scheme whereby investments such as those listed above are offered to those distributors prepared to accept ICL's high standards in value-added-resellers (Sasseen, 1992).

Despite the availability of specialists, many organizations prefer to manage their own logistics responsibilities. Most large organizations are developing an increasingly complex mix of marketing channels which go well beyond the traditional field sales force with specialist teams for major accounts, to include telemarketing, database marketing, direct mail, Internet sales, automatic ordering through EDI, together with a network of distributors, dealers, value-added-resellers and even retailers where appropriate. Some organizations are even acting as retailers in their own right (e.g. through 'factory shops' and mail order brochures). The potential for confusion as well as for synergies from this variety is clear, as Moriarty and Moran (1990) have pointed out, and they stress the need for hybrid marketing systems which make use of multiple channel strategies. Since the electronic channels are obviously not limited to large organizations it is presumably only a matter of time before smaller organizations begin to make more extensive use of these too; many are already proving more adept and innovative in their use of Internet selling methods (Samli, Wills and Herbig, 1997) and some large customers are demanding that all suppliers use EDI as a condition of business (Reekers and Smithson, 1996).

There is a tendency for textbook discussions of logistics to give an artificially simplified picture of logistics systems whereas the reality is usually a highly complex situation about which even those involved may have no clear or unanimous view despite apparently being in control of most of the relevant key variables. This is conveniently illustrated by Mini-case 5 which also gives some insight to the complexities of incoming logistics and associated internal systems (even before the use of electronic channels).

Finally, logistics is a huge and complex area where it is easy to overlook particular elements, such as packaging, in the sweep of more generalized discussions. So a brief illustration is provided in Mini-case 6 to remind the reader that detail is not only important in its own right for those charged with management responsibilities, but also crucial as the building blocks of strategic issues.

3.3 COMMUNICATIONS ISSUES

Organizational marketing tends to involve more direct methods of communication than consumer marketing where indirect mass media channels are used more often. This is because of the lower number of customers, the greater importance of person-to-person relationships, and the typically far larger size of individual orders in organizational marketing. With smaller and more tightly defined market segments, it is simply inefficient and wasteful, as a rule, to invest in mass media methods for organizational goods and services. Probably the most effective form of direct personal communication is through the field sales force which is discussed later; here the focus is more on preliminary and broader forms of marketing communication.

There are some obvious exceptions to the general disinclination of organizations to use mass media channels. For example, where the organization is seeking to develop a wider public perception of its strengths or contribution to society – reinforcing brand strengths or stressing societal contributions (e.g. both ICL and BP use TV advertising in this way in the UK though they are primarily industrial product manufacturers). Mass media such as newspapers and regional TV or radio may also be effective where the targeted organizational customers are relatively plentiful (e.g. small businesses in industrial areas; agricultural businesses in non-metropolitan Australia) or the offerings are generic in nature (e.g. office stationery) or where the customers share a tightly defined geographic location (e.g. the tendency for similar businesses to congregate as in science parks or in silicon 'valleys/glens'). It may also be the case that the relative lack of use of mass media is partly rooted in cultural differences since casual observation suggests that there seems to be somewhat greater use of mass media TV channels by organizational marketers in France, for example, than in the UK. Finally, as the cost of using electronic communication channels falls and their reliability and sophistication increase, it becomes increasingly sensible to invest in ways to use these novel channels effectively to communicate with customers (e.g. via the Internet), suppliers (e.g. via EDI), and even internally (e.g. via an intranet).

More typical perhaps is the use of print advertising, though organizational use of this medium has perhaps been more conservative and generally less elaborate than in many (though certainly not all) consumer markets and there seems scope for improvement in the quality and effectiveness of this means of communication (Clark, Kaminski and Brown, 1990), especially perhaps with respect to the print copy and style used by smaller organizations. The historically sexist nature of print advertising in industrial (especially manufacturing) markets seems somewhat on the decline though still inclined to portray women in subordinate, inferior, supportive or inappropriately sexual roles (Reese, Whipple and Courtney, 1987) – possibly reflecting the persistent male domination of the industrial purchasing function and equally persistent assumptions about how best to communicate with them.

For many organizations, especially perhaps in more conservative sectors, the preferred means of communication still seem to be personalized mail shots and, as appropriate, meetings with sales representatives. However, since purchase decisions can often be a collective responsibility it may be necessary to approach several individuals within each customer organization. On the other hand, once established as an approved supplier, the priorities shift from creating new relationships to the longer-term perspective of maintaining and developing relationships.

Thus suppliers' communications strategies fall into two broad categories relating to the degree of routine associated with the purchase. The switching costs of many rebuy situations and the insulating effect of evolving relationships between established suppliers and customers encourage suppliers to take the view that rebuy decisions may require less attention than new-task situations. Inevitably, this can also make rebuy situations vulnerable to competitors seeking to break into a complacent supplier–customer relationship. Nevertheless, the focus of suppliers' communications strategies seems to be on new-task purchasing and winning new accounts.

Generating interest in organizational markets can involve any of the channels associated with consumer markets though more targeted methods are generally used such as specialist publications (e.g. professional yearbooks and society membership listings, industry and technical magazines), trade shows and exhibitions such as the Frankfurt Book Fair, and technical or professional conferences (e.g. to launch new pharmaceutical products). Once leads have been generated, other issues can become very important such as the reputation of the supplier, recommendations or endorsements, and access to reference sites. Despite persistent recommendations in the literature, Tanner and Chonko (1995) found that organizations still use trade shows less often and less effectively than they might. Possible reasons might include pressure of other priorities, the disruptive need to involve senior managers if the full benefits of PR are to be achieved, lack of imagination concerning the potential for securing competitive intelligence (Sharland and

Balogh, 1996), and unwillingness to invest in the set-up costs (training, presentational facilities, time, expenses) (Williams *et al.*, 1993) and development costs involved (discounted offerings to encourage trialling, prospect data management, time to focus on follow-up).

With developments in IT several relatively new methods of communication are becoming increasingly used within organizational markets and established methods are becoming potentially more integrated and effective (Schultz, 1996). Large organizations have found the company newsletter – often a glossy magazine – to be an especially useful means of communication with external customers, potential customers or influential stakeholders (Vredenburg and Droge, 1987). Newsletters of this sort can now be produced internally with desktop publishing systems even by small organizations or those with limited resources (e.g. schools, charities). Other organizations are beginning to experiment with marketing communications based on using the Internet, where the difficulty of targeting specific customer groups is offset to some extent by the low costs involved.

Finally, some fresh approaches to marketing communications are emerging as researchers integrate the more sophisticated understanding of buyer behaviour and relationships which is emerging to the context of how members of the buying centre respond to different forms of communication (Gilliland and Johnston, 1997). However, it seems unlikely that any amount of electronic wizardry could challenge the force of the personal, informal, word-of-mouth recommendation or condemnation which has long been recognized as so influential both in consumer and organizational markets (Webster, 1970).

3.4 BRANDING ISSUES

While branding is well established as a research topic in consumer markets it is relatively unexplored in organizational markets (Egan, Shipley and Howard, 1992). Explanations of why organizational customers persistently favour one source over another when the offerings are virtually indistinguishable have tended to focus on buyer behaviour issues such as habit, entrenched processes, interpersonal relationships and switching costs (Hague and Jackson, 1994). While these are undoubtedly important factors, it is equally important to recognize the effect of a strong brand in competing against generic rivals. The combination of attention to customer relationships reinforced by personal interactions, responsiveness to customers, and a brand strengthened by appropriate investments can sustain significant price premiums even in commodity markets (Sinclair and Seward, 1988; Mudambi, Doyle and Wong, 1997).

Ideally, the effect of a strong brand is to reduce perceived risk, enhance anticipated satisfaction levels, provide quality assurances, guarantee post-purchase support services, and facilitate follow-on purchasing. In organizational markets – probably more so than in consumer markets – these risk reduction factors are often more influential than small pricing differences so there will often be scope to recoup the cost of investing in branding.

Differences in the motivation of buyer behaviour between consumer and organizational markets also raise implications for the design of brand names and of their associated attributes – there seems little reason to assume that the brand attributes that appeal to a consumer would be equally attractive to an organizational customer. For example, corporate-level branding seems often less important to consumers than product-level branding and this can be seen in label design and media advertising, while for organizational customers the reverse is probably true and corporate branding together with corporate reputation (the two are synergistic) can be more influential than sales presentations (Mudambi, Doyle and Wong, 1997). Probably the clearest example of this is the enormous value of the IBM brand in the 1960s and 1970s when it was commonly – and ruefully – acknowledged by IBM's rivals that many purchasers of computing systems chose IBM because 'nobody ever got fired for buying IBM . . .'.

It is self-evident that branding is already widely used (if not always effectively) for products in organizational markets, especially by larger organizations (Shipley and Howard, 1993); and since most markets seem to be increasingly competitive, with consequent erosion of product differentiation and shorter product life cycles, it seems reasonable to conclude that branding issues will become more important and will attract more research attention and consultancy specialization in the future. As Mudambi *et al.* conclude: 'The potential power of industrial brands is great, but remains largely unexplained and untapped' (Mudambi, Doyle and Wong, 1997, p. 445).

3.5 PRICING ISSUES

Pricing is usually a complex issue in marketing but especially so in organizational markets because of the need to agree not only a price for the particular contract – whether formal or informal – in question but also to agree a pricing structure and associated rules capable of application over the expected life of the product stream initiated by the particular contract. Obviously, prices can be adjusted, even radically adjusted, after the initial contract but unless this is done broadly in line with the initial agreement, it will constitute, to a greater or lesser extent, a failure of the original pricing agreement.

From the customer perspective this will mean negotiating an appropriate variable pricing structure to reflect the unique balance of supply/demand objectives in a particular exchange, while taking into account that neither side may know exactly how much of the stream will be consumed by the customer or in what volume at different stages in the relationship. From the supplier's perspective the pricing judgement will be affected also by awareness that the initial components of the product stream may be of greater or lesser significance – possibly even 'loss leaders' – compared to the possible future volume of associated goods and services consumed by the customer, or by other similar organizations, over the life of the relationship. The supplier will also be aware of the need to cover costs, generate profit, fund product development, and avoid setting precedents that may irritate other customers or deter potential prospects. In addition, all parties to the exchange (and there may well be more than two parties involved) will prefer to optimize pricing in line with their conflicting interests of profit maximization and cost reduction, to the extent that the balance of power between them allows.

Obviously, there are some one-off purchases where further relationships between customer and supplier are not anticipated (e.g. some specialist consultancy services such as counter-espionage or acquisition defence) or are unlikely to be influenced significantly by the previous purchase history (e.g. monopolist suppliers). But these situations are rare and the vast majority of purchases are of the sort which involve a relationship, though the significance of the relationship in the strategic priorities of either party can, of course, vary considerably. This relationship factor is rarely significant in pricing decisions for consumer markets where the typically much greater number of anticipated customers and the absence of relationship factors tend to result in a more precise, less flexible approach to pricing where market research data can be much more influential.

Market research data is, of course, important in organizational pricing decisions too but rather less so than in consumer markets. In organizational markets official prices (or 'list' prices) are often easily available and some rivals even routinely circulate their list prices, but the all-important discount structures are more difficult to acquire and the details of specific negotiated price agreements tend to be highly confidential (Blois, 1994). So market research for pricing is limited in scope, at least with respect to formal research – informal sources can provide rich information but this depends largely on the strength of the relationships through which the informal information is communicated.

Evidently, then, price negotiation is not simply a matter of arithmetic – it is dependent on judgement, forecasting, strategic perception, negotiation and relationships. But even the arithmetic can be problematic. In general terms, there are two fundamental approaches to the arithmetic of price calculation: cost-based pricing and market-based pricing (Morris and Joyce, 1988). Each has its problems in the real world.

As readers will recall from basic marketing principles, cost-based pricing assumes that it is possible to calculate all the fixed and variable costs specifically incurred in the production of a particular good or service (including distribution, marketing, and contribution to shared overheads). To this one adds the appropriate profit margin and this provides the price which is then adjusted according to market circumstances such as rival prices, exchange rate variance and the need to entice a customer through temporary discounts. There are obvious difficulties here in that, for example, variable costs depend crucially on production volume which in turn depends, to some extent, on market demand which is heavily affected by price. And it is clear that what constitutes 'appropriate profit' will always be an area for dispute (Connor and Hopkins, 1997). But there are less obvious problems also in that some production processes do not readily lend themselves to cost estimation. It surprises many students – but few with production line experience – that manufacturers may not be able to tell precisely how much it costs to make a product. Mini-case 7a provides an illustration of this problem, showing that this is not just a matter of how exactly to allocate shared costs such as capital investment and maintenance, labour, wastage, theft, etc., nor is it to do simply with covering the costs of corporate headquarters or brand investments or the sales force car fleet, it is also that the complexity of the paperwork can overwhelm the resources, patience and skill of the staff and it becomes too expensive or 'hassle-laden' to find out exact costs. In addition, genuinely innovative products at the start of their life cycle will offer little historic guidance as to projected cost data at different production volumes. The increasing use of computers is easing this problem to some extent but there remains in many organizations an absurd contradiction between calculations of standard labour down to fractions of a second alongside fudged guestimates of materials consumption at speculative future production levels.

In contrast, market-based pricing, or 'going-rate' pricing, seems to duck the issue of cost-allocation and therefore risks proving unprofitable. This approach to pricing also assumes that there are similar offerings in the market against which the 'going-rate' can be determined. This rather undermines the claims of the product to competitive differentiation and unique selling points. Even given the availability of a suitably comparable rival offering, differences in production volume, sourcing deals, profit expectations and strategic priorities make it very difficult to draw any conclusions for what is the appropriate price in a different manufacturing context. In short, strict adherence to market-based pricing can result in following rivals' strategies without the benefit of their strategic position. An example of this sort of decision is given in Mini-case 7b, providing a useful contrast to Mini-case 7a.

An alternative to either the cost-based or market-based approach is simply to haggle until you get the best deal possible on each occasion. There is a superficial logic to this in that it seems, by definition, to offer the highest available price and anticipates a similar self-interested behaviour from customers. Aggressive negotiation over price and terms may result in reduced costs for customers or higher profits for suppliers in the short term but again the real world is not as simple as this (Coe, 1990). For example, suppliers have many ways in which they can disguise costs at the tender stage only to reintroduce these costs later (see Mini-cases 2 and 9), just as customers have methods of recouping costs through rectification charges and parallel quotations from rival suppliers. Some of these realities of uncooperative supplier–customer relationships are well illustrated in Womack *et al.*'s (1990) famous analysis of the automobile manufacturing industry in the USA from which the material in Mini-case 8 is drawn.

In the absence of the sort of problems and irritations described in Mini-case 8, the supplier's increasing experience of the customer coupled with the effect of purchasing switching costs should act in favour of the established supplier. With this in mind, effective purchasing can be more to do with 'mutual satisfaction' than with price (Reichard, 1985). As the example of the hospital purchases suggests (see Mini-case

---

EXHIBIT 3.2

Some issues affecting pricing in organizational markets

Product/Service issues
- Degree of customization involved
- Customer's role in product development
- Service and support requirements
- Standards of quality and reliability stipulated
- Delivery arrangements (volume, timing, frequency)
- Packaging (form, configuration, special handling)
- *Solution* selling (integrated package of offerings)

Payment issues
- Volume (discount, need for specialized assets)
- Price discrimination (e.g. between different customers)
- Contract terms (e.g. cost+, fixed cost, rented access)
- Payment arrangements (credit, returns, counter-trade)

Process issues
- Negotiation process (role of people, professionalism)
- Mutual dependence (switching costs, reference sites)
- Competitive tendering (tender costs, future purchases)

Competitive issues
- Non-price competition (degree of value-added, availability of alternatives)

11), price may be less important in major purchases (within limitations, of course).

The issue of price in effective purchasing can also have important economic implications for the customer beyond the obvious depletion of financial resources (e.g. some prices may trigger make-or-buy decisions) and strategic implications for new business. For example, price can sometimes be discounted in order to secure prestigious suppliers (e.g. best-selling authors for publishers; well-known banks underwriting business ventures) or prestigious customers (e.g. Marks and Spencer; Rolls Royce; by 'royal appointment'), in anticipation that further suppliers or customers may be won on the strength of such credentials.

Obviously, pricing is not equally important in all purchasing situations. Logic would suggest that pricing issues are less complex in rebuy situations than in new-task purchasing because in rebuys fewer variables are involved and there are many more precedents and established relationships to ease negotiation. To understand the role of price in new-task buying situations it may be helpful to consider 'price' in two stages; first as an approximate benchmark to prospective suppliers, allowing them to decide whether they wish to tender for what may still be a loosely specified product; and secondly as the *balancing factor* which guides a purchasing decision in the final stages when short-listed offerings are broadly comparable. In most buying situations pricing is negotiable to an extent and will depend on customer requirements with respect, for example, to arrangements for delivery, packaging and service. Some of the factors potentially involved in new-task pricing decisions are suggested in Exhibit 3.2, and many will be relevant to other buying situations also, depending on the circumstances prevailing.

Laric (1980) argues that pricing is becoming more important as an issue in organizational marketing and, certainly, pricing is rarely an irrelevant factor in purchasing. Nevertheless, the literature on buying behaviour has shown that, depending on the situation, there are often many more important issues than price in organizational markets (Kelly and Coaker, 1976; Laric, 1980). It is also probably the case that more cooperative and open pricing negotiations are becoming the norm, and the old aggressive paradigm of zero-sum haggling is fading, as more collaborative patterns of supplier–customer relationships are adopted (Dion and Banting, 1988). Chapter 4 deals with these developments in more detail. If collaboration does become more common then pricing is likely to become less contested and so less of an issue in supplier–customer negotiations, possibly even leading to new opportunities for cost reduction such as target costing (Newman and McKeller, 1995) and activity-based costing (Gagne and Discenza, 1992). But it seems probable that for a long time yet there will be many organizations and many individuals for whom those aggressive, machismo-laden disputes over 'the bottom line' will be second nature.

3.6 SELLING AND SALES FORCE MANAGEMENT ISSUES

Direct personal selling is the traditional sales strategy in organizational markets because there are relatively few customers, compared to consumer markets, each with typically high average order value. Furthermore, as individual customers can often have significantly differing requirements in product specifications or terms of delivery, flexibility is essential to effective selling, which implies a direct sales force with discretionary powers (Weitz, Sujan and Sujan, 1986). Thus organizational selling is largely a process of information and persuasion conducted between individuals (though surprisingly little is known about how this interaction works – Schmitz, 1995) rather than indirectly through communications media, useful though the latter can be on occasion.

As has been emphasized before, this may well be the situation with respect to large-scale or complex organizational purchases but there are very many more instances when purchasing will be relatively routine, with little need for protracted negotiation or technical analysis. On these simpler occasions the sales force will act more as order-takers, in fact many organizations have separate personnel (often trainee or junior sales staff) for this sort of transaction. Many purchases of this simple 'rebuy' nature are managed through paperwork, phone calls or electronic order systems. So increasingly, the resource-hungry sales force is deployed towards specialist situations such as new accounts, major key accounts, or negotiations requiring particular technical or professional skills.

Naturally, there are advantages in using 'the personal touch' even in routine sales situations. Personal interaction tends to reinforce and develop the all-important relationship between the individuals involved, building customer satisfaction and switching costs. The direct involvement of the salesperson can also be surprisingly fruitful, on occasion, in yielding competitive intelligence and customer information which may lead to market benefits – though some research has suggested that sales staff are not necessarily a reliable source for customer analysis (Sharma and Lambert, 1994). For example, it is not unknown for the friendships between sales representatives and their customers to result in privileged access to confidential information such as prior notice of potential sales opportunities, warning of initiatives by rival suppliers, or even sight of tenders by rivals. Such favours can also be enticed, even solicited, by insidious incentives – to the extent acceptable to the ethical self-restraints of the individuals and cultures involved (Pitt and Nel, 1988; Mitchell et al., 1994).

But it should not be forgotten that just as this personnel-intensive approach involves significant additional costs to the supplier (to be reflected in prices), the purchasing function also incurs unnecessary costs from conducting such routine transactions in person rather than through electronic or clerical means. An illustration of customer reaction to these issues is given in Mini-case 9.

Although things may be changing in the 1990s, especially with the development of IT, for many years organizational marketing has tended to involve extensive use of an expensive direct sales force staff and this has attracted considerable attention from researchers and practitioners – though with limited theoretical consensus. Wotruba (1980) describes how during the 1970s selling in organizational markets became an increasingly professional function with sales staff often providing much more than an order-taking and delivery service. This trend continued in the 1980s and is probably inevitable given the cost of direct selling strategies, the growing competitive pressure on cost reduction, the increasing professionalism of the purchasing function and the technical sophistication of organizational users, coupled with growing recognition of the potential of interactive selling and professional purchasing to contribute to the competitiveness of organizations (Dion and Banting, 1988; Hise and Reid, 1994).

Nevertheless, developments in information and communications technologies have made it possible to automate and expedite many aspects of sales administration, for example through EDI systems, telemarketing, and portable computers equipped with modems (Hise and Reid, 1994; Fletcher, 1995). With appropriate investment in equipment and training, sales staff are now increasingly able to undertake managerial responsibilities such as customer relationship management and product development liaison, and to provide additional services such as staff training, basic system maintenance and market information collection (Wotruba, 1980; Shapiro, 1988).

Biong and Selnes (1996) have pointed out the continuing strategic and tactical contribution that sales representatives can offer even when ordering has become a routine clerical operation and the supplier–customer relationship is well established on a long-term contractual basis. They argue that the salesperson can reinforce and develop the supplier's reputation for reliability and support services, help to resolve problems and conflicts, facilitate the mutual exchange of useful information and generally build up the personal relationships which can raise perceived switching costs (Biong and Selnes, 1996). With increasing awareness of the competitive importance of customer service (Kyj, 1987; Donaldson, 1995; Johnston and Hewa, 1997), the role of the salesperson in this respect is especially valuable.

What is less clear is whether the salesperson, as traditionally conceived, is the appropriate person for such tasks – highlighting the older question of what exactly is it that sales representatives do (Moncrief, 1986, 1988). The skills involved in relationship development are somewhat different and the traditional sales training less directly applicable, so it may be that a new role of *relationship facilitator* is what is required in established strategic relationships. This revised role could then draw on additional organizational resources (such as technical advice, quality arbitration, product development analysis, competitive analysis) as and when necessary in support of existing and potential customers.

This sort of shift in management expectations of an organization's sales force would also require significant adjustments to the motivation systems and incentives through which sales force strategies are largely implemented. For example, the allocation of sales commission might have to be extended to and negotiated with other functional areas within the organization (e.g. R&D, marketing planning, product design) and sales incentives would have to encourage team selling approaches. Sales force remuneration systems have always been recognized as a particularly sensitive aspect of sales force management (Piercy *et al.*, 1998) and these shifts could well exacerbate these sensitivities, making organizations reluctant to develop innovative sales force strategies without clear evidence of their benefits.

Given the mutually supportive trends of selling *customer solutions* rather than products, and preferring single source partnerships to multiple source supply arrangements, the role of the salesperson seems likely to become increasingly significant, and increasingly specialized, in organizational marketing. An illustration of this trend, and of its implications for sales force management, is given in Mini-case 10.

The development of more specialized sales forces is likely to be facilitated by the parallel development of semi-automated, IT-intensive arm's-length sales support facilities such as the *Mielbon Vite* (Mini-case 9) illustration described above, and a reassessment of the role and skills of the sales representative. For example, IBM has found it useful to build customer assessment of sales staff into their incentive scheme on the logical basis that customers are best placed to determine how effective sales staff are when it comes to aspects such as relationship development (Lambert, Sharma and Levy, 1997). It is worth noting that the motivational consequences of this form of remuneration could be unpredictable in relationships that prove less collaborative than expected.

Another interesting development which reflects many of these dynamics is the use of 'selling alliances' where sales representatives from allied organizations (e.g. suppliers of computer systems, applications software packages and training services) cooperate in joint approaches to potential customers (Smith and Barclay, 1997; Smith, 1997). This has long been established practice in major capital projects where tenders typically involve coalitions of suppliers but the practice is becoming increasingly used in smaller-scale, technically complex purchasing. Puri and Korgaonkar (1991) advocate similar team-based selling strategies for individual organizations using internal resources from different functional departments in a 'selling centre' (analogous to the purchaser's buying centre), and reassigning the sales representative to the tasks of coordination and relationship development. Yet again, this reveals the spread of collaborative approaches in organizational marketing.

3.7 MARKETING PLANNING ISSUES

The logical first step in assessment of organizational markets is market research and the logical outcome, among other things, would be segmentation of these markets as the foundation for marketing mix policies. Whether this is realistic, as opposed simply to being logical, is another issue but it does suggest that these two areas are important topics for further attention here, especially as both have attracted considerable research attention in recent years.

3.7.1 Market research

Market research for organizational markets is less advanced than that for consumer markets, as a brief glance at the size of the two literatures will suggest. The differences between the two types of market provide some superficial explanation for the relative lack of attention to organizational market research. Key differences in this respect include, in organizational markets: the typically smaller number of potential customers; the greater personal interaction amongst customers, suppliers, competitors and intermediaries; the greater formality surrounding purchasing; the greater professionalism of customers; the relative importance of service aspects before and especially after the purchase decision; the higher levels of customer retention and perceived switching costs. All this encourages a continuity in supplier–customer relationships which, in general terms, should make competitive erosion more difficult and so less frequent. In which case market research would be less of a priority since suppliers would feel they know their customers well in any case, through frequent contact and rich long-standing relationships.

This may have been the case in some sectors, once, but it is unlikely to be a safe assumption now (and probably never was). Though the number of customers is usually less than in consumer markets their individual accounts are usually much larger, and this simply implies that the loss of even a single customer may jeopardize an organization's competitiveness. Frequent interaction amongst sector participants means that information (or prejudice) is being exchanged frequently and while this may seem to make formal market research less of a priority, it also means that informal market research is being conducted all the time. Nevertheless, a better understanding of customers can potentially make a considerable contribution to the improvement of a supplier's marketing (e.g. through product development) and this prospect should encourage greater formality and professionalism in market research. While high customer retention and switching costs may reduce the perceived need for greater customer understanding, these factors should equally increase the need to understand the needs and objectives of prospects, new segments in existing markets, new markets (Evans, 1993), and the customers of rivals. Finally, with increasing competitive pressure to lock-in customers through enhanced relationships there will be a growing need for market research to understand the dynamics of downstream derived demand – those who rely on immediate customers for an insight into downstream markets risk distorted or complacent perception (Peattie and Ratnayaka, 1992).

However, it is probably fair to conclude at a general level that organizations have perceived themselves as being sufficiently close to their markets and key customers to feel that, by and large, intuitive and informal methods of market research were sufficient for their needs. With typically low budgets for market research there was neither the inclination nor the resources to develop more rigorous information systems (Brown, Lilien and Ulvila, 1993).

Even if this was a fair picture of the past, which is arguable, it is certainly no longer accurate (Raphael and Parker, 1991). With increasing competitive pressures and heightened environmental volatility, organizations (some more enthusiastically and proactively than others) have sought ever more information on developments in markets, technologies and competitors' strategies – often from external sources. Consultancy services in strategic management, market research and competitive analysis are one of the few consultancy sectors showing consistent growth throughout the turbulent 1980s and 1990s, as successive surveys in *Management Consultancy* show. Organizations are now much more aware of the need for information and analysis on markets and competitors, though many seem to be leaving the more sophisticated analysis to specialist market research agencies (Jobber and Horgan, 1988; Raphael and Parker, 1991).

While empirical studies have not yet responded to these changes with the overall level of achievement evident in consumer market research, there have been some interesting studies on the more specific issue of competitor intelligence. This issue is one that may well become more controversial under the twin spotlights of competitive pressure and ethical concern (Beltramini, 1986; Schultz *et al.*, 1994), while it also provides some illustrations of the strengths and limitations of informal research methods (Cohern and Czepiec, 1988).

For those wishing to understand more about the application of market research in organizational markets, an excellent introduction is given by Chisnall (1995, pp. 106–154), while Hague (1992) provides a more detailed and comprehensive discussion.

3.7.2 Segmentation

Despite the modest literature on market research in organizational markets, there is a considerable body of work on organizational market segmentation, though one might expect segmentation to be based, at least to some extent, on market research. On the other hand, much of the literature on organizational market segmentation falls into two categories: descriptive studies of how organizations actually segment their markets (largely on the basis of operational practicality); and theoretical studies of how they could segment more effectively (largely on the basis of customer requirements and purchasing behaviour). In a recent extensive discussion of the segmentation literature, Mitchell and Wilson (1998) argue that the descriptive approach is sub-optimal but adequate where competitive pressures are low, and the market-oriented approach is idealistic but expensive and somewhat impractical for most situations. They recommend a mid-position where the needs for sophisticated segmentation are balanced with the costs involved, the competitive pressures prevailing, and the extent to which an understanding of customer requirements is derived from alternative sources such as relationship management experience.

Many of the issues involved in segmentation of consumer markets have relevance to organizational markets also, if only because of the ultimate importance of consumers in the derived demand of organizational markets. However, in organizational markets the principles of segmentation are significantly different, reflecting differences in buyer behaviour and purchasing processes.

Traditional bases for segmenting organizational markets included product lines, customer size and customer location, though it is probably fair to note that these criteria were more usually matters of convenience and experience rather than a positive strategy based on marketing planning or customer requirements. Building on research into buyer behaviour, it was established that segmentation might also be based on criteria of purchase classification (i.e. new task, modified rebuy, straight rebuy: Robinson, Faris and Wind, 1967), perception of risk (Luffman, 1974), and DMU composition and operation (Choffray and Lilien, 1980). And more recent competitive developments are providing fresh bases for segmenting, such as environmental awareness (Min and Galle, 1997) and ethical probity.

Cardozo suggests that segmentation of organizational markets is better thought of in terms of classification of buying situations, recommending a four-part classification which incorporates the findings of previous researchers, focusing on the features of the product itself, the familiarity of the buyer with the product (new/rebuy etc.), the perceived significance of the purchase to the organizational customer, and the degree of uncertainty surrounding the purchase situation (Cardozo, 1980).

Bonoma and Shapiro (1983) have developed the approach of Wind and Cardozo (1974) into a more comprehensive approach to segmentation which they refer to as the 'nested' approach. Each of the five successive 'nests', or layers in this approach, takes the segmentation process closer to the customer progressing *en route* through industry-wide demographics (referred to in the model as emporographics), competitive operating variables such as the use of technology and financial performance, organization-specific purchasing procedures, contract-specific factors such as the size and urgency of customer requirements, and eventually to specific personal variables such as motivation and risk perception (Bonoma and Shapiro, 1983). The more layers involved in the segmentation process, the more difficult and costly it is to obtain the necessary information and the more subtle and subjective the judgements involved. There will be few occasions when suppliers feel it necessary to engage with all five layers of the nested approach, especially with the innermost layers where access to the necessary information would surely be restricted to those suppliers already enjoying a close relationship with the customer. And since other models provide a more detailed approach to the standard outer layers of the 'nested' model, the nested approach may be more relevant as a theoretical model and teaching aid than as a prescriptive or normative contribution to segmentation and marketing planning.

Figure 3.2 shows an elaborated version of the original Bonoma and Shapiro model. This version starts with an additional layer entitled *environmental variables* to acknowledge that not all organizations are predisposed to segmentation in the first place (or even to marketing more broadly) and this may be a function, in large part, of the supplier's competitive situation, marketing competence and environmental pressures. There are also additional details to subsequent layers which serve to clarify and extend the logic of the original model. While the extra detail makes the model more useful for illustrative purposes, there is no specific empirical foundation for their inclusion.

Segmentation studies provide a convenient illustration of the contrast that is sometimes observable between the incessant pressurized reality faced by marketing managers looking for resource-effective ways to cope with complexity, and the theoretical recommendations of scholars which sometimes seem over-sophisticated and more concerned perhaps with demonstrating new complexities to fellow researchers than with helping practitioners to cope with existing difficulties. On the other hand, where complexities exist they are generally better revealed than concealed – and it is a mistake to assume that all research discussion in marketing should be oriented towards practitioner perspectives, even if this is the ultimate 'market' for research effort.

3.8   THE ROLE AND SIGNIFICANCE OF IT IN ORGANIZATIONAL MARKETING

There has been considerable research and discussion about the impact of developments in IT (especially EDI, MIS, the Internet and relational databases) on marketing in general, though less about the impact on organizational marketing and purchasing in particular (Bondra and Davis, 1996; Stump and Sriram, 1997; Leverick *et al.*, 1998). Nevertheless,

Figure 3.2 'Renesting' segmentation in organizational markets

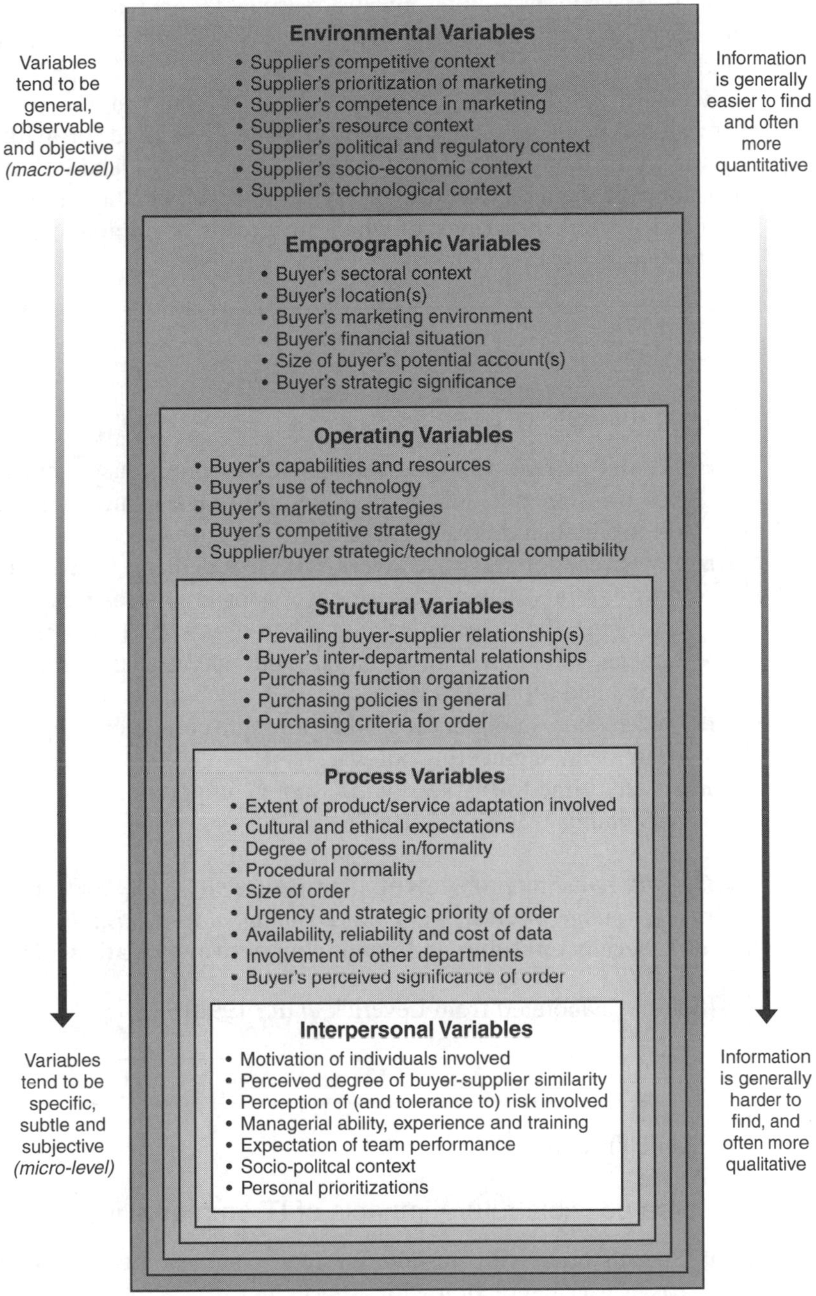

Variables
tend to be
general,
observable
and objective
(macro-level)

Environmental Variables

- Supplier's competitive context
- Supplier's prioritization of marketing
- Supplier's competence in marketing
- Supplier's resource context
- Supplier's political and regulatory context
- Supplier's socio-economic context
- Supplier's technological context

Information
is generally
easier to find
and often
more
quantitative

Emporographic Variables

- Buyer's sectoral context
- Buyer's location(s)
- Buyer's marketing environment
- Buyer's financial situation
- Size of buyer's potential account(s)
- Buyer's strategic significance

Operating Variables

- Buyer's capabilities and resources
- Buyer's use of technology
- Buyer's marketing strategies
- Buyer's competitive strategy
- Supplier/buyer strategic/technological compatibility

Structural Variables

- Prevailing buyer-supplier relationship(s)
- Buyer's inter-departmental relationships
- Purchasing function organization
- Purchasing policies in general
- Purchasing criteria for order

Process Variables

- Extent of product/service adaptation involved
- Cultural and ethical expectations
- Degree of process in/formality
- Procedural normality
- Size of order
- Urgency and strategic priority of order
- Availability, reliability and cost of data
- Involvement of other departments
- Buyer's perceived significance of order

Interpersonal Variables

- Motivation of individuals involved
- Perceived degree of buyer-supplier similarity
- Perception of (and tolerance to) risk involved
- Managerial ability, experience and training
- Expectation of team performance
- Socio-politcal context
- Personal prioritizations

Variables
tend to be
specific,
subtle and
subjective
(micro-level)

Information
is generally
harder to
find, and
often more
qualitative

[Source: elaborated from Bonoma, T.V. and Shapiro, B.P. (1983), *Segmenting the Industrial Market*, Lexington Books, Lexington, CT.]

what is clear from this discussion is that there continue to be wide-spread expectations – not always reasonable or realistic – about the allegedly revolutionary changes which IT will bring to all fields of marketing.

To illustrate these issues Exhibit 3.3 lists some of the principal perceived benefits and current applications of IT as used for marketing (based on the empirical work of Leverick *et al.*, 1998), and Exhibit 3.4 lists some of the anticipated future possible developments in IT which could affect marketing (most of which are already beginning to emerge).

EXHIBIT 3.3

IT in marketing: benefits

- Prompt or real-time interaction with suppliers/customers for ordering, receipt and payment (e.g. through using EDI, and electronic banking)
- Lower cost of service delivery, with less demand for personal staffing and 24-hour service access for crucial aspects (e.g. emergency help, technical advice based on expert systems)
- Greater integration of strategic and operational marketing (Good and Stone, 1995)
- Accelerated and iterative NPD through computer-integrated design and engineering software
- Faster time-to-market and, more importantly, *time-to-acceptance* (McKenna, 1995)

Overall: reducing problems of: *time, geography, complexity, ignorance, unimaginativeness, poor communication, cash flow* ... **and thereby enabling and enhancing network relationships.**

[Source: elaborated from Leverick *et al.*, 1998]

EXHIBIT 3.4

Some possible future impacts of IT on marketing

- Speech processing *technology* (e.g. for customer enquiries; easier user interaction with IT systems)
- Virtual reality *applications* (e.g. for design engineering; testing; experimenting)
- Database mining *techniques* (e.g. statistical process control data in manufacturing operations)

- Miniaturization (e.g. through neural/gene/laser designs for computer systems) allowing more extensive observation of system performance (e.g. for quality control and design improvement)
- Continuing reductions in costs, and so in price, through increased economies and efficiencies
- Increasing customer IT sophistication and growing expectation of IT sophistication amongst suppliers
- Greater integration of IT systems (generating internal efficiency and external networking)
- Competition based increasingly on IT-based assets (especially information-related assets/skills)
- The trends of globalization and customization in markets accelerated by IT developments
- Increasing global standardization of the technical foundations of IT systems, encouraging wider adoption, generating scale economies, lowering price, raising reliability, accelerating system development
- Alliancing to encompass all the aspects of technology demanded by key customers

[Source: elaborated from Leverick *et al.*, 1998]

Despite these attractive benefits, the adoption of IT applications in marketing has been generally disappointing (Fletcher, 1995). A recent survey of 111 UK organizations sought to clarify some of the barriers to more rapid adoption and usage of IT within marketing departments (Leverick *et al.*, 1998). The main findings of this research are summarized in Exhibit 3.5 and show the need for careful management of the IT adoption process.

EXHIBIT 3.5

Barriers to the adoption of IT in marketing

Technological barriers
- Limitations in available software and hardware for marketing applications
- The cost of hardware and software for marketing applications

Organizational barriers
- IT function not understanding marketing's requirements
- Marketing function is a low priority for IT investment
- Organizational and/or group culture of resistance to change in general

- Organizational and/or group culture of resistance to IT specifically
- Lack of senior management commitment to IT usage
- Lack of inter-functional communication and understanding in general

Personal barriers
- Lack of appropriate IT skills among marketing staff
- Lack of an IT 'champion' to drive forward the 'vision' of marketing IT
- Reluctance of other functions to share data with Marketing
- Resistance of marketing staff to adopting IT (either in principle or practice)
- Reluctance of marketing staff to share data with each other and with others

Other barriers
- Difficulty in obtaining access to relevant (and IT-compatible) information
- Unsuitability of creative marketing activities to data capture and to IT analysis
- Fast pace of change in the marketing environment (IT applications superseded)
- Customer reluctance to provide information or sensitivity over its use

[Source: elaborated from Leverick *et al.*, 1998]

It is worth reminding oneself that despite the awe-inspiring prospects offered by developments in IT, spending on IT systems does not automatically result in productive use of such systems, acquiring vast data processing power does not necessarily generate better analysis, having lots more data does not always equate to being wiser, and instantaneous global communication does not immediately spread enlightenment (Tsoukas, 1997). Unfortunately, we still seem perhaps too ready to ignore intuition in the face of reams of computer print-out – even though intuition may well reflect years of experience and unimaginable volumes of data, processed at inconceivable speed, in ways with which conventional computers cannot remotely compete (Parikh, Neubauer and Lank, 1994). It seems likely that the full potential of IT for marketing – and for management – must await the synergistic integration of IT and intuition, perhaps through such novel technologies as expert systems software, neural computing hardware and virtual reality systems.

3.9 CONCLUSION

All organizational marketing situations are complex if only because they involve interactions between individuals with divergent objectives and in separate organizational and competitive contexts. Even the most superficially straightforward examples, of which there are surprisingly few, become complex on closer examination. In this chapter various aspects of the marketing mix have been artificially broken out in order to examine them more directly, but any specific instance of organizational marketing will feature not only some of the factors addressed above but also additional issues and nuances arising from the multiple interactions of these, and other, dynamic factors.

All the elements of the marketing mix are interdependent, balanced and coordinated through marketing strategies which attempt to manipulate the mercurial whole in the rough direction of organizational objectives, while avoiding competitive ambushes and manoeuvring in and around environmental obstacles. If this sounds an impossible task, remember that organizations only have to be as competitive as their rivals – or rather, just a little bit more so than their chief rivals. No organization is judged by absolute standards of competitiveness and the ingredients and standards of competitive success will vary according to sector, region, and the limits that organizations impose on their own ambition.

As the competitive marketing environment gets more complex and seems to become less predictable and more dynamic, an increasingly attractive way of coping with this intractable situation is through collaboration, flexibility and the careful management of particular relationships with strategic customers, suppliers and even competitors. These issues provide the focus for the next chapter.

4 *Competitiveness and collaboration in organizational markets*

The purpose of marketing, whether in organizational or consumer markets, is to pursue the organization's objectives. Where these objectives are uncontested there is no logical need for marketing strategy or planning but this scenario can confidently be set aside. Therefore it could be argued that the aim of marketing is to enhance an organization's competitiveness.

At this point perhaps the term 'competitiveness' should be clarified since although it is used frequently, it is rarely defined. *Competitiveness is the capability to achieve contested objectives over time.* Some of the terms used in this definition may need a little further clarification. *Capability* refers to the resources and skills available to the organization, the extent of their differentiation from those of rivals, and the degree to which they can be sustained in the face of competitive adaptive behaviour. *Objectives* embraces organizational and sub-group objectives as well as their management and the means by which they are identified and prioritized. *Contested* emphasizes the point that competitiveness is a matter of comparative performance and becomes virtually meaningless if the organization's objectives are not contested (e.g. by rivals, stakeholder expectations, environmental constraints). Obviously, the extent and intensity of the contest will vary with time and in different arenas. *Over time* refers to the need for real competitiveness (i.e. not illusory or fleeting) to be sustained in the face of volatile shifts amongst the many variables involved, requiring attention to flexible strategies, resilient processes, and the ability to constantly refresh one's perspective.

Marketing is no different to the other organizational functions in its aim to improve competitiveness but this motivation has greater force for marketing since without competitive challenge or customer choice there would be little apparent role for marketing, while other functions would logically continue – pricing would become a financial matter, product development and packaging would be engineering and design issues, distribution would be an operational routine, and communications would be minimal. Furthermore, marketing is uniquely positioned amongst organizational functions to manage and interpret the interface between the organization and its multiple environments. For these reasons marketing is inextricably bound up with issues of competitiveness.

There is no shortage of books on marketing strategy, competitiveness and strategic management more broadly and despite the many debates in this field there is a surprising degree of consensus over the processes, techniques and general approaches relevant to strategic marketing planning (Cravens et al., 1997). The debate tends to be over which of these techniques and processes are more or less relevant and applicable in different circumstances (Greenley and Bayus, 1993), and why the process is undertaken at all (Mintzberg et al., 1986; Mintzberg, 1993).

However, there are a great many possible variables which could lead to recommendation of one approach over another, such as stage of the market (or product) life cycle, extent of government regulation, number and scale of competitors, ease of market segmentation, vulnerability to technological obsolescence, relative importance of fixed asset investment over current assets, balance of power between suppliers and customers, degree of competitive rivalry, etc. And, of course, there are also many organizational-level variables which could lead to variations of strategic perspective and methodology within whatever generic approach seems appropriate to the sector or market in question.

In addition, many scholars point out that some of the key assumptions behind these techniques and recommended strategy processes are themselves questionable – that managers are typically rational (as opposed to intuitive or emotional) and independent entities (as opposed to paradigm-driven socio-politically oriented peer groups) (de Chernatony et al., 1993); that strategic information is available, current, relevant, affordable and robust; that analysis of necessarily historic situations is applicable to future decisions; that strategic decisions are made and then implemented (as opposed to being remade through implementation); that the need to respond swiftly to competitive developments in a volatile environment leaves any significant room for strategic discretion (Mintzberg, 1993); that strategy formation is anything other than a social process played out between self-referential managers which the rest of the organization has to put up with as best it can while struggling to achieve its own disparate private and collective objectives.

While these are all interesting questions, and necessary for establishing the context of the following discussion, attention here is restricted to just six interrelated aspects which are particularly important for contemporary organizational marketing:

- strategic flexibility
- partnership sourcing
- network theory and interaction
- collaboration and strategic alliancing
- managing supplier–customer relationships
- internal collaboration.

These six aspects are highlighted here because of their particular relevance to the increasing competitiveness of organizational markets. Clearly, not all markets are increasing in their competitiveness at the same rate, just as not all economies and sectors are fully exposed to competitive dynamics, and not all marketing managers are equally imaginative, resourceful and competent. However, there is widespread acceptance that the spread of competitive pressures throughout most markets is forcing organizations to reconsider long-standing marketing assumptions and strategies.

It is also worth noting that if competition between organizations is viewed as a form of exchange (Hamel, Doz and Prahalad, 1989; Hodgkinson and Johnson, 1994; Spender, 1996), then logically competitive strategy is an aspect of (conceivably even a form of) marketing (Doyle, 1998). This, of course, distorts the situation by implying that competition is exclusively concerned with rival suppliers, as opposed to the markets involved, a criticism which could be applied to many analyses of competitive situations which become so involved in organizational analysis that they lose sight of the customers themselves. In a sense this is what is fundamentally wrong with the frequently used (and abused) military metaphor of marketing strategy which pictures warring competitors rampaging over battlefields (presumably 'markets') until one or the other (or both) are defeated (e.g. James, 1985; Ries and Trout, 1985). Where is the customer in this machismoid carnage? The logic of the metaphor seems to leave the customer as the victor's 'prize', or the target for unopposed triumphal plundering. Competition is about winning and retaining customers (organizations or consumers), not about vanquishing and pillaging them.

Once customers are brought back into the analysis it becomes increasingly apparent that collaboration has much to offer as a competitive strategy both to suppliers and to customers. Customers gain from increased product range, deeper skills, richer service and continuity in supply, even in uncertain and volatile environments. There are costs and problems of collaboration also and these are discussed below as well. Collaboration and competition are interdependent themes which run through all six of the aspects discussed below, reflecting the primacy of these twin dynamics of organizational marketing strategy.

4.1   STRATEGIC FLEXIBILITY

Many authors and practitioners have suggested that the unpredictability and uncertainty of contemporary markets make it foolhardy for any organization to commit itself exclusively to strategies based on a single view of the future. A degree of strategic flexibility is a necessary investment against the likelihood of surprise. The need for flexibility is also a major dynamic encouraging collaborative marketing strategies in particular. However, while many authors recommend strategic flexibility in one way or another, few specify what this means for practitioners. So the brief discussion below gives examples of what strategic flexibility can involve as well as touching on its limitations.

The purpose of strategic flexibility is to enable an organization to capitalize on unforeseen opportunities which are broadly consistent with its longer-term objectives – a capability which is increasingly important in volatile environments (Harrigan, 1985). No organization can take advantage of all the opportunities that present themselves, not even of those which are recognized in time for considered engagement. The opportunities that are prosecuted should conform to the over-arching strategic objectives of the organization (Hamel and Prahalad, 1989); and the development of a statement of strategic mission (for the short term) and vision (for the long term) will help in this analysis (Campbell, Devine and Young, 1990; Collins and Porras, 1991). It is equally important to avoid unforeseen threats and strategic flexibility can facilitate this also.

The importance of strategic flexibility is heightened in competitive environments where opportunities and threats arise more frequently, with shorter lead times and fleeting periods of access – what Abell (1978) refers to as 'strategic windows'. There is wide agreement that such volatile competitive environments are increasingly typical (Stacey, 1990; Boynton and Victor, 1991; Doyle, 1998), though neither universal nor permanent (Mintzberg, 1993), making a degree of strategic flexibility – or margin of strategic error – a necessary aspect of competitive marketing strategy for all organizations (Hooley and Jobber, 1986). Equally, the need for flexibility and close monitoring of the strategic environment is one of the few points of agreement in the multiple debates over the nature of strategic planning and management, though the proponents would probably differ in their approach to explaining how such 'flexibility' might be achieved.

Exhibit 4.1 offers some possible suggestions as to how strategic flexibility might be enhanced in organizations.

EXHIBIT 4.1

Strategic flexibility can have many dimensions

Financial: flexibility can be achieved through rapid access to finance (e.g. by means of near-liquid cash reserves; high international credit ratings; low debt gearing; low ratio of fixed to current assets; high retained earnings).

Collaborations: Olivetti prides itself on having over 250 'strategic and tactical alliances' which give it scope for flexible adjustment to unanticipated developments; small manufacturing firms can emulate large-scale operations through 'flexible manufacturing networks' (LaPlaca, 1993); multiple technological expertise can be achieved through networks of 'virtual companies' (Goldman and Nagel, 1993).

Markets: monitor a range of potential segments and markets for entry/growth opportunities; be alert to fresh applications and potential substitutes; develop strong branding (to facilitate product/brand extension); treat marketing as a mutually educative process in which intermediaries and customers have much to contribute through feedback.

Production: avoid dedicated manufacturing operations by use of OEM, joint marketing, sub-assembly and component sourcing, subcontracting and outsourcing, and especially through investment in computer-integrated manufacturing and flexible manufacturing systems (Talaysum, Hassan and Goldhar, 1987; De Meyer *et al.*, 1989; Parthasarthy and Sethi, 1992).

R&D: monitor developments in a variety of potentially important avenues through journals and professional conferences etc., and through shared-cost exploratory studies such as joint R&D with commercial partners and sponsorship of university R&D projects.

Recruitment: where practicable, recruit personnel with experience/skills which are also compatible with markets, technologies and competitors of possible future relevance; encourage a degree of eccentric (i.e. unconventional and unusual) thinking as a stimulus to others.

Remuneration: encourage flexibility and innovativeness amongst staff at all levels (e.g. through productivity incentive schemes, performance-related pay, schemes based on customer satisfaction measures, staff share schemes, staff suggestion schemes); good working conditions are also conducive to this as is sensitivity to corporate sub-cultures and awareness of industry norms and rivals' offerings.

Organization: a flatter organizational hierarchy with delegated responsibility can encourage a more entrepreneurial and innovative culture (Johannessen, Olsen and Olaisen, 1997) (e.g. IBM used spin-offs and joint ventures to develop entrepreneurial new products outside the 'Big Blue' bureaucracy) but beware that this can also undermine cultures and smother innovativeness through over-burdening managers (Willmott, 1994).

Work practices: encourage multi-functionism (through training and recruitment) and anti-demarcation (perhaps through single-union arrangements) for flexibility in production strategy; quality circles and suggestion schemes can also help; clear staff

communications channels and internal marketing are also important to ensure a commonality of perspective.

Information: make use of informal sources (e.g. as early warning systems concerning technology, new rivals, contracts) and
invest in environmental scanning systems (Brownlie, 1995).

Training: develop current staff (generally cheaper than recruitment) and encourage self-development (e.g. via part-time and
open learning programmes) with career incentives.

IT: apart from the many IT-related suggestions above, IT systems
are increasingly necessary to coordinate, process and analyze the
data available from multiple sources (Boynton, 1993).

Management: inculcate project management skills; use cascade
communications to ensure wide dissemination of sense of strategic mission; where appropriate, encourage project/task orientation (not functional) and team management (not line).

Strategic planning: avoid excessively detailed planning systems
and encourage devil's advocacy; provide goals and broad directions while sanctioning pragmatic opportunism within this framework (with clear discretionary guidelines); consider informal and
exceptional information in analysis/discussion; continually assess
competitors and market environments.

It should not be forgotten that strategic flexibility can also have associated costs and risks, such as the risk of seeming ambiguous in commitment to customers and suppliers (all of the suggestions in Exhibit
4.1 require investment). It will also be necessary to convince influential
stakeholders of the need for cautious flexibility and alertness rather than
the sanguine single-minded pursuit of the latest populist 'guru' rhetoric.
In short, the helter-skelter of fast-moving competitive markets may
make it difficult to keep up a stance requiring uncommitted assets
(waste?), peripheral vision (distractions?) and a broader analysis of the
environment (dilution of competitive attention?).

4.2 PARTNERSHIP

It is increasingly accepted that there can be considerable scope for
benefits on both sides of the purchasing exchange relationship if a
collaborative atmosphere prevails rather than the more traditional perception of purchasing relationships as necessarily competitive and even
antagonistic (Chisnall, 1995; Han *et al.*, 1993). From this general
principle of increasingly collaborative purchasing relationships, the idea
of exclusive long-term purchasing partnerships has emerged – generally

referred to as partnership sourcing – and many sectors (especially manufacturing sectors such as the automobile industry) have adopted extensive partnership sourcing arrangements (Matthyssens and Van den Bulte, 1994). The strategic advantages of partnership sourcing are summarized in Table 4.1 which is based on the experiences of a major supplier of electrical components to the automotive industry.

Something of the logic behind partnership sourcing is illustrated in the IBM/*Dove Computers* examples in Mini-case 11. Despite the decade separating the two examples, there are marked similarities, not least the collaborative approach to marketing taken by the supplier and customer involved, and the success this generated for both parties.

Collaborative approaches are recommended by the findings of a growing number of researchers in marketing. For example, Dion and Banting (1988) conducted research in the USA which suggested that a collaborative approach to supplier–buyer negotiations was more typically associated with high overall performance than an approach focusing on winning price concessions. There is also considerable anecdotal and academic evidence to suggest that managing logistics relationships as partnerships, whether upstream or downstream, can generate significant competitive advantages for both partners (Johnston and Lawrence, 1988; Naurus and Anderson, 1986; Lamming, 1993).

It might be argued that long-term customer–supplier relationships could reduce the supplier's scope for selling to other customers in the same sector through being seen to be too closely tied (or even dependent) on a particular customer. But research by Kalwani and Narayandas (1995) shows this marginal disadvantage to be more than offset by reduced marketing expenditure and lower inventory, not to mention

Table 4.1 Key benefits of strategic partnership sourcing

Customer benefits	Mutual benefits	Supplier benefits
Fair and long-term pricing agreement	Equitable pricing (using an agreed model)	Fair and predictable margin (eases cash-flow and forecasting)
No multiple tooling costs	Scale economies (in purchasing and in relationship costs)	Increased volume (facilitates future investment planning)
Fewer sourcing variables (or hassles)	Better quality and closer customization	Clearer awareness of supplier's requirements
Lower life-time costs of purchases	Longer-term perspective and easier planning	Supportive climate for investment
Better supplier response and support	Increased mutual dependence and support	Not forced into subservient role

[Source: adapted from research material in Davies, 1996]

the public endorsement of the supplier implicit in such a long-term relationship and the financial stability arising from guaranteed sales streams. However, it may well be the case that partnership arrangements have significant potential disadvantages for smaller suppliers unable to afford the start-up costs of partnering (Ramsay, 1996), or those in generic markets (where switching costs are low and opportunistic purchasing is attractive to customers), or those vulnerable to exploitation in long-term commitments (e.g. small organizations with key expert staff susceptible to poaching by a partner, or at risk of acquisition) (Pilling and Zhang, 1992). Low (1996) points out that there are important costs in relationships that fail, including litigation and exit costs. Some superficially attractive partners can be operating to hidden agendas, or may deteriorate with changing circumstance, and just as successful relationships can raise a supplier's reputation (Leuthesser, 1997), so failures can prove disastrous and exit from entrenched relationships may be far from straightforward (Low, 1996, 1997).

Arguably, there are also many macro-environmental and competitive factors beyond short-term commercial gain which could be regarded as stimuli to interorganizational relationships, such as acceleration of the widely recognized phenomena of globalization, increasing competition, environmental complexity and escalating R&D costs (Littler and Wilson, 1992). Under these pressures a routine purchasing relationship can evolve into a strategic alliance, especially as the foundation for such relationships may have as much to do with mutual familiarity and trust as it does with strategic logic. This encourages a much wider understanding of the scope and significance of 'buying behaviour' in organizational markets than has generally been recognized and emphasizes the importance of understanding such relationships in their long-term dynamic and strategic context rather than, perhaps, as a series of recurring exercises in cost control (Turnbull and Valla, 1987). Research into the process of how such relationships develop over time, the typical problems and costs involved, and the implications arising for marketing management is therefore increasingly relevant to organizations seeking to develop their competitiveness through strategic alliances. Many of these aspects are addressed by research into collaboration more broadly (see Section 4.4 below for a brief discussion) and many of the findings of collaboration research can be applied to the narrower context of partnership sourcing.

4.3 NETWORK THEORY AND INTERACTION

The IMP Group's extensive research into European buyer–seller purchasing relationships has generated significant insights into how such relationships develop. The Group describes these relationships in what has become known as the *interaction approach* to organizational marketing. The buyer behaviour implications of the interaction approach were discussed earlier (see Section 2.6 above) but it may be helpful briefly to recapitulate the main points here to save cross-referencing.

In essence, the approach regards purchasing in organizational markets as a multi-faceted and dynamic phenomenon where specific purchases are understood as 'exchange episodes' in the evolving relationship between buyer and seller organizations, and also between individuals within these organizations. The approach emphasizes the stability and continuity of markets which are evolving through many interrelated buyer–seller relationships, even where a superficial analysis may suggest greater volatility. It is also implied that the textbook dichotomy between 'marketing' (by suppliers) and 'purchasing' (by customers) is not a helpful way to describe what is essentially a seamless and iterative process. Nor are such interactions limited to purchasing relationships since purchasing can overlap seamlessly with product development, production management and marketing planning (Håkansson and Eriksson, 1993).

The interaction approach prefers a view of organizational marketing as, in effect, *the management of buyer–seller relationships* where it is more appropriate to differentiate participants in terms of power, expertise, experience and cultural affiliation rather than broad organizational membership. This approach also emphasizes the importance of 'atmospherics' such as personal objectives and expectations, interpersonal familiarity and levels of cooperation and dependence in understanding specific 'exchange episodes'.

Interactions build up patterns of behaviour which over time become recognizable as relationships, each one subtly different to the others, reflecting the personal and contingent variables involved. Similarly, patterns of interorganizational relationships form networks. The IMP Group has developed an analysis of networks (network theory) which highlights the dynamics created by three clusters of variables: *actors*, *activities* and *resources*. These three variables are briefly elaborated in Exhibit 4.2.

EXHIBIT 4.2

Network theory – actors, activities and resources

Actors
- Perform and control activities
- Develop relationships with other actors
- Control resources (directly and/or indirectly)
- Are goal oriented (e.g. to gain influence over network resources through relationships)
- Have different levels of knowledge (about activities, resources, relationships, actors, network dynamics)

■ Have multiple roles in simultaneous, inter-influential, networks of relationships

Activities
■ Involve actors activating resources (generally by means of transformation and subsequent transfer)
■ This transformation and transfer is referred to as an activity *cycle*
■ Successive related *cycles* form an activity *chain*
■ One activity may form a part of many different *cycles* and *chains*
■ The learning process and context surrounding activities tends to routinize them into relatively stable and institutionalized SOPs (standard operating procedures)

Resources
■ Activities of transformation and transfer consume resources
■ Actors control all resources (either directly or indirectly, singly or collectively)
■ Resources are heterogeneous and multi-dimensional and so have very varied usage possibilities
■ Novel resource combinations tend to generate novel learning, experience and knowledge

Network theory and the interaction approach have significant implications for organizational marketing, some of which are summarized in Exhibit 4.3.

EXHIBIT 4.3

Implications of network theory and the interaction approach for organizational marketing

■ Focus strategic marketing planning on key customers and key channel partners in target markets (including foreign markets) rather than just on products and contracts.
■ Develop systems to identify and monitor strategic relationships for planning purposes.
■ Develop product design and technology based on an understanding of customer requirements (Walsh *et al.*, 1992) and channel partner requirements (Gassenheimer *et al.*, 1995).
■ Closely monitor 'independent' or 'arm's-length' operations and be prepared to collaborate in them if necessary (e.g. distributors, export operations, subcontracted functions).

- Develop integrated team selling (Hutt *et al.*, 1985; Smith and Barclay, 1993) with multi-functional representation as appropriate, possibly including channel representatives (e.g. where they cover service aspects).
- Appoint managers to coordinate all aspects of key customer relationships (Ford, 1980b; Weeks and Stevens, 1997).
- Try to learn from the wider experience available within sectoral supplier groups and markets (e.g. by joining sectoral associations, subscribing to sectoral publications).
- Try to integrate the customer's purchasing function more closely with the supplier's marketing function (Hutt *et al.*, 1985).
- Encourage key customers, suppliers and channel agents to become involved in product/service development; and seek to make reciprocal contributions.
- Invest in retaining personnel who are relationship facilitators and 'nodes', perhaps by giving them relationship management responsibilities and designing remuneration systems that reward relationship development.

Many of these suggestions are compatible with the recommendations of the literature on the management of collaborations and strategic alliances, which is not surprising given the collaborative nature of networks. Much of the following discussion of collaboration management will therefore also be relevant to the management of networks and interactions.

4.4 COLLABORATION AND STRATEGIC ALLIANCING

The increasing research attention being devoted to collaborative relationships and strategic alliances in organizational markets raises important issues concerning how such relationships should be managed. This has been the focus of recent research in which respondents to a UK survey were asked to identify factors apparently influencing the success and failure of collaborative product development relationships (Littler *et al.*, 1998). Exhibit 4.4 lists some of the main problems experienced by partnerships as identified by Kanter (1989) and Figure 4.1 summarizes the findings of Littler *et al.*'s research with respect to the factors affecting the outcome of collaborations aimed at product development.

These findings are consistent with earlier research into partnership sourcing (Kanter, 1989; Han *et al.*, 1993) and with research by Ford (1980b) which described the process of adaptation between partners in an interorganizational relationship as, ideally, one of benign adjustment in the best interests of the parties involved, and founded crucially on mutual trust (Morgan and Hunt, 1994). As Ford suggests, it is important

EXHIBIT 4.4

The problems of partnerships

- Changes in business conditions leading to reprioritization and re-evaluation of collaborative investments (e.g. downgrading or even exit)
- Disagreements over the direction, scope, pace and timing of strategic decisions owing to differences in strategic objectives and perspectives
- Power imbalances owing to unequal commitments and inequitable contributions – benefits must seem broadly in line with contributions
- Creeping dependency as one partner grows more involved and focused on the partnership (this can be a result of success in the relationship activities or of failure in other activities)
- Uncertainty about ownership of information and jointly developed assets/operations
- Mutual suspicion – trust is vital but emerges slowly, not only because interpersonal respect takes time to develop but also due to the need for appropriate procedural safeguards
- Conflicting loyalties (to the parent organizations and also to the partnership itself)
- Insufficient partnership identity (e.g. lack of dedicated assets, staff, budget, framework, authority) so undermining credibility and capability
- Divergent career and motivation patterns amongst partners leading to seconded partnership staff facing inconsistent incentives and influences.

[Source: adapted from Kanter, 1989]

to have modest expectations at the start and not to allow short-term tactical issues to eclipse long-term strategic interests. To ensure that this does not happen, Ford recommends the appointment of a relationship manager in the supplier, with responsibilities comparable to those attributed earlier by Webster and Wind (1972) to the professional buyer in the customer organization.

It is also worth noting that successful collaborations can bring unexpected problems, with further implications for managing the relationships between organizations and collaborating individuals. Fisher, Maltz and Jaworski (1997) recognize that the cultural and professional links between individuals collaborating from similar functional orientations

Figure 4.1 Factors affecting the outcome of collaborative product development relationships

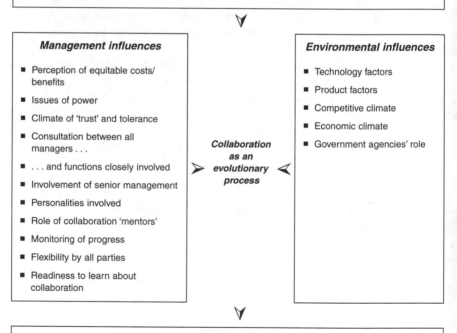

Inputs

- Assessment of mutual compatibility with respect to cultures and modes of operation
- Clear strategic goals, objectives and responsibilities mutually defined, understood and accepted
- Establishment of collaboration limits (to avoid breach of mutual confidentiality)
- Past experience of collaborations (and ability to learn from this experience)
- Close relationship of collaboration activities with existing operations of all partners
- Establishment of accountability and control
- Establishment of collaboration 'milestones'
- Avoidance of exclusively financial measures of progress
- Allocation of sufficient resources (determined flexibly)
- Relatively long-term perspective of benefits expected to be realized

Management influences

- Perception of equitable costs/ benefits
- Issues of power
- Climate of 'trust' and tolerance
- Consultation between all managers . . .
- . . . and functions closely involved
- Involvement of senior management
- Personalities involved
- Role of collaboration 'mentors'
- Monitoring of progress
- Flexibility by all parties
- Readiness to learn about collaboration

Collaboration as an evolutionary process

Environmental influences

- Technology factors
- Product factors
- Competitive climate
- Economic climate
- Government agencies' role

Outcomes

- Effect on products/services in question
- Learning about collaboration management
- Effect on customers and end-users
- Effect on suppliers and channel intermediaries
- Effect on partners' reputations
- Effect on competitive structures
- Effect on rivals and other observers
- Effect on other key stakeholders

[Source: adapted from Littler, Leverick and Wilson, 1998]

(technological, sales, financial, marketing) but based in separate collaborating organizations may, in well-established collaborations, generate closer affinities and affiliations than they have with their employing organizations. The collaboration entity itself (e.g. the joint venture or the project) may elicit internal staff loyalties which super-sede loyalties to the parent organizations, especially where staff are hired externally (as may well be the case where particular expertise is thought necessary).

This cumulative body of research into collaboration is already very extensive and still under vigorous development but in this book our attention is limited to what this research means for organizational mar-keting. The research has built up a persuasive and broadly consistent picture of organizational buying and selling as a complex, multi-layered area of practical marketing where clear-cut distinctions between suppli-ers, customers, tasks, roles, phases and even organizations may be mis-leading, and where mutual trust, equitable gains and consensus are the precursors to success (Morgan and Hunt, 1994; Spekman, Salmond and Lambe, 1997). In other words, what emerges is a relationship between suppliers and customers, characterized by mutual strategic exchange advantages rather than by short-term contractual obligations. The impli-cations for managing such interorganizational marketing relationships are considered next.

4.5 MANAGING CUSTOMER–SUPPLIER RELATIONSHIPS

It is a truism that suppliers are crucial to any organization's operations and to its continued survival. The reverse is equally obvious. With increasing collaboration in logistics channels the question arises of how to manage the mutually dependent and increasingly integrated relation-ships involved. Is it better to adopt a rigorous control approach with extensive legal contracts and performance mechanisms to insure and protect against the possibility of things going wrong but which might also force all those involved to spend much of their attention in moni-toring adherence to some inflexible control system? Or is it better to adopt a *laissez-faire* 'empowered' approach that would allow all those involved to follow their view of mutual best interests but which lacks coordination and accountability?

The management of the relationship *in principle* will be determined by the broad strategies adopted by the supplier and the customer, which are in turn a reflection of the competitive circumstances, cultural norms and paradigm perspectives of both organizations. But the manage-ment of the relationship *in practice* will also depend both on how the individual managers responsible perceive these strategies, and also on how they relate to each other in the everyday routine of purchasing, delivery, quality management and purchase accounting. Practice will also depend, of course, on how much discretion the managers are granted (and with what resources) together with the effectiveness of any monitoring and reporting procedures.

Generally, the development of effective collaborative supplier–customer relationships will involve investing time, corporate resources and managerial commitment. These investments can be demanding and may be easily underestimated so Exhibit 4.5 elaborates a little further what might be involved.

EXHIBIT 4.5

Investing in collaborative supplier–customer relationships

1 Time

- Encourage purchasing and selling staff to be willing to make more frequent visits, when appropriate.
- Develop records of meetings (but not simply in 'tick-box' format) so that the relationship is not so dependent on individuals.
- Encourage occasional mutual attendance at appropriate planning meetings so each understands the others' policies and objectives.
- Broaden relationship scope with visits by staff of production, quality, product engineering, service, etc., and by senior managers – on a reciprocal basis (consider using short-term secondments or shadowing arrangements to increase mutual insight).
- Aim for continual rather than sporadic communication, and for long-term cooperative relationships with fewer suppliers rather than short-term relationships with many suppliers.

2 Resources

- Budget for the costs of investing staff and time as described above.
- Be prepared to invest in improved supplier facilities and training to make the supplier more competitive, thereby enhancing the value of the supplier to the customer (e.g. in quality control, commitment, reliability) – this should still be on a commercial basis.
- Offer access to IT, experience and technical expertise in the general improvement of the suppliers' business operations (e.g. provide advice on accounting and management systems; encourage adoption of mutually compatible ICT systems to enhance manufacturing, ordering and payment systems).

- Allow staff of partnering organizations mutual access to each other's facilities (e.g. social, recreational, training) to encourage individual relationships and mutual trust.

3 Commitment

- Involve senior executives more in the relationship signalling the perceived value of the relationship and facilitating the integration of purchasing and product development policies in strategic marketing planning.
- Consider long-term sole supply contracts, especially where product development continuity is important and product development is likely to involve strategic or sensitive investments (Comer and Zirger, 1997).
- Allow mutual access to costing and profitability data of relevant products/services to ensure fair rewards and the perception of equitable treatment.
- Be prepared to spend time and attention in building mutually comfortable relationships, not least through mutual hospitality (McCracken and Callahan, 1996).

Once a long-term collaborative relationship has been established through such investments, it may be in the strategic interests of both parties to encourage the development of the other, for example into fresh markets or through new business ventures. For the supplier, this can produce production economies (from expanded sales) or increased R&D (from increased turnover), both of which can feed back into reduced costs and/or improved offerings to strategic customers. For the customer, such expansion can result in increased demand for the suppliers' offerings or for a wider range of offerings. Where such mutual advantages do arise it may be worth considering more formal collaborations such as joint venturing options ranging from buyer investment in the supplier's production facilities to joint development of new geographic markets.

So these relationships may deliver for both parties not only the short-term purchasing benefits initially anticipated, but also potential longer-term strategic benefits. It is therefore wise to treat these relationships as important strategic opportunities and to manage them accordingly as collaborative strategic alliances.

Ford (1984) reinforces this point when he argues that skill in the management of interorganizational relationships can itself become a strategic asset and an important factor in the selection of interorganizational partners, possibly even providing a useful basis for segmentation.

The design and development of collaborative supplier–customer relationships – both upstream and downstream – can also be seen as part of the emerging strategy of relationship marketing which Grönroos defines thus:

> Marketing is to establish, maintain, and enhance . . . relationships with customers and other partners, at a profit, so that the objectives of the parties involved are met . . . [through] mutual exchange and fulfilment of promises.

(Grönroos, 1994)

While this definition does give some useful pointers to what relationship marketing is about, some difficulties do remain. Logically, for example, the reference to profit is redundant since achieving objectives supersedes this. Also, this definition (like most other definitions of marketing) implies that where objective achievement is absent (or partial or unilateral) then somehow marketing is not what is going on. In other words, Grönroos is defining 'successful marketing', or the objectives of marketing rather than the activity itself. Even excellent marketing is not necessarily successful, and a definition which excludes less-than-successful marketing would probably address only a small fraction of the phenomenon under examination. Clearly then, the concept of relationship marketing is still very much under development, but it does hold much promise for a reconceptualizing of marketing.

4.6   INTERNAL COLLABORATION

Much has been said about collaboration with external organizations. Many have also pointed out that since no organization is independent of other organizations (Håkansson and Snehota, 1989) in the pursuit of its objectives then we need to reconsider what we mean by 'an organization' and where its boundaries might be (Badaracco, 1991). If so, it would be logical to extend collaborative strategies not only to 'external' agencies such as suppliers, customers and rivals but also to 'internal' functions which are in exchange relationships with each other.

For example, there are many exchanges between marketing and manufacturing and R&D, whether in purchasing, or product development, or quality management, or customer service (Song et al., 1997). Traditionally, these exchanges have been seen as potentially awkward because of the conflicting cultural traditions associated with the different functional activities (Griffin and Hauser, 1996; Song et al., 1997). It is tempting to assume that these internal collaborations will somehow take care of themselves because of shared organizational objectives, procedures, hierarchical structures, motivations and competitive pressure (Song et al., 1997). However, extensive research has demonstrated that this is not so and that interpersonal and interdepartmental rivalry, suspicion and hostility can be surprisingly common in intra-organizational relationships (Mast and Hawes, 1986; Frankwick,

Walker and Ward, 1994). Applying the principles of collaboration management to internal relationships, with appropriate adaptations, can help to improve the effectiveness and productivity of many internal processes, especially product development and design (Barczak and Wilemon, 1992; Song, Neeley and Zhao, 1996), purchasing (Wagner, 1987; Watts, Kim and Hahn, 1992), quality management (Kohoutek, 1988; Gobeli and Brown, 1993), and strategic planning and management (Dibb, 1997; Maltz, 1997).

The relevance of this issue for organizational marketing is twofold. First, the entire organization (or network of sub-organizations) needs to coordinate and integrate its resources and capabilities if these assets are to be managed for optimal productivity. The way in which the organization engages with its environment – the essence of marketing – is inevitably much affected by the ability of the organization (howsoever demarcated) to direct its energies and assets towards its shared objectives. The organization's portfolio of offerings is not simply the actual goods and services it markets but also, especially perhaps in organizational markets, the organizational systems of design, development, production and servicing which generate these offerings. Marketing the organization's offerings must therefore entail some responsibility for nurturing appropriate systems for effective generation of future offerings.

Second, all individuals within an organization can have an effect on the organization's reputation within its markets. Few things are as effective in destroying the perceived value of a product as a damning comment from someone involved in its manufacture – someone who 'knows the inside story'. Word of mouth then multiplies the damage many times over and far more rapidly and effectively than any remedial action by the organization. The example of Gerald Ratner's casual jocular remark that his company's mass-market jewellery products were trivial and worthless led in short order to a huge slump in company sales, and stock, followed promptly by his own departure. One approach to addressing this potential problem is 'internal marketing' in which marketing programmes are designed for consumption by internal employees and, by extension, staff from other organizations involved in the sourcing, augmentation and delivery of the organization's offerings. Mini-case 12 gives an illustration of internal marketing and internal collaboration. See also Harrell and Fors (1992) for their recommendations of how to manage a broadly comparable situation.

What is important to remember here is that organizational marketing is not only about how the organization engages with its external environment, especially as most organizations are now so seamlessly enmeshed in their environments that it becomes tricky to say what is truly external and what is internal. Organizational marketing is also about how the organization engages with its internal environment – where this affects the relationship with the external environment.

Internal marketing is particularly fraught with potential for inter-departmental strife and needs a very delicate managerial touch in which a collaborative approach is essential.

4.7 CONCLUSION

Despite the extensive research into collaboration between suppliers and customers in organizational markets, and the many examples of successful collaboration, there is still considerable uncertainty about the circumstances in which this approach is appropriate, the mechanisms which drive it towards success or failure, and the appropriate management processes and network structures (Sharma and Sheth, 1997). Bresnen (1996) has pointed out that much of the research is concentrated in specific sectors (manufacturing and technology-intensive sectors), it still suffers from the traditional implicit assumptions of managerial rationality in so much of marketing research, and it has yet to take into account fully the perceptual, processual and interpersonal influences which can make such a difference between otherwise similar organizations. In addition, little is understood about the external dynamics of network evolution, other than that there are very many complex factors and interactions involved (Osborn and Hagedoorn, 1997) or about the internal dynamics of managerial perceptions and paradigms (Beyer *et al.*, 1997), other than that they are both difficult to 'manage' and highly influential in the management and success of collaborations. Research into collaboration management continues to be a priority for marketing, not least because it will be impossible to evaluate the full significance of relationship marketing as a potential basis for reconceptualizing marketing, as many suggest, until we know a great deal more about collaboration and its association with competitiveness.

Finally, with respect to research into organizational competitiveness, the recommendations of academic research studies sometimes risk losing sight of the daily pressures on managers of in-trays, deadlines, bosses, importunate clients, personal preoccupations, fatigue, limited competence, frustration and desperation. This is all the more surprising since academics themselves are scarcely immune to such factors. As a result, recommendations of 'best practice' can overlook the reality that organizational competitiveness is measured against that of rivals (or against historical performance) rather than against absolutes. Put simply, being competitive is about doing better than others, not about being perfect. It is perhaps too easy to forget the cost in time, attention and resources involved in establishing and managing so-called 'best practice', let alone the problems of deciding what best practice is in any specific practical (as opposed to theoretical) situation (Mitchell and Wilson, 1998).

Conclusion

Six themes in particular emerge from the discussion above which reflect some of the more important dynamics currently changing our understanding of organizational marketing. The themes are:

- the increasing significance of marketing strategy for the overall competitiveness of organizations;
- the emerging 'spanning' role of the marketing function integrating with other functional areas . . .
- . . . and with different organizations through relationship marketing, partnership, collaboration and other forms of strategic alliancing;
- organizational marketing as the continual management of interorganizational relationships (rather than as preparing and negotiating individual purchasing 'deals');
- the increasing complexity of organizational marketing responsibilities and the significance of information technology (IT) in managing this complexity (e.g. in facilitating segmentation and communication);
- the convergence of marketing theory with respect to organizational and consumer markets (important differences of emphasis notwithstanding).

There is considerable continuing research in all these areas and the prospects for further advances are bright. But there is also a need at the end of such a discussion to stand back from the mass of detail and consider the broader picture and here it may be helpful to reconsider some of what Charles Ames said in a hugely influential paper nearly 30 years ago (Ames, 1970).

Our discussion started with the claim that organizational marketing can be seen not only as *the marketing of products and services between organizations* but more widely as *the management and development of exchange relationships between organizations.* By now it should also be clear why management of a portfolio of such exchange relationships can provide strategic competitive benefits and therefore why, in Ames' words, 'marketing in the industrial world is much more a general management responsibility than it is in the consumer-products field.' (Ames, 1970).

Ames also pointed out that organizations seem to find it relatively easy to adopt the 'trappings' of marketing, as illustrated by senior management declarations in speeches and annual reports, or by the introduction of formal marketing planning systems; but that this can be very different to a genuine 'marketing orientation', which is revealed more by a 'willingness to require cooperation from all functions, to invest for long-term goals, and to face up to deficiencies in product, price or service' (Ames, 1970). Ames suggests that what is needed to achieve this marketing orientation in practice, as opposed to appearance, is: 'qualified people, reliable market and economic information, and planning to ensure the right strategic focus for the business' (Ames, 1970). So while there are many new challenges to organizational marketing, many of the major challenges remain similar to those of three decades ago.

On the other hand, it could be argued that much of the theory of organizational marketing is actually a theory of the more important occasions of organizational marketing – of new-task purchasing and major accounts, of complex customer requirements and competitive markets. It should not be forgotten that much of organizational marketing, probably even most of it, is concerned with routine purchasing in relatively familiar circumstances and with few immediate implications for overall competitive positions or strategic dynamics. And this sub-strategic organizational marketing management is conducted amongst all the pressures and privations of contemporary managerial practices, with limited resources and conflicting priorities, by hard-worked individuals with career aspirations and private preoccupations. On such occasions the application of the processes and principles discussed above remains relevant but is likely to be mediated through compromises based on experience, work priorities and common sense. There is a clear need for more research on the routine and low-profile activity of organizational marketing, for research which explores the realities of organizational marketing at the middle and junior management levels rather than always focusing on the senior and executive levels.

While Ames calls for organizational marketing managers to improve their skills and routine operations through greater familiarization with theory and good practice, perhaps we can now also recognize the need to improve theory and recommended practice through greater familiarization with the routine work of organizational marketing managers. In this respect at least, the readers of this book have a great deal to offer.

A *note on research directions in organizational marketing*

Students looking for dissertation topics might wish to consider some research priorities in organizational marketing which, like many other facets of marketing, is rich with research challenges and opportunities, not the least of which is the cornucopia of research issues blossoming from relationship studies.

Möller and Wilson (1995) identify the following as current priority issues for organizational marketing, though they give surprisingly little explicit attention to relationship aspects considering their own contributions to this area:

- better tools for customer portfolio management, especially the development of appropriate databases to facilitate novel segmentation methods and identification of innovative prospects;
- database marketing which allows detailed customer information to be stored and processed in ways which can hugely increase the supplier's understanding of customer needs and their ability to identify incremental and new opportunities within customers;
- the coordination and integration of multiple marketing channels in 'hybrid marketing systems';
- coordinating and integrating the multiple contacts between organizations (especially between a supplier and their customers) which can involve several different functions and may generate confusion and inconsistency;
- the adaptation (and even reinvention) of marketing and sales practices for the context of single source relationships.

Many other research priorities will be apparent from the discussion so far, for example into segmentation, collaboration management, buyer behaviour, purchase classification, logistics management, purchase decision making, sourcing decisions, partnership purchasing, Internet and intranet communications, industrial branding, sales staff motivation, mapping networks, the impact and potential of IT for marketing practice, and so on.

There is also a need for more attention to the differences in marketing between larger and smaller organizations (Sashittal and Wilemon,

1996), between private and public businesses (File, 1995), to the real objectives of commercial organizations (if they are not adequately captured by 'profit generation' then what are they and how does this affect strategy?), and between organizations embedded in different cultures or in multiple cultures. And there is also an urgent need for research into how practitioners themselves respond to the findings of academic research, what difference these recommendations make, how best to communicate the findings of research, and what implications there may be for the design of future research.

But perhaps the most fundamental research challenge in the field of organizational marketing is the question of whether the field itself has any future, or whether it should be merged with consumer marketing. Exhibit 5.1 provides a summary listing of the main differences which are claimed to distinguish organizational markets from consumer markets.

EXHIBIT 5.1

The principal differences claimed between organizational and consumer markets

- The derived nature of demand
- The means and timing of payment
- The purchasing expertise and bargaining power of organizational customers
- The smaller number of customers
- The typically larger size and scale of orders
- The more direct means of selling, often through a field sales force
- The negotiability of terms of purchase and supply
- The greater regulation of the purchasing process in organizational markets
- The complexity of purchasing decision processes
- The greater significance and detail of technical specifications
- The importance of repeat purchasing flows to all parties
- The crucial importance of reliability and quality of goods/services
- The importance of delivery timing, units, packaging and other logistics arrangements
- The importance of suppliers' financial and competitive viability into the future
- The significance of the reputation both of suppliers and of customers
- The influence of risk perception and risk tolerance both at an organizational and an individual level

- The greater professionalism of purchasing in organizational markets
- The greater flexibility of suppliers in dealing with organizational customers
- The collaboration often found between suppliers and customers in organizational markets
- The greater importance and influence of interorganizational and interpersonal relationships in organizational markets

[Source: This summary listing is developed from the listing provided by Gross *et al.* (1993, pp. 16–34) which is probably the most comprehensive listing of these differences available in the literature.]

Few have challenged this distinction between organizational and consumer markets and so between organizational and consumer marketing, with the notable exception of Fern and Brown (1984), though most writers regard the differences as being relative rather than absolute. Given the many changes to both forms of market in recent years, and given developments in marketing theory, it seems sensible to reassess the basis for the distinction.

For example, many of the claimed differences relate more to new-task buying situations and to technically complex offerings than to rebuy purchasing and routine situations, which tend to be more representative of the bulk of organizational buying. Many other differences are reducing in significance under the combined dynamics of increasing competitive pressures, developments in IT, shifting consumer loyalty patterns (driven in part by increasing consumer affluence and sophistication), market deregulation, growing consumer protection legislation, and so on.

If it is debatable whether there remains a sufficient or worthwhile basis for continuing these distinctions in marketing at a theoretical level, this is not necessarily the case at a practical level. The distinction between organizational and consumer marketing (and other comparable distinctions) helps to structure what would otherwise be excessive complexity, and has an intuitive appeal which is difficult to resist (e.g. for educational purposes). Meanwhile, perhaps it is time to develop a research emphasis which asks what are the similarities between organizational and consumer marketing, rather than what are the differences.

References

Abell, D.F. (1978), 'Strategic Windows', *Journal of Marketing*, 42(3), July, pp. 21–26

Ames, B.C. (1970), 'Trappings vs. Substance in Industrial Marketing', *Harvard Business Review*, 48(4), July/August, pp. 93–102

Anderson, E. and Weitz, B. (1986), 'Make-or-Buy Decisions', *Sloan Management Review*, 27(1), Spring

Badaracco, Joseph, L., Jr. (1991), *The Knowledge Link – How Firms Compete Through Strategic Alliances*, Harvard Business School Press, Mass.

Baily, P.J.H. and Farmer, D. (1990), *Purchasing Principles and Management*, 6th edition, Pitman, London

Baily, P.J.H., Farmer, D., Jessop, D. and Jones, D. (1994), *Purchasing Principles and Management*, 7th edition, Pitman, London

Baker, M.J. (1996), *Marketing: an Introductory Text*, 6th edition, Macmillan, London

Barczak, G. and Wilemon, D. (1992), 'Successful New Product Team Leaders', *Industrial Marketing Management*, 21(1), February, pp. 61–68

Beard, C. and Easingwood, C. (1996), 'New Product Launch: Marketing Action and Launch Tactics for High-Technology Products', *Industrial Marketing Management*, 25(2), March, pp. 87–103

Beltramini, R.F. (1986), 'Ethics and the Use of Competitive Information Acquisition Strategies', *Journal of Business Ethics*, 5, pp. 307–311

Bettis, R.A., Bradley, S.P. and Hamel, G. (1992), 'Outsourcing and Industrial Decline', *Academy of Management Executive*, 6(1), February, pp. 7–22

Beyer, J.M., Chattopadhyay, P., George, E., Glick, W.H., Ogilvie, D.T. and Pugliese, D. (1997), 'The Selective Perception of Managers Revisited', *Academy of Management Journal*, 40(3), pp. 716–737

Biemans, W.G. and Brand, M.J. (1995), 'Reverse marketing: a synergy of purchasing and relationship marketing', *International Journal of Purchasing and Materials Management*, 31(3), Summer, pp. 29–37

Biong, H. and Selnes, F. (1996), 'The Strategic Role of the Salesperson in Established Buyer–Seller Relationships', *Journal of Business-to-Business Marketing*, 3(3), pp. 39–78

Birou, L.M. and Fawcett, S.E. (1993), 'International purchasing: Benefits, requirements, and challenges', *International Journal of Purchasing and Materials Management*, 29(2), Spring, pp. 27–37

Blenkhorn, D.L. and Banting, P.M. (1991), 'How Reverse Marketing Changes Buyer–Seller Roles', *Industrial Marketing Management*, 20(3), August, pp. 185–191

Blois, K.J. (1994), 'Discounts in Business Marketing Management', *Industrial Marketing Management*, 23(2), April, pp. 93–100

Bondra, J.C. and Davis, T.R.V. (1996), 'Marketing's role in cross-functional information management', *Industrial Marketing Management*, 25(3), May, pp. 187–195

Bonoma, T.V. (1982), 'Major Sales: Who *Really* Does the Buying?', *Harvard Business Review*, 60(3), May/June, pp. 111–119

Bonoma, T.V. and Shapiro, B.P. (1983), *Segmenting the Industrial Market*, Lexington Books, Lexington, MA

Boynton, A.C. (1993), 'Achieving dynamic stability through information technology', *California Management Review*, 35(2), Winter, pp. 58–77

Boynton, A.C. and Victor, B. (1991), 'Beyond Flexibility: Building and Managing the Dynamically Stable Organization', *California Management Review*, 34(1), Fall, pp. 53–66

Bresnen, M. (1996), 'An Organizational Perspective on Changing Buyer–Supplier Relations: a Critical Review of the Evidence', *Organization*, 3(1), pp. 121–146

Brockner, J. (1992), 'The Escalation of Commitment to a Failing Course of Action: Toward Theoretical Progress', *Academy of Management Review*, 17(1), January, pp. 39–61

Brown, M. (1997), 'Outsourcery', *Management Today*, January, pp. 56–60

Brown, R.V., Lilien, G.L. and Ulvila, J.W. (1993), 'New Methods for Estimating Business Markets', *Journal of Business-to-Business Marketing*, 1(2), pp. 33–60

Browning, J.M. and Zabriskie, N.B. (1980), 'Professionalism in Purchasing: a Status Report', *Journal of Purchasing and Materials Management*, 16, Fall, pp. 2–10

Brownlie, D. (1995), 'Environmental Scanning', in Baker, M.J. (ed.), *The Marketing Book*, 3rd edition, Heinemann, 1995, pp. 139–192

Buttle, F. (ed.) (1996), *Relationship Marketing: Theory and Practice*, Paul Chapman Publishing Ltd, London

Campbell, A., Devine, M. and Young, D. (1990), '*A Sense of Mission*', The Economist Books, Hutchinson, London

Cardozo, R.N. (1980), 'Situational Segmentation of Industrial Markets', *European Journal of Marketing*, 14(5/6), pp. 264–276

Carter, J.R. and Narasimhan, R. (1994), 'The role of purchasing and materials management in total quality management and customer satisfaction', *International Journal of Purchasing and Materials Management*, 30(3), Summer, pp. 3–13

Chisnall, P.M. (1995), *Strategic Business Marketing*, 3rd edition, Prentice-Hall, Englewood Cliffs, NJ

Choffray, J.M. and Lilien, G.L. (1978), 'Assessing Response to Industrial Marketing Strategy', *Journal of Marketing*, 42(2), April, pp. 20–31

Choffray, J.M. and Lilien, G.L. (1980), 'Industrial Market Segmentation by the Structure of the Purchasing Process', *Industrial Marketing Management*, 9, pp. 331–342

Christopher, M., Payne, A. and Ballantyne, D. (1991), *'Relationship Marketing'*, Butterworth Heinemann, Oxford

Clark, G.L., Kaminski, P.F. and Brown, G. (1990), 'The Readability of Advertisements and Articles in Trade Journals', *Industrial Marketing Management*, 19(3), August, pp. 251–260

Coe, B.J. (1990), 'Strategy in Retreat: Pricing Drops Out', *Journal of Business and Industrial Marketing*, 5(1), Winter/Spring, pp. 5–25

Cohern, W. and Czepiec, H. (1988), 'The Role of Ethics in Gathering Corporate Intelligence', *Journal of Business Ethics*, 7, pp. 199–203

Collins, J.C. and Porras, J.I. (1991), 'Organizational Vision and Visionary Organizations', *California Management Review*, 34(1), Fall, pp. 30–52

Comer, J.M. and Zirger, B.J. (1997), 'Building a Supplier–Customer Relationship Using Joint New Product Development', *Industrial Marketing Management*, 26(2), March, pp. 203–211

Connor, P.E. and Hopkins, R.K. (1997), 'Cost plus what? The importance of accurate profit calculations in cost-plus agreements', *International Journal of Purchasing and Materials Management*, 33(2), Spring, pp. 35–40

Cooper, R.G. (1975), 'Why new industrial products fail', *Industrial Marketing Management*, 4, pp. 315–326

Cooper, R.G. (1980), 'Project NewProd: Factors in New Product Success', *European Journal of Marketing*, 14(5/6), pp. 277–292

Cooper, R.G. (1984), 'New Product Strategies: What distinguishes the Top Performers', *Journal of Product Innovation Management*, 2, pp. 151–164

Cooper, R.G. (1996), 'Overhauling the New Product Process', *Industrial Marketing Management*, 25(6), November, pp. 465–482

Cooper, R.G. and Kleinschmidt, E.J. (1988), 'Resources Allocation in the New Product Process', *Industrial Marketing Management*, 17(3), August, pp. 249–262

Cooper, R.G. and Kleinschmidt, E.J. (1995), 'Performance Typologies on New Product Projects', *Industrial Marketing Management*, 24(5), October, pp. 439–456; also Cooper, R.G. and Kleinschmidt, E.J. (1995), 'Benchmarking the firm's critical success factors in new product development', *Journal of Product Innovation Management*, 12(5), November, pp. 374–391

Cravens, D.W., Greenley, G., Piercy, N.F. and Slater, S. (1997), 'Integrating Contemporary Strategic Management Perspectives', *Long Range Planning*, 30(4), pp. 493–506

Dale, B.G. and Cunningham, M.T. (1983), 'The Purchasing/Manufacturing Interface in the Make or Buy Decision', *Journal of Purchasing and Materials Management*, 19(1), pp. 11–18

Dale, B.G. and Cunningham, M.T. (1984), 'The Importance of Factors other than Cost Considerations in Make and Buy Decisions', *International Journal of Operations and Production Management*, 4(2), pp. 43–54

Davies, M. (1998), *Understanding Marketing*, Prentice Hall, Hemel Hempstead, UK

Davies, R. (1996), 'Collaboration and Competitiveness in the Automotive Components Industry', *unpublished MSc (Marketing) thesis*, Manchester School of Management, UMIST, Manchester

de Chernatony, L., Daniels, K. and Johnson, G. (1993), 'A Cognitive Perspective on Managers' Perceptions of Competition', *Journal of Marketing Management*, 9(4), October, pp. 373–381

De Meyer, A., Nakane, J., Miller, J.G. and Ferdows, K. (1989), 'Flexibility: the Next Competitive Battle: the Manufacturing Futures Survey', *Strategic Management Journal*, 10(2), pp. 5–144

Dibb, S. (1997), 'How Marketing Planning Builds Internal Networks', *Long Range Planning*, 30(1), February, pp. 53–63

Dion P.A. and Banting P.M. (1988), 'Industrial Supplier–Buyer Negotiations', *Industrial Marketing Management*, 17(1), February, pp. 43–48

Dion, P.A., Banting, P.M., Picard, S. and Blenkhorn, D.L. (1992), 'JIT Implementation: a Growth Opportunity for Purchasing', *International Journal of Purchasing and Materials Management*, 28(4), Fall, pp. 32–38

Donaldson, W.G. (1995), 'Manufacturers Need to Show Greater Commitment to Customer Service', *Industrial Marketing Management*, 24(5), October, pp. 421–430

Doyle, P. (1998), *Marketing Management and Strategy*, 2nd edition, Prentice Hall, Hemel Hempstead, UK

Drumwright, M.E. (1994), 'Socially Responsible Organizational Buying: Environmental Concern as a Noneconomic Buying Criterion', *Journal of Marketing*, 58(3), July, pp. 1–19

Egan, C., Shipley, D. and Howard, P. (1992), 'The Importance of Brand Names in Industrial Markets', in Baker, M.J. (ed.), *Perspectives on Marketing Management*, Vol. 2, 1992, Wiley, Chichester, UK

Ellram, L.M. (1993), 'Total Cost of Ownership: Elements and Implementation', *International Journal of Purchasing and Materials Management*, 29(4), Fall, pp. 3–11

Ellram, L.M. and Carr, A. (1994), 'Strategic Purchasing: a History and Review of the Literature', *International Journal of Purchasing and Materials Management*, 30(2), Spring, pp. 10–18

Evans, R.H. (1993), 'Analyzing the potential of a new market', *Industrial Marketing Management*, 22(1), February, pp. 35–39

Fern, E.F. and Brown, J.R. (1984), 'The Industrial/Consumer Marketing Dichotomy: a Case of Insufficient Justification', *Journal of Marketing*, 48, Spring, pp. 68–77

File, K.M. (1995), 'Is There a Trillion Dollar Family Business Market?', *Industrial Marketing Management*, 24(4), August, pp. 247–255

Fisher, R.J., Maltz, E. and Jaworski, B.J. (1997), 'Enhancing Communication Between Marketing and Engineering: the Moderating Role of Relative Functional Identification', *Journal of Marketing*, 61, July, pp. 54–70

Fletcher, K. (1995), *Marketing Management and Information Technology*, 2nd edition, Prentice Hall International (UK) Ltd, London

Ford, D. (1980a), 'Introduction' [Editor's introduction to the special edition on *Developments in Industrial Marketing*], *European Journal of Marketing*, 14(5/6), pp. 235–238

Ford, D. (1980b), 'The Development of Buyer–Seller Relationships in Industrial Markets', *European Journal of Marketing*, 14(5/6), pp. 339–353

Ford, D. (1984), 'Buyer–Seller Relationships in International Industrial Markets', *Industrial Marketing Management*, 13, pp. 101–112

Ford, D. (ed.) (1997), *Understanding Business Markets: Interaction, Relationships and Networks*, 2nd edition, Dryden Press, London

Ford, D., Cotton, B., Farmer, D. and Gross, A. (1993), 'Make-or-buy decisions and their implications', *Industrial Marketing Management*, 22(3), August, pp. 207–214

Ford, D. and Farmer, D. (1986), 'Make or Buy: a Key Strategic Issue', *Long Range Planning*, 19(5), October, pp. 54–62

Frankwick, G.L., Walker, B.A. and Ward, J.C. (1994), 'Belief structures in conflict: Mapping a strategic marketing decision', *Journal of Business Research*, 31(1,2), October/November, pp. 183–195

Frazier, G.L., Spekman, R.E. and O'Neal, C.R. (1988), 'Just-in-Time Exchange Relationships in Industrial Markets', *Journal of Marketing*, 52(4), October, pp. 52–67

Gagne, M.L. and Discenza, R. (1992), 'Accurate Product Costing in a JIT Environment', *International Journal of Purchasing and Materials Management*, 28(4), Fall, pp. 28–31

Gassenheimer, J.B., Calantone, R.J. and Scully, J.I. (1995), 'Supplier involvement and dealer satisfaction: implications for enhancing channel relationships', *Journal of Business and Industrial Marketing*, 10(2), pp. 7–19

Gentry, J.J. (1993), 'Strategic alliances in purchasing: Transportation is the vital link', *International Journal of Purchasing and Materials Management*, 29(3), Summer, pp. 11–17

Gilliland, D.I. and Johnston, W.J. (1997), 'Toward a model of business-to-business marketing communications effects', *Industrial Marketing Management*, 26(1), January, pp. 15–29

Gobeli, D.H. and Brown, D.J. (1993), 'Improving the Process of Product Innovation', *Research-Technology Management*, 32(2), March/April, pp. 38–44

Goldman, S.L. and Nagel, R.N. (1993), 'Management, technology and agility: the emergence of a new era in manufacturing', *International Journal of Technology Management*, 8(1/2), pp. 18–38

Good, D.J. and Stone, R.W. (1995), 'Computer technology and the marketing organization: an empirical investigation', *Journal of Business Research*, 34(3), November, pp. 197–209

Greatorex. M., Mitchell, V.-W. and Cunliffe, R. (1992), 'A Risk Analysis of Industrial Buyers: the Case of Mid-Range Computers', *Journal of Marketing Management*, 8, pp. 315–333

Greenley, G.E. and Bayus, B.L. (1993), 'Marketing Planning Decision Making in UK and US Companies: an Empirical Comparative Study', *Journal of Marketing Management*, 9, pp. 155–172

Griffin, A. and Hauser, J.R. (1996), 'Integrating R&D and Marketing: a Review and Analysis of the Literature', *Journal of Product Innovation Management*, 13, pp. 191–215

Grönroos, C. (1994), 'Quo Vadis, Marketing? Toward a Relationship Marketing Paradigm', *Journal of Marketing Management*, 10, pp. 347–360

Gross, A.C., Banting, P.M., Meredith, L.N. and Ford, I.D. (1993), '*Business Marketing*', Houghton Mifflin, Boston, Mass.

Gummesson, E. (1987), 'The New Marketing: Developing Long-Term Interactive Relationships', *Long Range Planning*, 20(4), August, pp. 10–20

Hague, P. (1992), *The Industrial Market Research Handbook*, 3rd edition, Kogan Page, London

Hague, P. and Jackson, P. (1994), *The Power of Industrial Brands*, McGraw-Hill, London

Håkansson, H. (1987), 'Product development in Networks', in Håkansson, H. (ed.), *Industrial Technological Development – a Network Approach*, 1987, Croom Helm, pp. 84–128 *[also in Ford, 1997, pp. 475 496]*

Håkansson, H. and Eriksson, A.-K. (1993), 'Getting Innovations Out of Supplier Networks', *Journal of Business-to-Business Marketing*, 1(3), pp. 3–43

Håkansson, H. and Snehota, I. (1989), 'No Business is an Island: the Network Concept of Business Strategy', *Scandinavian Journal of Management*, 4(3), pp. 187–200

Hamel, G., Doz, Y. and Prahalad, C.K. (1989), 'Collaborate with Your Competitors – and Win', *Harvard Business Review*, 67(1), January/February, pp. 133–139

Hamel, G. and Prahalad, C.K. (1989), 'Strategic Intent', *Harvard Business Review*, 67(3), May/June, pp. 63–76

Han, S-L., Wilson, D.T. and Dant, S.P. (1993), 'Buyer–Supplier Relationships Today', *Industrial Marketing Management*, 22, pp. 331–338

Harrell, G.D. and Fors, M.F. (1992), 'Internal Marketing of a Service', *Industrial Marketing Management*, 21(4), November, pp. 299–306

Harrigan, K.R. (1985), *Strategic Flexibility: a Management Guide for Changing Times*, D.C. Heath and Co., Lexington Books

Harrison, A. (1992), *Just-in-time Manufacturing in Perspective*, Prentice-Hall, London

Hart, S.J. (1993), 'Dimensions of Success in New Product Development: an Exploratory Investigation', *Journal of Marketing Management*, 9, pp. 23–41

Heinritz, S. *et al.* (1991), *Purchasing: Principles and Applications*, 8th edition, Prentice-Hall, London

Hill, R.W. and Hillier, T.J. (1977), *Organizational Buying Behaviour*, Macmillan, London

Hise, R.T. and Reid, E.L. (1994), 'Improving the Performance of the Industrial Sales Force in the 1990s', *Industrial Marketing Management*, 23(4), October, pp. 273–279

Hodgkinson, G.P. and Johnson, G. (1994), 'Exploring the mental models of competitive strategists: the case for a processual approach', *Journal of Management Studies*, 31(4), July, pp. 525–551

Hooley, G.J. and Jobber, D. (1986), 'Five Common Factors in Top Performing Industrial Firms', *Industrial Marketing Management*, 15(2), May, pp. 89–96

Howard, N. and Sheth, J. (1969), *Consumer Buyer Behavior*, John Wiley, New York

Hutt, M.D., Johnston, W.J. and Ronchetto, J.R. (1985), 'Selling Centers and Buying Centers: Formulating Strategic Exchange Patterns', *Journal of Personal Selling and Sales Management*, 5, May, pp. 33–40

Jackson, R.W. and Cooper, P.D. (1988), 'Unique Aspects of Marketing Industrial Services', *Industrial Marketing Management*, 17(2), May 1988, pp. 111–118

James, B.G. (1985), *Business Wargames: Business Strategy for Executives in the Trenches of Market Warfare*, Penguin Books, Harmondsworth

Jobber, D. and Horgan, I.G. (1988), 'A Comparison of Techniques Used and Journals Taken by Marketing Researchers in Britain and the USA', *Service Industries Journal*, 8(3), July, pp. 277–285

Johannessen, J.-A., Olsen, B. and Olaisen, J. (1997), 'Organizing for Innovation', *Long Range Planning*, 30(1), February, pp. 96–109

Johnson, P.F. and Leenders, M.R. (1997), 'Make-or-Buy Alternatives in Plant Disposition Strategies', *International Journal of Purchasing and Materials Management*, 33(2), Spring, pp. 20–26

Johnston, R. and Lawrence, P.R. (1988), 'Beyond Vertical Integration – the Rise of the Value-Added Partnership', *Harvard Business Review*, 66(4), July/August, pp. 94–101

Johnston, T.C. and Hewa, M.A. (1997), 'Fixing Service Failures', *Industrial Marketing Management*, 26(5), September, pp. 467–473

Johnston, W.J. (1994), 'Organizational buying behavior – 25 years of knowledge and research', *Journal of Business and Industrial Marketing*, 9(3), pp. 4–5

Johnston, W.J. and Bonoma, T.V. (1981), 'The Buying Centre: Structure and Interaction Patterns', *Journal of Marketing*, 45, Summer, pp. 143–156

Johnston, W.J. and Lewin, J.E. (1997), 'Advances in Industrial Marketing

Theory and Research from the *Journal of Business and Industrial Marketing*, *Journal of Business Research*, 38, pp. 199–209

Jones, T.C. and Ridley, D.W. (1987), 'Using Inventory for Competitive Advantage Through Supply Chain Management', *International Journal of Physical Distribution and Materials Management*, 17, pp. 94–104

Kalwani, M.U. and Narayandas, N. (1995), 'Long-Term Manufacturer–Supplier Relationships: Do They Pay Off for Supplier Firms?', *Journal of Marketing*, 59(1), January, pp. 1–16

Kanter, R.M. (1989), *When Giants Learn to Dance – Mastering the Challenges of Strategy, Management and Careers in the 1990s*, Simon and Schuster, NY

Katrichis, J.M. (1998), 'Exploring Department Level Interaction Patterns in Organizational Purchasing Decisions', *Industrial Marketing Management*, 27(2), pp. 135–146

Kelly, P.J. and Coaker, J.W. (1976), 'The Importance of Price as a Choice Criterion for Industrial Purchasing Decisions', *Industrial Marketing Management*, 5, October, pp. 281–292

Kennedy, A. (1983), 'Buyer Behaviour', in Baker, M.J. (ed.), *Marketing Theory and Practice*, 2nd edition, Macmillan, 1983

Kistner, L.J., di Benedetto, C.A. and Bhoovaraghavan, S. (1994), 'An Integrated Approach to the Development of Channel Strategy', *Industrial Marketing Management*, 23(4), October, pp. 315–322

Kohoutek, H.J. (1988), 'Coupling Quality Assurance Programs to Marketing', *Industrial Marketing Management*, 17(3), August, pp. 177–188

Krause, D.R. (1997), 'Supplier Development: Current Practices and Outcomes', *International Journal of Purchasing and Materials Management*, 33(2), Spring, pp. 12–19

Kyj, M.J. (1987), 'Customer Service as a Competitive Tool', *Industrial Marketing Management*, 16(3), August, pp. 225–230

Lambert, D.M., Sharma, A. and Levy, M. (1997), 'What Information can Relationship Marketers Obtain from Customer Evaluations of Salespeople?', *Industrial Marketing Management*, 26(2), March, pp. 177–187

Lamming, R. (1993), *Beyond Partnership*, Prentice Hall, Hemel Hempstead, UK

LaPlaca, P.J. (1993), 'Editorial', *Journal of Business and Industrial Marketing*, 8(2), pp. 3–4

Laric, M.V. (1980), 'Pricing Strategies in Industrial Markets', *European Journal of Marketing*, 14(5/6), pp. 303–321

Leenders, D. and Blenkhorn, D.L. (1988), *Reverse Marketing: the New Buyer–Seller Relationship*, Free Press, New York

Lehmann, D.R. and O'Shaughnessy, J. (1974), 'Differences in Attribute Importance for Different Industrial Products', *Journal of Marketing*, 38, April, pp. 36–42

Leuthesser, L. (1997), 'Supplier Relational Behavior: an Empirical Assessment', *Industrial Marketing Management*, 26(3), May, pp. 245–254

Leverick, F., Littler, D.A., Bruce, M. and Wilson, D.F. (1998), 'Using

Information Technology Effectively: a Study of Marketing Installations', *Journal of Marketing Management*, 14(8), pp. 927–962

Lichtenthal, J.D. and Butaney, G. (1991), 'Undergraduate Industrial Marketing: Content and Methods', *Industrial Marketing Management*, 20, pp. 231–239

Lichtenthal, J.D., Wilson, D.T. and Long, M.M. (1997), 'Scientific Contributions to the Field from the *Journal of Business-to-Business Marketing*', *Journal of Business Research*, 38, pp. 211–233

Littler, D.A., Leverick, F. and Wilson, D.F. (1998), 'Collaboration in New Technology Based Product Markets', *International Journal of Technology Management*, 15(1/2)

Littler, D.A. and Wilson, D.F. (1991), 'Strategic Alliancing in Computerized Business Systems', *Technovation*, 11(8), pp. 457–473

Littler, D.A. and Wilson, D.F. (1992), 'Globalization and Customization: the Role of Collaboration', paper presented at the Twelfth Annual Strategic Management Society Conference, Amsterdam

Low, B.K.H. (1996), 'Long-Term Relationships in Industrial Marketing: Reality or Rhetoric?', *Industrial Marketing Management*, 25(1), January, pp. 23–35

Low, B.K.H. (1997), 'Managing Business Relationships and Positions in Industrial Networks', *Industrial Marketing Management*, 26(2), March, pp. 189–202

Luffman, G.A. (1974), 'The Processing of Information by Industrial Buyers', *Industrial Marketing Management*, pp. 363–375

Lunn, A. (1986), 'Segmenting and Constructing Markets', in Worcester, R.M. and Downham, J. (eds.), *Consumer Market Research Handbook*, 3rd edition, McGraw-Hill, London, pp. 387–423

Magrath, A.J. (1990), 'The Hidden Clout of Marketing Middlemen', *Journal of Business Strategy*, 11(2), March/April, pp. 38–41

Maltz, E. (1997), 'An Enhanced Framework for Improving Cooperation Between Marketing and Other Functions: the Differential Role of Integrating Mechanisms', *Journal of Market Focused Management*, 2(1), pp. 83–98

Mansfield, E. and Rapoport, J. (1975), 'The Costs of Industrial Product Innovation', *Management Science*, August, pp. 1380–1386

Mast, K.E. and Hawes, J.M. (1986), 'Perceptual Differences Between Buyers and Engineers', *Journal of Purchasing and Materials Management*, 22(1), Spring, pp. 2–6

Matthyssens, P. and Van den Bulte, C. (1994), 'Getting closer and nicer: Partnerships in the supply chain', *Long Range Planning*, 27(1), February, pp. 72–83

McCracken, G.K. and Callahan, T.J. (1996), 'Is there such a thing as a free lunch?', *International Journal of Purchasing and Materials Management*, 32(1), Winter, pp. 44–50

McDonald, M.H.B. (1989), 'Ten barriers to marketing planning', *Journal of Marketing Management*, 5(1), Summer, pp. 1–18

McKenna, R. (1995), 'Real-time marketing', *Harvard Business Review*, 73(4), July/August, pp. 87–95

Min, H. and Galle, W.P. (1997), 'Green purchasing strategies: Trends and implications', *International Journal of Purchasing and Materials Management*, 33(3), Summer, pp. 10–17

Mintzberg, H. (1993), 'The pitfalls of strategic planning', *California Management Review*, 36(1), Fall, pp. 32–47

Mintzberg, H., Brunet, H.P. and Waters, J.A. (1986), 'Does planning impede strategic thinking: Tracking the strategies of Air Canada from 1937 to 1976', in Lamb, R.B. and Shrivastava, P. (eds), *Advances in Strategic Management*, vol. 4, JAI Press, Greenwich, CT, pp. 3–41

Mitchell, A., Puxty, A., Sikka, P. and Willmott, H.C. (1994), 'Ethical statements as smoke-screens for sectional interests: the case of the UK accountancy profession', *Journal of Business Ethics*, 13(1), January, pp. 39–51

Mitchell, V.-W. and Wilson, D.F. (1998), 'Balancing Theory and Practice: a Reappraisal of Business-to-Business Segmentation', *Industrial Marketing Management*, 27(5), pp. 429–445

Mohr, J. (1998), 'Managing a Total Quality Orientation: Factors Affecting Customer Satisfaction', *Industrial Marketing Management*, 27(2), pp. 109–125

Möller, K. and Wilson, D.T. (1995), 'Business Marketing', in Baker, M.J. (ed.), *Companion Encyclopedia of Marketing*, Routledge, London, pp. 803–817 (*pages 815–816 refer*)

Moncrief, W.C. (1986), 'Ten Key Activities of Industrial Salespeople', *Industrial Marketing Management*, 15(4), November, pp. 309–317

Moncrief, W.C. (1988), 'Five Types of Industrial Sales Jobs', *Industrial Marketing Management*, 17(2), May, pp. 161–167

Monczka, R.M., Nichols, E.L. and Callahan, T.J. (1992), 'Value of Supplier Information in the Decision Process', *International Journal of Purchasing and Materials Management*, 28(2), Spring, pp. 20–30

Monczka, R.M. and Trent, R.J. (1992), 'Worldwide Sourcing: Assessment and Execution', *International Journal of Purchasing and Materials Management*, 28(4), Fall, pp. 9–19

Morgan, N.A. and Piercy, N.F. (1992), 'Market-Led Quality', *Industrial Marketing Management*, 21(2), May, pp. 111–118

Morgan, R.M. and Hunt, S.D. (1994), 'The Commitment–Trust Theory of Relationship Marketing', *Journal of Marketing*, 58(3), July, pp. 20–38

Moriarty, R.T. and Moran, U. (1990), 'Managing Hybrid Marketing Systems', *Harvard Business Review*, 68(6), November/December, pp. 146–155

Morris, M.H. and Joyce, M.L. (1988), 'How Marketers Evaluate Price Sensitivity', *Industrial Marketing Management*, 17(2), May, pp. 169–176

Mudambi, S.M., Doyle, P. and Wong, V. (1997), 'An Exploration of Branding in Industrial Markets', *Industrial Marketing Management*, 26, pp. 433–446

Naurus, J. and Anderson, J. (1986), 'Turn Your Industrial Distributors into Partners', *Harvard Business Review*, 64(2), March/April

New, C.C. and Myers, A. (1986), '*Managing Manufacturing Operations in the UK, 1975–1985*', British Institute of Management, Corby, UK, pp. 56

Newman, R.G. and McKeller, J.M. (1995), 'Target pricing – a challenge for purchasing', *International Journal of Purchasing and Materials Management*, 31(3), Summer, pp. 13–20

O'Neal, C.R. (1989), 'JIT Procurement and Relationship Marketing', *Industrial Marketing Management*, 18(1), February, pp. 55–64

Oakland, J.S. (1995), 'Total Quality Management', in Baker, M.J. (ed.), *Companion Encyclopedia of Marketing*, Routledge, London, pp. 953–978

Olson, E.M., Walker, O.C. and Ruekert, R.W. (1995), 'Organizing for Effective New Product Development: the Moderating Role of Product Innovativeness', *Journal of Marketing*, 59(1), January, pp. 48–60

Osborn, R.N. and Hagedoorn, J. (1997), 'The Institutionalization and Evolutionary Dynamics of Interorganizational Alliances and Networks', *Academy of Management Journal*, 40(2), pp. 261–278

Parikh, J., Neubauer, F. and Lank, A. (1994), *Intuition: the New Frontier of Management*, Blackwell, Oxford

Parkinson, S.T. (1982), 'The Role of the User in Successful New Product Development', *R&D Management*, 12(3)

Parkinson, S.T. (1991), 'World Class Marketing: From Lost Empires to the Image Men', *Journal of Marketing Management*, 7(3), July, pp. 299–311

Parkinson, S.T. and Baker, M.J. (1986), *Organizational Buying Behaviour: Purchasing and Marketing Management Implications*, Macmillan, Basingstoke, UK

Parthasarthy, R. and Sethi, S.P. (1992), 'The Impact of Flexible Automation on Business Strategy and Organizational Structure', *Academy of Management Review*, 17(1), Jan, pp. 86–111

Patton, W.E. (1997), 'Individual and Joint Decision-Making in Industrial Vendor Selection', *Journal of Business Research*, 38, pp. 115–122

Peattie, K. and Ratnayaka, M. (1992), 'Responding to the Green Movement', *Industrial Marketing Management*, 21(2), May, pp. 103–110

Peters, T.J. and Waterman, R.H. Jnr. (1982), *In Search of Excellence – Lessons from America's Best-run Companies*, Harper and Row, NY

Piercy, N.F., Cravens, D.W. and Morgan, N.A. (1998), 'Salesforce Performance and Behaviour-Based Management Processes in Business-to-Business Sales Organizations', *European Journal of Marketing*, 32(1/2)

Pilling, B.K. and Zhang, L. (1992), 'Cooperative Exchange: Rewards and Risks', *International Journal of Purchasing and Materials Management*, 28(2), Spring, pp. 2–9

Pitt, L.F. and Nel, D. (1988), 'The Wearer's Merit – A Comparison of the Attitudes of Suppliers and Buyers to Corruption in Business', *Industrial Marketing and Purchasing*, 3(1), pp. 30–39

Plank, R.E. (1997), 'Theory, Practice, and Empirical Development Contributions: Advances in Business Marketing and Purchasing', *Journal of Business Research*, 38, pp. 235–241

Porter, M.E. (1980), *Competitive Strategy: Techniques for Analysing Industries and Competitors*, Free Press, NY

Porter, M.E. (1985), *Competitive Advantage – Creating and Sustaining Superior Performance*, Free Press, NY

Puri, S.J. and Korgaonkar, P. (1991), 'Couple the Buying and Selling Teams', *Industrial Marketing Management*, 20(4), November, pp. 311–317

Ramsay, J. (1996), 'The Case Against Purchasing Partnerships', *International Journal of Purchasing and Materials Management*, 32(4), Fall, pp. 13–19

Raphael, J. and Parker, I.R. (1991), 'The Need for Market Research in Executive Decision Making', *Journal of Business and Industrial Marketing*, 6(1/2), Winter/Spring, pp. 15–21

Reekers, N. and Smithson, S. (1996), 'The Role of EDI in Inter-Organizational Coordination in the European Automotive Industry', *European Journal of Information Systems*, 5, pp. 120–130

Reese, N.A., Whipple, T.W. and Courtney, A.E. (1987), 'Is Industrial Advertising Sexist?', *Industrial Marketing Management*, 16(4), November, pp. 231–240

Reichard, C.J. (1985), 'Industrial Selling: Beyond Price and Resistance', *Harvard Business Review*, 63(2), March/April

Ries, A. and Trout, J. (1986), *Marketing Warfare*, McGraw-Hill International, Singapore

Robinson, P.T., Faris, C.W. and Wind, Y. (1967), *Industrial Buying and Creative Marketing*, Allyn and Bacon, Boston, Mass.

Samli, A.C., Wills, J.R. and Herbig, P. (1997), 'The Information Superhighway Goes International: Implications for Industrial Sales Transactions', *Industrial Marketing Management*, 26(1), January, pp. 51–58

Sashittal, H.C. and Wilemon, D. (1996), 'Marketing Implementation in Small and Midsized Industrial Firms: an Exploratory Study', *Industrial Marketing Management*, 25(1), January, pp. 67–78

Sasseen, J., (1992), 'Delivering the Goods', *International Management*, September, pp. 72–75

Schmitz, J.M. (1995), 'Understanding the Persuasion Process Between Industrial Buyers and Sellers', *Industrial Marketing Management*, 24(2), March, pp. 83–90

Schultz, D.E. (1996), 'The inevitability of integrated communications', *Journal of Business Research*, 37(3), November, pp. 139–146

Schultz, N.O., Collins, A.B. and McCulloch, M. (1994), 'The Ethics of Business Intelligence', *Journal of Business Ethics*, 13, pp. 305–314

Segal, M.N. (1989), 'Implications of Single vs. Multiple Buying Sources', *Industrial Marketing Management*, 18(3), August, pp. 163–178

Shapiro, B.P. (1988), 'Close Encounters of the Four Kinds: Managing Customers in a Rapidly Changing Environment', *Harvard Business Review*, 66

Shapiro, B.P. *et al.* (1992), 'Staple Yourself to an Order', *Harvard Business Review*, 70(4), July/August, pp. 113–122

Sharland, A. and Balogh, P. (1996), 'The value of non-selling activities at international trade shows', *Industrial Marketing Management*, 25(1), January, pp. 59–66

Sharma, A. and Lambert, D.M. (1994), 'How Accurate are Salespersons' Perceptions of Their Customers?', *Industrial Marketing Management*, 23(4), October, pp. 357–365

Sharma, A. and Sheth, J.N. (1997), 'Supplier Relationships: Emerging Issues and Challenges', *Industrial Marketing Management*, 26(2), March, pp. 91–100

Sheth, J.N. (1973), 'A Model of Industrial Buyer Behavior', *Journal of Marketing*, 37(4), October, pp. 50–56

Shipley, D. and Howard, P. (1993), 'Brand-Naming Industrial Products', *Industrial Marketing Management*, 22(1), pp. 59–66

Sinclair, S.A. and Seward, K.E. (1988), 'Effectiveness of Branding a Commodity Product', *Industrial Marketing Management*, 17(1), February, pp. 23–33

Smith, J.B. (1997), 'Selling Alliances: Issues and Insights', *Industrial Marketing Management*, 26(2), March, pp. 149–161

Smith, J.B. and Barclay, D.W. (1993), 'Team-Selling Effectiveness: a Small Group Perspective', *Journal of Business-to-Business Marketing*, 1(2), pp. 3–32

Smith, J.B. and Barclay, D.W. (1997), 'The Effects of Organizational Differences and Trust on the Effectiveness of Selling Partner Relationships', *Journal of Marketing*, 61(1), January, pp. 3–21

Song, X.M., Montoya-Weiss, M.M. and Schmidt, J.B. (1997), 'Antecedents and Consequences of Cross-Functional Cooperation: a Comparison of R&D, Manufacturing, and Marketing Perspectives', *Journal of Product Innovation Management*, 14(1), January, pp. 35–47

Song, X.M., Neeley, S.M. and Zhao, Y. (1996), 'Managing R&D – Marketing integration in the new product development process', *Industrial Marketing Management*, 25(6), November, pp. 545–553

Spekman, R.E., Salmond, D.J. and Lambe, C.J. (1997), 'Consensus and Collaboration: Norm-Regulated Behaviour in Industrial Marketing Relationships', *European Journal of Marketing*, 31(11/12), pp. 832–856

Spender, J.-C. (1996), 'Making Knowledge: the Basis of a Dynamic Theory of the Firm', *Strategic Management Journal*, 17, Winter, pp. 45–62

Stacey, R.D. (1990), *Dynamic Strategic Management for the 1990s: Balancing Opportunism and Business Planning*, Kogan Page, London

Strauss, G. (1964), 'Work-Flow Frictions, Inter-Functional Rivalry and Professionalism: a Case Study of Purchasing Agents', *Human Organizations*, 23, pp. 137–149

Stump, R.L. and Sriram, V. (1997), 'Employing Information Technology in Purchasing: Buyer–Supplier Relationships and Size of the Supplier Base', *Industrial Marketing Management*, 26(2), March, pp. 127–136

Talaysum, A.T., Hassan, M.Z. and Goldhar, J.D. (1987), 'Uncertainty Reduction Through Flexible Manufacturing', *IEEE Transactions on Engineering Management*, EM–34(2), May, pp. 85–91

Tanner, J.F. (1996), 'Buyer Perceptions of the Purchase Process and its Effect on Customer Satisfaction', *Industrial Marketing Management*, 25(2), March, pp. 125–133

Tanner, J.F. and Chonko, L.B. (1995), 'Trade Show Objectives, Management, and Staffing Practices', *Industrial Marketing Management*, 24(4), August, pp. 257–264

Tsoukas, H. (1997), 'The Tyranny of Light: the Temptations and Paradoxes of the Information Society', *Futures*, 29(9), pp. 827–843

Turnbull, P.W. (1994), 'Business-to-Business Marketing: Organizational Buying Behaviour', in Baker, M.J. (ed.), *The Marketing Book*, 3rd edition, Heinemann, pp. 216–237

Turnbull, P.W. and Valla, J.-P. (eds) (1986), *Strategies for International Industrial Marketing*, Croom Helm, Beckenham, UK

Turnbull, P.W. and Valla, J.-P. (1987), 'Strategic Planning in Industrial Marketing: an Interaction Approach', *European Journal of Marketing*, 121(5), pp. 5–20

Turner, G.B., Taylor, G.S. and Hartley, M.F. (1994), 'Ethics policies and gratuity acceptance by purchasers', *International Journal of Purchasing and Materials Management*, 30(3), Summer, pp. 43–47

Venkatesan, R. (1992), 'Strategic Sourcing: To Make or Not To Make', *Harvard Business Review*, 70(6), November/December, pp. 98–107

Venkatesh, R., Kohli, A.K. and Zaltman, G. (1995), 'Influence Strategies in Buying Centers', *Journal of Marketing*, 59, October, pp. 71–82

Von Hippel, E. (1978), 'Successful Industrial Products from Customer Ideas', *Journal of Marketing*, 42(1), January, pp. 39–49; and 'A Customer-Active Paradigm for Industrial Product Idea Generation', *Research Policy*, 7, 1978, pp. 240–266

Vredenburg, H. and Droge, C. (1987), 'The Value of Company Newsletters and Magazines', *Industrial Marketing Management*, 16(3), August, pp. 173–178

Wagner, W.B. (1987), 'The Changing Price Dimension in Purchasing', *European Journal of Marketing*, 21(1), pp. 5–13

Walsh, V., Roy, R., Potter, S. and Bruce, M. (1992), '*Winning by Design: Technology, Product, Design and International Competitiveness*', Basil Blackwell, Oxford

Watts, C.A. and Hahn, C.K. (1993), 'Supplier development programs: an empirical analysis', *International Journal of Purchasing and Materials Management*, 29(2), Spring, pp. 10–17

Watts, C.A., Kim, K.Y. and Hahn, C.K., (1992), 'Linking Purchasing to Corporate Competitive Strategy', *International Journal of Purchasing and Materials Management*, 28(4), Fall, pp. 2–8

Webster, F.E. (1970), 'Informal Communication in Industrial Markets', *Journal of Marketing*, 7, May, pp. 186–89

Webster, F.E. and Wind, Y. (1972), *Organizational Buying Behavior*, Prentice-Hall, Englewood Cliffs, NJ; *see also* Webster, F.E. Jr. and Wind, Y., 'A General Model of Organizational Buying Behavior', *Journal of Marketing*, 36(2), April 1972, pp. 12–19

Weeks, W.A. and Stevens, C.G. (1997), 'National account management sales training and directions for improvement: a focus on skills/abilities', *Industrial Marketing Management*, 26(5), September, pp. 423–431

Weitz, B.A., Sujan, H. and Sujan, M. (1986), 'Knowledge Motivation and Adaptive Behaviour: a Framework for Improving Selling Effectiveness', *Journal of Marketing*, 50, October

Welch, J.A. and Nayak, P.R. (1992), 'Strategic Sourcing: a Progressive Approach to the Make-or-Buy Decision', *Academy of Management Executive*, 6(1), February, pp. 23–31

Williams, A.J. and Smith, W.C. (1990), 'Involving Purchasing in Product Development', *Industrial Marketing Management*, 19(4), November pp. 315–319

Williams, J.D., Gopalakrishna, S. and Cox, J.M. (1993), 'Trade show guidelines for smaller firms', *Industrial Marketing Management*, 22(4), November, pp. 265–275

Willmott, H.C. (1994), 'Business process re-engineering and human resource management', *Personnel Review*, 23(3), pp. 34–46

Wilson, D.F. (1994), '*Competitiveness in a Volatile Environment: Marketing Strategy in the UK Computer Industry*', *unpublished PhD thesis*, Manchester School of Management, UMIST, Manchester

Wind, Y. (1978), 'Issues and Advances in Segmentation Research', *Journal of Marketing Research*, 15, August, pp. 317–337

Wind, Y. and Cardozo, R. (1974), 'Industrial Market Segmentation', *Industrial Marketing Management*, 3, pp. 153–166

Womack, J.P., Jones, D.T. and Roos, D. (1990), *The Machine that Changed the World*, Rawson Macmillan, NY

Wotruba, T.R. (1980), 'The Changing Character of Industrial Selling', *European Journal of Marketing*, 14(5/6), pp. 293–302

Yip, W.R.W.Y. (1993), 'Segmentation and Strategic Analysis: Principles and Practice', *unpublished MSc (Marketing) thesis*, Manchester School of Management, UMIST, Manchester

—PART II
Readings

Introduction

The first of the four readings (LaPlaca, 1997) is taken from a special issue of the *Journal of Business Research* (*JBR*) which focused on the contributions to the field of organizational marketing by four of the leading periodicals in this area. The contributions of *Industrial Marketing Management* (*IMM*), the longest established of these periodicals, form the bulk of this literature and LaPlaca's article (he is *IMM*'s editor) provides a convenient and valuable summary of the cumulative wealth of studies published by *IMM* over the last 24 years. However, readers are also encouraged to explore the three further main articles in the special edition of *JBR* which summarize the contributions of the *Journal of Business and Industrial Marketing* (Johnston and Lewin, 1997), the *Journal of Business-to-Business Marketing* (Lichtenthal *et al.*, 1997), and of the less frequent periodical specializing in longer articles, *Advances in Business Marketing and Purchasing* (Plank, 1997).

1 LaPlaca, P. (1997), 'Contributions to Marketing Theory and Practice from *Industrial Marketing Management*', *Journal of Business Research*, 38, pp. 179–198

The remaining readings address different practical and theoretical aspects while sharing a common perspective of successful organizational marketing as the effective management of collaborative exchange relationships, both within and between organizations, aimed at the prosecution of mutually compatible objectives.

The second reading relates to purchasing issues, probably the most important specific aspect of organizational marketing whether seen from the customer's perspective (as purchasing) or from the supplier's perspective (as marketing). It is, of course, crucial for effective organizational marketers to have a clear perception of the customer's purchasing perspective. The reading gives a clear picture of how professional purchasing is managed and of the underlying principles which are driving a more collaborative approach to this crucial strategic issue for the competitiveness of all organizations.

2 Gadde, L.-E. (1995), 'Purchasing Management', in Baker, M.J. (ed.), *Companion Encyclopedia of Marketing*, Routledge, London, pp. 187–201

The third reading addresses another vital competitive issue – product development – which is especially problematic in uncertain and fast-moving environments, and is increasingly approached in organizational markets through collaborative strategies, both between functional areas and between organizations. Cooper gives a clear and vigorous analysis of the practical problems and sensible responses involved in managing product development, based on his extensive empirical research over many years.

3 Cooper, R.G. (1996), 'Overhauling the New Product Process', *Industrial Marketing Management*, 25(6), November, pp. 465–482

The fourth reading discusses the challenging contributions of the interaction approach to a better understanding of organizational marketing. It is this theoretical background, reflecting the collective research of the IMP Group, that gives much of the conceptual credibility to the current interest in collaborative strategies and relationship management in organizational marketing.

4 The IMP Group (1997), 'An Interaction Approach', in Ford, D. (ed.), *Understanding Business Markets: Interaction, Relationships and Networks*, Dryden Press, London, 2nd edition, pp. 3–22 [first published in Håkansson, H. (ed.) (1982), *International Marketing and Purchasing of Industrial Goods – an Interaction Approach*, John Wiley, New York, pp. 7–26]

The last reading is a brief extract from Hodgkinson (1996) which can be linked to many different aspects of organizational marketing though marketing was probably not what Hodgkinson had in mind when he wrote it. The extract reminds us that marketing is part of organizational management and administration, and so part of our general and specific social interaction as individuals, each with multiple organizational allegiances. Astute readers will recognize the potential for applying an understanding of marketing to various aspects of interpersonal and interorganizational exchanges (such as career management) beyond the contexts which have dominated our attention so far. In short, Hodgkinson provides a salutary warning not to place too much reliance on the elaborate strategies we construct for ourselves and our organizations in our attempts to manipulate collective and individual exchanges towards the achievements of distant personal and organizational objectives.

EXTRACT FROM HODGKINSON, 1996

Policy making – that is, the formulation and implementation of policy – cannot occur *tabula rasa*. Each policy maker arrives at the table already prejudiced and predisposed. Any myth of impartiality is akin to the illusion of scientific objectivity. Any decision entails values and any single decision maker embodies an a priori value complex. When policy is being formed or, in other words, when organizational philosophy is being established, what happens is that a factual scenario is *re*presented to the policy makers with more or less logical consistency and empirical accuracy. Included in this representation, explicitly or tacitly, is a projection of hypothetical future states of affairs. This is then subjugated to the value considerations of the policy making administrators. That is, to their desires, wills and intentions. Thus, through complex and subtle processes, as well as simple and direct mechanisms, agendas conflict and interact, and via dialogue, dialectic, and power the purposes, aims, objectives, and goals of the organization come to be formulated. An actual organizational value complex evolves which, regardless of the formulation or verbalization or rhetoric in which it is couched, becomes the mundane, quotidian philosophy that is translated into the realities and events of the workaday world through managerial processes.

(Source: Hodgkinson, C. (1996), *Administrative Philosophy:*
Values and Motivations in Administrative Life,
Pergamon, Elsevier Science Ltd, Oxford, p. 11)

1 Contributions to marketing theory and practice from industrial marketing management

Peter J. LaPlaca
UNIVERSITY OF CONNECTICUT
EDITOR-IN-CHIEF, *INDUSTRIAL MARKETING MANAGEMENT*

During its first twenty-four years of publication, *Industrial Marketing Management* has been at the forefront of development of marketing thought applied to industrial, high-tech, and business-to-business market environments. Over 900 articles have appeared concerned with topics such as: marketing strategy and planning, marketing management, industrial buyer behavior, sales and sales management, marketing research, product development, pricing and others. As its name implies, over thirty percent of *Industrial Marketing Management*'s articles have focused on the management of marketing and sales functions. This article presents highlights of outstanding articles from *IMM*'s past arranged by major topical area: marketing management, market segmentation, strategic marketing planning, selling and sales management, purchasing and industrial buying behavior, global and international industrial, researching industrial markets, innovation and new product development, distribution, pricing, and promotions and advertising.
©1997 Elsevier Science Inc. *J Busn Res* 1997. 38.179–198

Industrial Marketing Management (IMM) was started as the official publication of the European Association for Industrial Marketing

Address correspondence to Peter J. LaPlace, Department of Marketing, University of Connecticut, 368 Fairfield Road, U-41-M, Storrs, CT 06269-2041.

Journal of Business Research 38, 179–198 (1997)
© 1997 Elsevier Science Inc.
655 Avenue of the Americas, New York, NY 10010

Research. Since the first issue of *IMM* appeared in 1971, there have been 915 articles published dealing with industrial buyer behavior, sales and sales management, marketing research, product development, pricing, and other topics. The three editors, R. Derek Medford (editor from 1971–1973), James D. Hlavacek (editor from 1974–1993), and Peter J. LaPlaca (editor since 1994), have following the same editorial philosophy for acceptance of articles submitted by authors. Under the theme of 'scholarly applied research,' submitted papers are judged by the standards of making a contribution to the field of industrial marketing, demonstrating useful practical applications to marketing managers, synthesizing existing research, or presenting accepted marketing thought in an innovative manner.

Table 1 shows the distribution of articles that have appeared in the first 23 years of publication (from 1971–1994). The single most common subject of an article published in *IMM* has been management of the marketing function, including articles focusing on strategic marketing planning, marketing control, organizing the marketing function, decision systems, product planning, segmentation, and developing and implementing marketing plans. I will discuss some of the major findings presented in *IMM* in each of the above topical areas.

MARKETING MANAGEMENT

Segmentation and marketing planning have been the two most frequent topics covered under the generic heading of marketing management. One of the earliest management articles by Fluitman (1973a) looked at the most profitable way of handling the product mix and concluded that many companies have too many products in their product line (have things changed any in the ensuing 22 years?) and that the sales force misallocates its time with the firm's past or current products rather than the products that will ensure the firm's future stability. Wasson (1976) demonstrated how the product life cycle can be used to develop a dynamic marketing strategy (and its components) as the product moves from introduction through to maturity to eventual elimination. Stiff and Khera (1977) provided a useful explanation of how industrial marketing managers can use changes in price, quality, service, and delivery to develop better fits with different market segments. That same year Evans (1977) looked at the need for obtaining direct input from the salesforce before a final decision to eliminate a product due to poor financial results. Several authors revisited the issue of product elimination including an article by Avlonitis (1984), which described a multistage process using financial, marketing, resources released, and managerial considerations in selecting products for elimination from the company's product offering.

That companies succeed or fail as total entities rather than as individual components was clearly demonstrated in an excellent article by

Table 1 Distribution of articles published by topic

General topics	Total	Percent
Management	146	15.90
Sales management	134	14.60
Global marketing	123	13.40
Buyer behavior	113	12.31
Marketing research	102	11.11
Product development	88	9.59
Distribution	41	4.47
Promotions	38	4.14
Pricing	26	2.83
Other topics, case stories	326	35.51
	1137	123.86

Total exceeds 100% due to multiple topics with many articles (of 915 articles published)

Blois (1985). He shows that the new manufacturing capabilities can be used to create distinctive competence only if marketing teams are aware of these capabilities and can translate them into effective selling propositions aimed at specific market needs. For example, marketing can input customer needs into a computer-aided design unit as the front end of a computer-integrated manufacturing system. Product design and development works with this information to rapidly design potential products. These designs can be linked with rapid prototyping technologies to produce samples for customer and manufacturing evaluation, drastically reducing the entire product development cycle. Whereas this article focused on an offensive type of marketing strategy, numerous articles in *IMM* have dealt with defensive strategies. For instance, Calantone and di Benedetto (1990) use a derivative of the Defender Model (1983) to develop alternative strategies to counter a variety of competitive attacks. This article investigated those conditions under which product improvements might be more effective than price modifications or promotional strategies.

In addition to the impact of technology on the process of marketing such as the link between marketing and product design and manufacturer caused by CAD-CAM-CIM, there have been many changes in the business world which have impacted a variety of industrial marketers. One such change has been the development of Just-In-Time (JIT) inventory and materials systems. In 1990 Dion, Banting, and Hasey (1990) discuss a wide variety of impacts of JIT systems on development and implementation of marketing strategies including price and cost reductions, quicker deliveries and reduced inventories, and increased profits. Mitchell, Quinn, and Percival (1991) present six strategies useful for marketing of mature products. The first strategy looks at a secondary takeoff whereby minor technological improvements in the product are used to promote more frequent purchase by existing customers and the attraction of new customers. Dynamic adaptation, the second strategy discussed, uses marketing mix variations to hold market share by blunting competitive actions. Recycling strategies prolong the life of the product by image enhancement through advertising or packaging. A fourth strategy, product rejuvenation, uses minor or secondary product features and benefits to attract new market segments. Secondary stretching and harvesting are useful when there is little competitive pressure to accelerate product decline. The final strategy is regeneration by product-based strategies or the use of new technologies borrowed from other products to enhance the appeal of the original product (for example emphasizing the environmentally friendly nature of the product which is now made of a biodegradable material.) Sousa de Vasconcell (1991) also reported that whereas the critical success factors for mature industrial products varied from product to product, advertising, sales promotion, and customer financing are never seen as greatly important and may be deemed universal non-critical success factors.

Perrien and Richard (1995) look at the development of relationships between buyers and sellers in an industrial context. They find that while the relationship has different meanings to the buyer and to the seller, both view marketing relationships as advantageous and as a way to make the entire exchange process more efficient.

Market segmentation

Market segmentation has been a frequent subject for *IMM* authors over the years. Cardozo and Wind (1973) presented *IMM*'s first article on this important topic. They show that the principal use of market segmentation had been to explain the results of marketing strategy rather than to plan marketing strategies. The a priori approach that the authors recommended is to conduct a two-stage segmentation of markets. The first stage, or macro stage, defines segments based on characteristics of the buying organization and the buying situation, and the second, or micro stage, divides the macrosegments into microsegments based on the characteristics of the decision-making units. This technique has become the principal way industrial companies segment their markets. The approach was expanded upon by Choffray and Lilien (1980) to include the structure of the purchasing process and the level and type of involvement by different people or organizations in this process. For example some firms might use an outside consultant to provide input to the evaluation of alternative product offerings (especially for complex, technical products), whereas others will use only in-house personnel. Each situation will require a different approach by the seller.

Boyd and Headen (1978) applied the concept of market segmentation to product portfolio analysis by asking the simple question of

Figure 1 An approach to segmentation of organizational markets

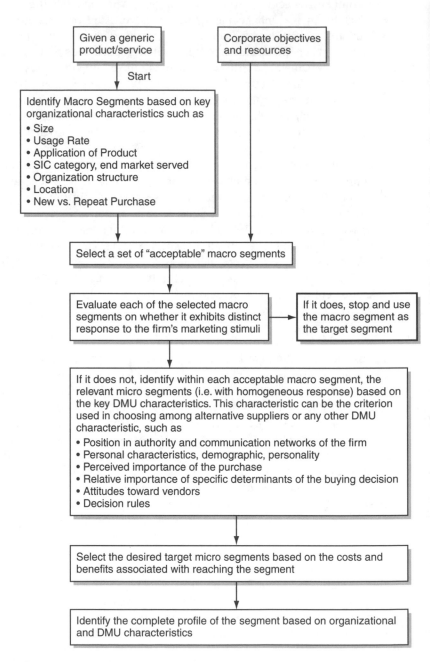

Adapted from Cardozo. Richard, and Wind, Yoram, Industrial Market Segmentation. *IMM* 3(3) (1973): 156

'relative share of what?'. Alternative segmentation strategies and measurements can yield greatly differing conclusions for strategic decisions. Depending on the definition of the market, what was once considered a 'cash cow' could become a 'dog' or since different market segments could be growing at different rates, a 'cash cow' could be reclassified as a 'star' with quite different investment requirements and expectations. Parasuraman (1980) extended the application of market segmentation to segmentation of vendors by matching characteristics of vendor performance (e.g., speed of delivery, quality, etc.) with needs of specific customer segments. In this way vendors noted for rapid delivery would be used when serving market segments with the same requirement and slower vendors (at a lower cost) could be used when dealing with market segments where speed of delivery was not as important a factor.

Wind, Robertson, and Fraser (1982) demonstrated the need to develop multiple estimates of market penetration for new products aimed at segmented markets. Separate forecasts of sales for each segment were recommended rather than the traditional use of a single diffusion model for the entire market. Using examples from medical technology, the authors show that overall forecasts are more accurate when developed as a composite of forecasts for distinct segments. Bonoma and Shapiro (1984) look at the cost of implementing various segmentation strategies and the benefits that managers can derive from each. They recommend that marketing managers use more economical methods of market segmentation before using more costly modifications of marketing mix components. They also caution against oversegmenting a market due to the high costs involved.

Planck (1985), in a review of over 30 articles dealing with industrial market segmentation from 1964 to 1984, concluded that segmentation is more of a strategic problem of resource allocation rather than a statistical analysis of market data. Almost all segmentation approaches fall into one of three categories. The first is the single stage approach (customer characteristics, product dimension, type of distribution, etc.) where only one variable is used to define market segments. The second group uses two tiers to macro segment followed by a micro segmenting of the market, for example, an initial cut using SIC codes combined with type of purchase decision-making to refine initial segmentation strategies. The third category of segmentation approaches is the nested approach whereby several levels of segmentation criteria are used to fine tune marketing strategies for maximum effectiveness. Laughlin and Taylor (1991) develop market segments by looking at responses to controllable marketing variables. In this way segments that are homogenous in their response to marketing variables are identified. In a similar vein Dibb and Simkin (1994), using international examples, conclude that segmentation paradigms based on market behavior are more useful than product-based segments widely used by industry.

Strategic marketing planning

From the very first issue of *Industrial Marketing Management*, market-ing planning has been a strong component of the articles published. Far-rer (1971) applied the product life cycle to analyzing the military market to plan marketing approaches. Farrer modeled the entire life cycle of a weapons system purchased by the U.S. Army and showed that marketing strategies must be dynamic throughout the entire life cycle for maximum effectiveness.

Spitz (1975) investigated the product planning process and found that numerous legal, technological, social, and other factors seriously impede progress in developing new products. He recommended that industry-based teams educate public agencies on the negative impact of regulation on new product development. He also discussed some of the popular new product development models of the time such as STRATOP, NEWPROD, and GERTS. In the same issue of *IMM*, C. Davis Fogg (1975) outlined a comprehensive approach to developing new business plans. This included proper goal setting for new products, identification of opportunities in the marketplace, and careful entry strategies. As shown in Figure 2, the initial step in developing an entry strategy for a new business is to develop the goals of the company and of the program. The scope of the business will place limits on where management should look for opportunities. Objectives should be spe-cific in terms of sales, profits, market penetration, and market share. The third step is to define strategy – how will the objectives be met and what strategies are open to follow (aggressive pricing, extensive distribution, heavy promotions, etc.) Once the goals are set, the fourth step is to iden-tify potential opportunities that may meet stated goals. Fifth, each opportunity must be examined to see if it will meet stated objectives and

Figure 2 The process of planning

I. GOAL SETTING

• Define scope
• Define objectives
• Define strategies

II. OPPORTUNITY IDENTIFICATION

• Identify opportunities

III. ENTRY PLANNING

• Conduct specific market research
  and planning
• Plan actual entry

Adapted from Fogg, C. Davis. The New Business Planning Process. *IMM* 4(6) (1975): 295.

if there is a practical strategy for entering the market. Finally, the sixth step is to plan the actual entry into those businesses that survive this rigorous screening. Fogg also described the various types of market, competitive, technology, and financial information necessary to adequately plan for new business development. Doyle (1975) demonstrated the need for systematic review of all products offered by multiproduct firms to assure that the product line did not become overly complex with resources being devoted to products with minimal returns and potential long-range winners being starved for adequate resources. Doyle (1975) showed the need to look at demand and cost interactions, sales covariance, and risk covariance before eliminating specific products based on data that only pertain to its sales and profits.

Market environments are undergoing a period of transition from long-term stability to an unstable and unpredictable era. Marketers are concerned with the ability to adapt to increasing rates of change as well as concern for accountability and productivity of the marketing function, especially when faced with the diversity resulting from broadening of the market base. Citing the need to adapt planning systems to these dynamic environmental considerations, Hempel and LaPlaca (1975) developed 10 guidelines for the strategic planner:

1   The key to effective planning is adequate information.
2   Planners should develop models to facilitate adaptability in a period of transition.
3   A systems perspective is essential for effective strategic planning.
4   New planning styles are needed to improve flexibility in dealing with uncertainty and unanticipated changes.
5   Specific goals and evaluative criteria need to be specified as primary considerations to focus planning decisions.
6   Planning horizons should be flexible parameters of the planning process.
7   Successful strategic planning requires broad-based organizational support and involvement.
8   Planners should stress the concept of marketing productivity, especially as it pertains to the attainment of both corporate and societal objectives.
9   Effective planning in a period of transition requires a revitalization of the marketing concept.
10 The concept of positioning provides a useful orientation for achieving balance in the planning process.

Hopkins (1977) described several of the planning tools used by industrial companies. These included the PIMS model, the General Electric planning matrix, the Boston Consulting Group's Growth-Share Matrix, and the Arthur D. Little strategy center matrix. Shah and LaPlaca (1981) showed the importance of incorporating analysis of marketing, competitive, financial, business portfolio, technological, and regulatory risks in developing comprehensive marketing and business plans. In two separate articles, Jackson and Cooper (1988) and Woodside, Sanderson, and Brodie (1988) look at the unique aspects of marketing industrial services. Jackson and Cooper (1988) presented a new paradigm for classifying industrial services as well as industrial products that incorporate service as a major component of the customer's purchase. Woodside, Sanderson, and Brodie (1988) described a system for testing the acceptance of industrial services at different levels of distribution.

SELLING AND SALES MANAGEMENT

Articles dealing with selling and sales management are the second most common to have appeared in *Industrial Marketing Management* during the past 24 years. From the very first issue where Hudson (1971) called on better integration of buying and selling functions (as a harbinger of integrated partnerships between buyers and seller in the 1990s), *IMM* has attracted many leading sales scholars and published over 130 articles dealing with some aspect of the sales function. Mattson (1973) describes how system selling (a combination of products and services offered by a single seller providing more extended fulfillment of customer needs and increasing the customer's dependence on the seller) can be used to increase barriers to switching and to market entry. Hannaford (1976) delineated the benefits of system selling for both buyers and sellers. He also provided tools and suggestions for system design and selecting the correct type of system to offer to satisfy higher level strategic needs as well as routine needs of purchasing function.

Rink and Dodge (1980) showed that changes in sales operations and management styles are necessary at different stages of the product life cycle. They use the four stages of the product life cycle to categorize 64 selling strategies and tactics. They also point out that the product life cycle does not relate to diversified companies where no one product or product line dominates the company's sales volume.

Gwinn and Perreault (1981) developed a model for sales call planning that optimizes the productive time spent in selling relative to call planning, administrative duties, traveling, waiting, and office time. Ferguson (1980) developed a heuristic algorithm to solve the problem of planning sales calls (the classic traveling salesman problem.) Plank and Dempsey (1980) presented a comprehensive model of personal selling based on five earlier models (stimulus-response, AIDA, needs-satisfaction, the grid system, and the depth approach.) The model covers the complexities of selling to industrial organizations and can serve as the basis for effective sales training as well as development of strategic selling strategies (see Figure 3).

Several articles have dealt with the problems of selecting members of the sales team. Johnston and Cooper (1981), Meidan (1982), Johnston

Figure 3 An organizational selling model

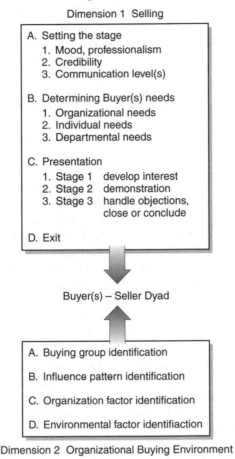

Dimension 1 Selling

A. Setting the stage
   1. Mood, professionalism
   2. Credibility
   3. Communication level(s)

B. Determining Buyer(s) needs
   1. Organizational needs
   2. Individual needs
   3. Departmental needs

C. Presentation
   1. Stage 1   develop interest
   2. Stage 2   demonstration
   3. Stage 3   handle objections,
                 close or conclude

D. Exit

Buyer(s) – Seller Dyad

A. Buying group identification

B. Influence pattern identification

C. Organization factor identification

D. Environmental factor identifiaction

Dimension 2 Organizational Buying Environment

Adapted from Plank, Richard, and Dempsey. William. A Framework for Personal Selling to Organizations. *IMM* 9(2) (1980): 145.

and Shields (1983), Bellizzi and Cline (1985), Powers (1987), Sager (1991), and Mehr (1992) all presented articles concerned with the selection, training, and evaluation of direct salespeople or independent sales reps. Mehr (1992) showed how to build an effective rep organization by redefining target accounts for the company, identifying rep firms currently selling those accounts, and leveraging company strengths with those reps to build strength in the marketplace. With costs of recruiting and training sales people approaching $30,000, effective systems for salesforce retention are critical. Sager (1991) describes the use of bio-data to select salespeople with high levels of commitment. Powers (1987) addresses the difficult task of switching from a rep network to direct sales people. Whereas sales potential is the most important factor to consider, fixed and variable salesforce costs versus rep commissions must also be factored into the decision process.

Bellizzi and Cline (1985) discuss the dilemma faced by many technology-oriented companies: should you hire people with sales backgrounds and train them in the technology of your products or should you hire people well versed in the technology and train them to be salespeople? They show that the greater the degree of technical information sought by the customer, the greater the benefit from hiring technically competent people and providing sales training. In these instances, the salesperson becomes an outside technical expert for the customers. Analysis of the cost of each type of person is required to determine the best mix of technical versus nontechnical people to have in the salesforce. Johnston and Shields (1983) showed that patterns of sales can exert a greater influence on evaluation of new sales people than the absolute sales levels. They caution about the use of sales trends when evaluating new sales hires especially when the salesperson has some degree of latitude in reporting when sales are logged.

Median (1982) presented a methodology for determining the optimal number of salespersons. He contrasted simulations, linear programming techniques, dynamic techniques, and return on time invested methods and concluded that no single technique was ideal for this problem but rather a combination approach yielded the best results.

As important as the proper selection process, sales managers are interested in determining the causes of salesperson failure. Ingram, Schwepker, and Hutson (1992) reported on a survey of 126 sales executives as to why salespeople fail. The six major reasons were: (1) poor listening skills, (2) failure to concentrate on top priorities, (3) lack of sufficient effort, (4) inability to determine customer needs, (5) lack of planning for sales presentations, and (6) inadequate product/service knowledge.

Several articles have looked at the problem of salesforce motivation and compensation. Demirdjian (1984) argued for a motivational program that addressed social and self-fulfillment needs in addition to economic needs. Conversely, Tyagi and Block (1983) see monetary compensation as the principal motivator of increased sales performance. They discuss numerous caveats for effective use of money as a motivator and present the pros and cons of open versus private pay policies. In a similar vein, Winer (1976) describes a monetary sales compensation program that ties the structure of the compensation (salary, commission, and bonus) to sales potentials in different sales regions. He argues that straight commission or uniform compensation programs that do not take into account differences in sales potential or necessity for expenses (e.g., excessive travel in sparsely populated sales territories) often lead to frustration, disappointment, turnover, and other negative consequences rather than to the increased performance and stability that are the goals of most motivational programs. Darmon (1982) showed the use of conjoint analysis to match salesmen's objectives with those of the company. A variety of sales compensation plans with differing levels of salary, commission, and bonus, but with the same overall level of compensation yielded different results in the salesmen's attainment of company objectives. Dalrymple, Stephenson, and Cron (1981) analyzed sales compensation programs based on product gross margins rather than sales levels. They found that gross margin plans do increase wages, they do not necessarily improve the profit contribution of the firm. Wotruba, Macfie, and Colletti (1991) examined the impact of sales force recognition programs in over 250 firms and found that some commonly perceived understandings for such programs (such as top management involvement, presenting awards at special events, and recognition in the presence of family and friends) are quite valid, whereas others (such as restricting the awards to the top third of the sales force) actually have undesired effects.

Barrett (1986) describes the methods for and benefits of establishing a separate sales force for major accounts. Major accounts represent the most important customers of the firm. A separate national accounts sales force is helpful in improving relationships between buyer and seller, increasing sales and share of purchases from national accounts, improving communication between buyers and sellers, coordinating sales from centralized purchase centers with deliveries to remote locations, and establishing a better dynamic balance between the buyer and seller. Narus and Anderson (1986) looked at the emerging roles of distributor sales forces composed of inside and outside salespersons. Industrial manufactures are increasingly relying on outside distributor salespersons to conduct prospecting for new accounts and acting as the first line interface between the customer and the manufacturer. These outside sales people are viewed by many customers as the product specialist to whom they turn for information about product use. Slatter (1987) looks at the unique roles of sales people in industries that typically operate in competitive bidding situations. These salesmen are tasked with increasing the credibility of the selling firm, undertaking marketing research about customers and competitors, influencing design and specifications to give the selling firm a competitive advantage, and establishing and maintaining a communication linkage between the two organizations before, during, and after the bidding process.

PURCHASING AND INDUSTRIAL BUYING BEHAVIOR

The foundation of all successful marketing is a firm understanding of customers and their needs, how they make buying decisions, and how purchasing is actually implemented. In the past 24 years over 100 articles dealing with industrial buyer behavior or the industrial purchasing process have appeared by many of the leading buyer behavior

Figure 4 Generalized model of the industrial purchasing situation

Marketing effort of supplying company

Marketing research	Product planning
Pricing and financial services	Technical services
Delivery services	Packaging
Advertising through varied media	Direct mail selling
Personal selling and aids	Public relations

1. Buying stages over time

1 Anticipation or recognition of a problem and a general solution	6 Acquisition and analysis of proposals
2 Determination of characteristics and quality of needed items	7 Evaluation of proposals, negotiation, price, performance parameters
3 Description of characteristics and quality of needed items	8 Selection of supplier, placing patronage
4 Determination of whether to make or buy	9 Selection of an order routine
5 Search for and qualification of potential sources	10 Performance feedback and evaluation payment for goods

2. Factors affecting buying behaviours

Product consideration, technology essentially value
Psychological and sociological factors affecting individual and group behaviours
Novelty of purchase
Reasons for purchase
Organizational environment

3. Possible functional areas involved in the buying decision

Marketing	Engineering
General management	Finance including budgetary control and accounting
Quality control	Purchasing
Industrial engineering production control	Research & development
Production	Factory receiving stores, control and shipping

A range of industrial purchases

Buildings	Capital equipment
Maintenance and R&D items	Raw and processed materials
Price parts	Trade components
Sub-assemblies	Consumables
Packaging	Services

Adapted from Hill, Roy W., The Nature of Industrial Buying Decisions, *IMM*, 2(1) (1972): 52.

researchers in the United States and Europe. In *IMM*'s first year, Wind and Webster (1972) boldly proclaimed that the study of organizational buying was as important as the study of household buying and presented a framework for the study of industrial buying behavior that served as the standard for researchers for many years. They said that the generalized models of consumer research would have to be modified and made more specific to the problems being studied by organizational buying researchers. Hill (1972) developed one of the earliest generalized models of the industrial buying process (see Figure 4). This model factored in the marketing efforts of the selling organization, a 10-stage buying process, environmental factors impacting the buying process, and the roles of different organizational components as the buying process progressed. He further looked at this process over a range of industrial product and service situations. Grønhaug (1975) developed a model to describe and predict autonomous vs. joint decisions in organizational buying. The key variables identified by the discriminant analysis were organizational size, goods used in the production process, size, and novelty of the purchase.

The development of a research approach to the study of organizational buying was further advanced by Zaltman and Bonoma (1977) in their summary of a focus group of leading organizational buying researchers. They proposed a structure which looked at a 2×2 matrix of corporate locus (intrafirm vs. interfirm influences) and departmental locus (intradepartmental vs. interdepartmental influences). One of the conclusions that was identified is that word-of-mouth communication among buying firms is greatly underestimated by selling organizations. They also provided a list of suggested research foci, which stimulated organizational buying research for many years. Nicosia and Wind (1977) presented an analysis of the general factors that were being incorporated into organizational buying models (see Figure 5). These included general characteristics of the buying firm (SIC, size, economic and financial resources, nature of operations and technology, location, and others), situation-specific organizational characteristics (amount and type of purchase, criteria for vendor selection, composition of the buying center, buying situation, etc.), general characteristics of the individual decision-maker (age, sex, position and authority, personality, etc.), and situation-specific characteristics of the decision-maker (attitudes toward vendors, loyalty to vendors, response to marketing stimuli, etc.) Current thinking of organizational buying behavior includes purchasing/marketing models (focusing on purchasing activities), economic models (such as minimum initial price or minimum life-cycle cost), and interdisciplinary models (which combine perspectives of economics, organizational theory, sociology, and psychology.)

Grønhaug (1977) used the example of a firm purchasing a computer to describe how firms undertake the purchase of complex products. In all but one case the process was initiated by the buyer rather than the

Figure 5 Traditional approaches to the study of interorganizational processes

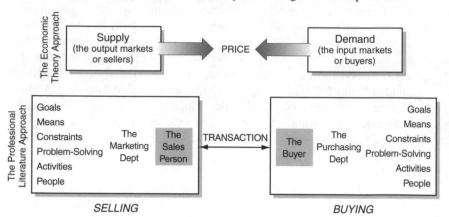

Adapted from Nicosia, Francesco. and Wind, Yoram, Emerging Models of Organizational Buying Processes. *IMM* 6(5) (1977): 365.

seller. He also found that senior officials were involved in three quarters of the cases studied. Robey and Johnston (1977) studied the impact of lateral influences and vertical authority in organizational buying decisions. Among the hypotheses supported by their research were the following:

- the larger the size of the organization, the greater the extent of lateral influences on buying decisions
- the more variety and the more uncertainty in the organization's environment, the greater the extent of lateral influences on buying decisions
- size is not related to the vertical distribution of influence on buying decisions; however, increasing size is related to the way in which the influence is exercised
- environmental uncertainty is related to greater discretion of lower levels in the buying process
- the greater the complexity of a purchase, the greater the extent of lateral influences and the greater the discretion of lower levels in buying decisions
- the newer the purchase, the greater the extent of lateral influences and the greater the discretion of lower levels in buying decisions.

One of the most widely recognized models of organizational buying behavior is the BUYGRID model (1967). Ferguson (1979) performed an elaborate statistical test of two of the model's components (modified rebuy and straight rebuy) and found that the model could *not* be supported by empirical evidence. Bellizzi and McVey (1983) also performed a test of this model and found a similar lack of empirical support for BUYGRID, especially when extended to determine the influence of marketing variables or environmental factors on the buying process. One of the components of the organizational buying model contained in BUYGRID is the concept of the buying center. Thomas (1984) found that expertise was the strongest factor in exerting influence upon the buying center. This factor was more than twice as important as the second most influencing factor: authority. Mattson (1988) also looked at the composition and influence of the buying center and found that as the purchase needs category was higher (e.g., capital equipment rather than component materials) or the dollar amount was higher, higher levels of management tended to constitute the buying center for that decision and tended to exert greater influence on the purchase decision. DeRose (1991) showed that selling messages which focused on value selling (lower costs, higher sales, or greater profits) have a positive influence at all levels in the buying center. This is especially true when the buying center is composed of cross-functional teams (purchasing, engineering, manufacturing, marketing, quality control, etc.) and the value message is developed from the buyer's perspective.

Personality traits among salespersons have been studied by many researchers, and numerous articles concerning this aspect of selling have appeared in *IMM*. Dion, Easterling, and Miller (1995) present an interesting perspective on this topic when they compare personality traits between buyers and sellers in the purchase dyad. They found that perceived similarities (rather than measured similarities) are linked to both buyer trust of a salesperson as well as to sales performance.

Another aspect of the organizational buying process is that of the purchasing function. Numerous articles have appeared in *IMM* investigating various aspects of the purchasing process. An analysis of the role of purchasing across the stages of the product life cycle was presented by Fox and Rink (1978). They found that purchasing provides different inputs to marketing decisions, depending on the stage of the life cycle. For example, during the design of new products purchasing agents can frequently link ideas from suppliers to the product development process; indeed suppliers can initiate product modifications by introducing new concepts through the purchasing department. During product launch, purchasing can reduce the firm's risk by minimizing long-term purchase commitments or leasing equipment. During the growth phase, purchasing can help reduce or eliminate component and materials shortages that can occur in high growth situations, and during maturity the critical role of purchasing is to stabilize materials commitments and assure timely shipments of production inputs. Finally, during decline the purchasing function can ease the firm's exit from the marketplace with careful matching of buying orders with sales forecasts to minimize work-in-process and finished goods inventories. Blenkhorn and Banting (1978) demonstrated that a broader concept of the purchasing function to include all aspects of organizational materials management provides for a better understanding of purchasing processes and can increase the benefits of the purchasing function on the firm. Bellizzi and Walter (1980) found that whereas purchasing agents are heavily involved in many stages of the purchasing process such as selection of the order routine, they are much less involved with other stages such as post-sale performance.

Of key concern to industrial sellers is the impact of dealing with a centralized purchasing department. Woodside and Samuel (1981) used the purchasing function of a large electronics firm to describe the benefits of coordinated purchasing on overall cost of purchased components for all five of the firm's business units. They developed models of all four of the coordinated purchasing system components: (1) development and analysis of purchase requirements, (2) preparing RFQs and analyzing quotations, (3) committee-supplier negotiations, and (4) post-purchase evaluation and reporting. Bellizzi and Belonax (1982) also studied the factors that influence whether or not centralized or decentralized buying methods were used and found that neither geographic nor communications separation were significantly related to centralized or decentralized forms of purchasing.

With increasing interest in JIT inventory systems, *IMM* authors turned their attention to the JIT process. Giunipero and O'Neal (1988) found six major barriers to implementing a JIT procurement system: type of production process (job shop vs. continuous production), frequency of schedule changes, lack of supplier benefits, distance from suppliers, focus on price vs. costs, and lack of role models to follow. They also provide marketers with specific responses to each of these barriers. O'Neal (1989) expanded this study to find support for six specific hypotheses: a desire for JIT will cause suppliers' marketing centers to (1) develop longer term relationships with those customers they wish to serve, (2) exercise greater care in the choice of industrial customers to serve, (3) develop a more extensive marketing center, encompassing a larger number of functional units, (4) develop a higher degree of interaction between the marketing center and the customer's buying center, (5) experience a greater degree of openness in communicating with the customer's buying center, and (6) provide a higher level of customer support activities for the OEM customers served.

GLOBAL AND INTERNATIONAL INDUSTRIAL MARKETING

From its beginnings in the European and United States market arena, *Industrial Marketing Management* has always incorporated a global perspective. Although global or international marketing has not been the central focus of *IMM*, over 13% of all articles that have appeared in the first 24 years of *IMM* have dealt with some aspects of international marketing. Some of these have been general in nature and others have explored specific industries in specific countries. In one of *IMM*'s first articles dealing with international marketing, Eid (1972) looked at the economic development role of marketing and the obstacles faced by firms from highly developed countries doing business in undeveloped countries. These obstacles include the absence of such institutions as grading systems, standard weights and measures, an adequate legal code covering rights and obligations under contracts, weak and ineffective distribution systems, shortages of managerial talent, and imbalances between economies of scale for production and distribution. The role of technology in successfully marketing to developing countries was discussed by Roman (1974). Roman pointed out that by the year 2000 80% of the world's 6.5 billion people will be living in developing countries and thus represent a tremendous market opportunity. He views technology transfer systems as the key approach to successfully establishing relationships in developing countries.

Dutch economist Andre van Dam (1976) warned industrial marketers to expect the unexpected and plan for scarcities in raw materials, components, and other necessities of production. He discussed the global scarcities that impacted global markets in 1972 through 1975 and presented suggestions for anticipating and coping with them. Brasch (1978) looked at the difficulties in forecasting sales when dealing with developing countries. Not only are reliable data sources scarce or not available, but unpredictable changes in economic activity, political upheaval, and institutional changes can wreak havoc on forecasts and the plans based upon these forecasts. The impact of changing technological bases in developing countries was discussed by Pal and Bowonder (1979). Because they can borrow technologies from more developed countries, technology life cycles in developing countries tend to be shorter than similar curves in advanced countries. Market windows of opportunity are therefore of shorter duration and payback of investments must of necessity be realized in a compressed time frame. Dawson (1987) also concluded that the best technologies for export to developing countries involve agricultural technologies (such as new seed strains or growing technologies) and infrastructure technologies (communication and energy transmission technologies) as these are most closely aligned with the needs of these markets and can experience the greatest growth rates. She also described the channels for technology transfer: direct knowledge transfers (direct investment, licensing and joint ventures, or free donations), and product introductions (including current products and simplified products.)

Exhibiting at trade shows would seem to be closely linked to exporting; however, because much exporting is actually done through representatives and middlemen, export opportunities at trade shows frequently are not explored. Bello and Barksdale (1986) discuss how firms that exhibit at trade shows can target foreign attendees and expand on export opportunities. Although there is difficulty in evaluating the credit of foreign buyers, a carefully trained staff and a firm committed to increasing export activities can overcome this problem. Firms must be committed to discovering export opportunities at many of the major trade shows in the United States (such as those in New York, Las Vegas, Chicago, and other major cities) and must develop effective protocols for staff attending the show. Trade missions are another vehicle for increasing export activity. Seringhaus (1987) discusses the use of trade missions and the necessity of having a management oriented to exporting to achieve the greatest benefit from participating in trade missions. He found that firms that participate in trade missions also are more systematic in market research, planning, and preparation for market entry than are firms that do not use trade missions as part of their export strategy. Herbig and Kramer (1992) point out that there are numerous differences between perceptions of American negotiators and those from foreign countries. Saving face, for example, is much more important in most countries than it is in the United States, and the concept of compromise is viewed by many as a sign of weakness. They present many examples of do's and don'ts that impact negotiation strategies and tactics when dealing with foreign business people. These factors are involved with national negotiating styles, differences in decision-making, status and protocol, social aspects of negotiations, attitudes toward time, personal relationships, and nonverbal communications. The article concludes with seven specific recommendations to improve the success of cross-cultural negotiations.

During the past 10 years researchers have paid more and more attention to the issue of countertrade. Shipley and Neale (1987) contrast domestic and international countertrade practices among large British companies. They estimate that countertrade accounts for between 20 and 30% of all international trade. Among the advantages they cite are the entry into difficult markets, increasing company competitiveness, overcoming currency control and exchange problems, and increasing sales volume. The biggest drawbacks of countertrade are lack of an in-house use for the goods and difficulties with resale. Reisman, Fuh, and Li (1988) discuss the various advantages of countertrade, depending upon the level of economic development (agrarian, developing, developed) of both the home country and the trading partner's country. They also describe types of countertrade including barter, counterpurchase, offset, switch (transfer of goods to another country or party), swap (redirecting of goods to another country), clearing (agreement between two countries to exchange specific amounts of goods over a specified time period), cooperation agreements (involving three or more parties for exchange of goods), and joint ventures. Reisman, Aggarwal, and Fuh (1989) describe a method of identifying profitable countertrade opportunities by analyzing the demand and supply of countertraded goods, applying probability measures to estimate the likelihood of profits to direct the firm to those opportunities with the greatest expected profit potential.

Articles in *IMM* have provided specific examples of international trade with many countries and areas of the world including: Australia, Belgium, Brazil, China, Czechoslovakia, Germany, Great Britain, India, Indonesia, Iran, Ireland, Japan, Korea, Kuwait, Nigeria, Sweden, Saudi Arabia, South Africa, Taiwan, Yugoslavia, Far East, Middle East, and Latin America. Specific countertrade examples have been presented dealing with China (Palia and Shenkar, 1991), Japan (Palia, 1993), and Australia (Leisch, 1994).

RESEARCHING INDUSTRIAL MARKETS

When the first article concerning research for industrial markets first appeared in *IMM* in 1973 (Fluitman, 1973), there was considerable confusion as to exactly what marketing research was, how to go about doing it, and what were the real benefits of this new science applied to industrial markets. Fluitman shed considerable light on this issue by showing that industrial marketing research does improve profitability, provides excellent input to the product design process, and can reduce the amount of time required to bring a successful product to market. Hall (1975) also visited the issue of the value of marketing research and found reduced risk was a major component to the value of the dollars spent on marketing research projects. Adler (1975) presented 12 procedures to reduce the cost of marketing research and get more return for dollars invested. Some of these included: (1) fully exhausting secondary sources before conducting primary research, (2) simplify complex research designs, (3) don't overspecify the degree of precision designed into the sampling plan, (4) use low cost methods for screening for low incidence respondents, (5) reduce overly long questionnaires, and (6) plan tabulations in advance.

Cox and Dominguez (1979) conducted an extensive comparison of marketing research procedures between consumer and industrial products. They found many problems using published secondary data including (1) timeliness of data collected only every five years, (2) need for finer SIC classifications than published data provides, (3) multiproduct establishments classified by their primary output, and (4) inaccuracies due to captive plants. They also found that industrial marketing researchers were rapidly adopting multivariate techniques used by consumer market researchers. According to Penn (1978), one of the problems with conducting industrial marketing research is the fact that many marketers want to rush to do the job without careful definition of the problem being investigated. Rather than focusing on symptoms, Penn urges industrial marketing researchers to develop a well-formulated problem statement with a full understanding of the implications of possible outcomes of the research. He proposes a generalized problem formulation process comprised of six steps: (1) discussion of the problem as given to the research department with the originator as well as with other divisions of the company that are involved with the question; (2) thinking the problem through, especially as to the nature of the real question and its implications to the firm; (3) preparation of a written statement of the problem or question and identification of the researchable aspects; (4) review with the originator to obtain agreement and approval of the statement, modified as necessary to satisfy his needs; (5) consideration of the hypotheses that can be developed to lead to approaches to the research effort and estimation of the costs of the effort; and (6) submission of written project proposal with the problem stated as agreed and with cost estimates for the work involved, both money and time. Gentry and Hailey (1981) raised the question about the representativeness of industrial samples and cautioned about the statistical analysis of survey data without first determining that there is no nonresponse bias in the sample by conducting a second sample taken from the nonrespondents to the first survey. Comparisons should be made on respondent (individual and company) demographics.

The use of focus groups and qualitative research techniques were presented in articles by Welch (1985) and Wallace (1984). Welch presented an excellent methodology for conducting focus groups including the planning of the entire process, recruiting process, selecting the moderator, costs incurred, and several common problems. Wallace described the use of qualitative research to fill in the 'why' and 'how' that is frequently not uncovered in quantitative surveys. She correctly pointed out the need for a much higher skill level for interviewers for qualitative research.

Several articles focused on techniques for improving sales forecasts. Many companies use the salesforce composite technique. Cox (1989) describes a system that improves the accuracy of salesforce sales forecasts. He lists five steps which should be taken including: (1) providing the salesforce with information that might affect the forecasts such as economic data, political considerations, changes in company policies, etc.; (2) provide salespeople with enough time to get the job done; (3) provide incentives for accuracy; and (4) formally adjust the salesperson's forecast based on past accuracy.

One area of marketing research, which has appeared numerous times in *IMM*, is concerned with ways to increase responses to mail surveys. Pressley (1980) provided numerous suggestions for generating routine response rates between 50 and 70%. Among these hints were: prenotification, high quality envelopes and stationary, yellow colored return envelope, current commemorative stamps, personalized cover letter incorporating benefits to the respondent of completing the questionnaire, and make the questionnaire easy to complete. Hansen, Tinney, and Rudelius (1983) may have stated the frequently overlooked but obvious, when they point out that sending the survey to the right person at the company will increase response rates. This should be done by a combination screening and prenotification telephone call.

In a survey to 1,000 sales executives, Skinner, Dubinsky, and Ingram (1983) found that the inclusion of humor in a survey had no impact on response rates. Duhan and Wilson (1990) and Murphy, Dalenberg, and Daley (1990) demonstrated that prenotification had positive impacts on response rates, response speed, and quality of the data. Jobber (1986) and Haggett and Mitchell (1994) also found that prenotification increased response rates; he also reported that both monetary and non-monetary incentives and follow-up contacts also increased response rates, although the use of colored questionnaires did not. Armstrong and Yokum (1994) found that a one-dollar incentive significantly increased response rates from members of professional groups. Chawla, Balakrishnan, and Smith (1992) also support the notion that incentives increase response rates among distributors. They also reported that university sponsorship resulted in higher response rates—a finding similar to that reported by Greer and Lohtia (1994) and Faria and Dickinson (1992). Chawla and Nataraajan (1994) found that surveys that included a Christian-sounding name as the sponsor yielded higher response rates than surveys sponsored by people with non-Christian-sounding names. Kallis and Giglierano (1992) found that the use of express mail was cost effective when trying to survey hard-to-reach executives. Ford, McLaughlin, and Williamson (1992) found that certified mail increased response rates for lengthy questionnaires but not for short ones.

Perhaps the two most comprehensive articles dealing with response rates for industrial surveys were by Diamantopoulos, Schlegelmilch, and Webb (1991) and by Walker, Kirchmann, and Conant (1987). Diamantopoulos, Schlegelmilch, and Webb looked at the process of industrial mail surveys based on the framework of communications theory. Using this structure, they examine all aspects of the survey process including the message, sponsorship, the cover letter and questionnaire, promise of anonymity and confidentiality, prenotification and follow-up, type of postage, monetary, and nonmonetary incentives. Walker, Kirchmann, and Conant presented a system called Total Design method, which focuses on the reasons people respond to surveys and provides a systematic means of optimizing all aspects of the survey process.

INNOVATION AND NEW PRODUCT DEVELOPMENT

The development and successful marketing of new products is the lifeblood of any firm. For 24 years, *Industrial Marketing Management* has welcomed submissions dealing with the new product process and approximately 10% of all published articles focus on some aspect of innovation and the new product development process. That we can learn from successes and failures alike is demonstrated by Briscoe (1973). With two examples of failed products in the plastics and steel industries, Briscoe shows that failures are the result of combinations of factors rather than a simple blunder. Cooper (1975) also looked at failed products and found that combinations of factors also were responsible for failure. He pointed out that a significant majority of these factors were market-based, yet firms spend relatively little on marketing research as opposed to technology research. Link (1987) also found that market factors were critical in most new product failures, including unforeseen competitive responses, inadequate marketing research, negligible savings or benefit to customers, improper promotional, selling, and distribution strategies.

Several *IMM* articles have dealt with the overall new product development process. Phelps (1977) was one of the first to point out the need for marketing and research people to work together to make new products more responsive to customer needs. Souder (1978) compared several new product management methods including: new products department, product committees, commercial project manager (the most common and most successful), commercial line manager (most likely to fail), technical project manager, technical line manager, commercial one-man show, technical one-man show, and dyad. The technically oriented management systems have a failure rate four times as high as the commercially (market) oriented systems.

Marketing managers are very concerned with the problem of new product development and introduction and with reducing the failure rate of products which enter the marketplace. Of key concern is the selection of which new product projects to pursue given limited resources and uncertainty in the market. Merrifield (1978) developed a screening model that looked at several business attractiveness factors (sales/profit potential, growth rate, competitive forces, opportunity to restructure a stagnant industry, distribution of risks, etc.) and company fit or strength factors (capital availability, in-house marketing and manufacturing capabilities, strength of technological basis, etc.) Rochford (1991) investigated 22 methods for generating new product ideas and described several screening methods and criteria. Cooper and de Brentani (1984) analyzed 86 screening items used by managers and reduced them to an 11-factor representation. The principal factors were: financial potential, corporate synergy, technology and production synergy, and product differential advantage. These factors were further elaborated on in a follow-up article that analyzed three key dimensions of product success: financial performance, market impact, and opportunity window (Cooper and Kleinschmidt, 1987). Cooper (1979) reported on a study of 102 new product successes and 93 failures to determine those factors that explained these results. As part of Project NEWPROD, he identified 15 factors that differentiated between success and failures. Among these were: (1) proficiency executing the launch—selling, promoting, and distributing; (2) a new product that is clearly superior in meeting customer needs than competitors' products; (3) a product that exceeds quality standards of competitive products; (4) having the sales force and/or distribution effort well targeted at the right customers, etc. In a follow-up study, Cooper (1982) also found the majority of industrial products that reach the market actually succeed. This contradicts earlier studies that estimate much lower success rates.

Miaoulis and LaPlaca (1982) developed a three-dimensional (product, technology, and market) systems approach for developing new high technology products. This system was divided into three stages: assessment, development, and execution. Cooper and Kleinschmidt (1991) studied the new product process at IBM, 3-M, General Motors, Northern Telecom, and Emerson Electric, firms noted for continued success in new product development (see Figure 6). These firms have new product development processes that are formal but flexible and involve cross-functional teams. Kortge and Okonkwo (1989) developed a methodology for simultaneous development of both the new product and the marketing strategy used for its launch (see Figure 7). This increases the likelihood of product success as well as reduces the time to market. They provide guidelines for development of the marketing strategy that parallels the new product development cycle of idea generation, screening, development, testing, and commercialization. Specific strategies are provided for product or service, promotion, distribution, and pricing concerns at each stage of product development. Vesey (1992) also visited the issue of decreasing time-to-market and concluded that the better integration of marketing and design teams and the use of concurrent engineering can greatly reduce the time it takes to get a product from concept to the marketplace.

Due to their exposure to outside suppliers and vendors and their centralized location with respect to the flow of information into the company, Williams and Smith (1990) encourage the incorporation of a firm's purchasing department as a member of the new product team. Nickolaus (1990) demonstrated the importance of involving distributors with the planning and launching of new products, especially for firms that market a substantial proportion of their sales through independent distributors. It is important to design the new product program to protect the distributor's investments as well as those of the manufacturer. Herbig and Golden (1994) contended that the movement from negligence to strict liability has hindered the development of new products. From pharmaceuticals to small piston aircraft to small companies, new ventures, and entrepreneurs, product liability has increased the cost of innovation, delayed the introduction of new products while repetitive testing is undertaken, and placed U.S. companies at a global disadvantage.

DISTRIBUTION

Distribution research has not been as evident in marketing literature as has research dealing with many other aspects of marketing theory and

Figure 6 Overview of a typical stage-gate new product system

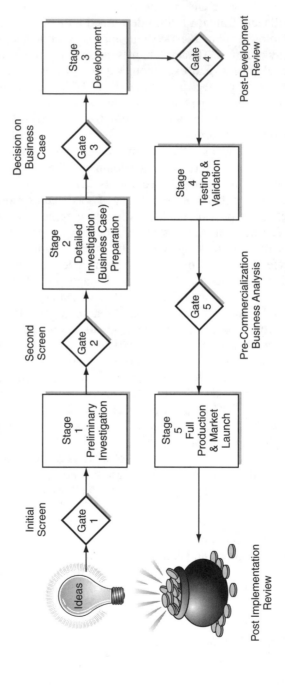

Adapted from Cooper, Robert G., and Kleinschmidt, Elko J. New Product Processes at Leading Industrial Firms. *IMM* 20(2) (1991): 138

Figure 7 The product development life cycle

Product Development Process	Idea Generation	Screening	Development	Testing	Commercialization
Strategy Development Process	Mission	Objective	Planning	Programs	Tactics

MARKETING STRATEGY					
Target Market	Marketing Research	Accessibility	Segmentation	Targeting	Positioning
Product/ Service	Opportunities Consistency	Complement Fit	Specifications Prototype Branding Packaging	Uses/ Applications Pre- and Post- Sales Services	Guarantee Warranty Financial Services Repair and Parts Service
Promotion	Assessment	Feasibility	Advertising Personal Selling Sales Promotion Image	Theme Media Message Effectiveness	Selection Sales Force Manufacturer's Representative
Distribution	Reachable	Alternatives	Channel Availability Transportation	Functional Separation Customer–Service Level Transportation Modes	Channel Management Inventories Warehousing Transportation Rates Channel Selection
Price	Value	Consistency Pricing Policy	Cost/Revenue Analysis Breakeven Analysis	Profitability Target Return Pricing Terms	List Price Discounts Allowances Geographic

Adapted from Kortge, G. Dean, and Okonkwo, Patrick A., Simultaneous New Product Development: Reducing the New Product Failure Rate. *IMM* 18(4) (1989): 303

management. *Industrial Marketing Management* has had about the same frequency of published articles dealing with distribution as have the other general marketing journals. Those articles that have appeared have provided valuable insight to industrial marketing managers. Rosenbloom (1978) discussed a general program aimed at motivating independent distribution channel members. This program involved: (1) finding out the needs and problems of channel members, (2) offering support to channel members that is consistent with their needs and problems, and (3) providing the necessary leadership to institute the motivational program. He illustrated his article with examples of effective distributor motivation programs from Armstrong Floor Division and from Libby, Owens, Ford. One of the factors that increase the longevity of industrial marketing channels is stability. Shipley (1984) also studied the techniques used to motivate channel members and found that distributor margins and profits were the most common techniques. He also stated that manufacturers should investigate additional motivational techniques. Distributor motivation and support was discussed by Magrath and Hardy (1989). Effective support for distributors includes items such as aggressive direct mail programs designed to provide sales leads for distributor sales people, a liberal co-op advertising program, quarterly product promotions, and extensive training seminars for distributor reps. These should not be forced on distributors but offered to those who want to take advantage of them.

Ford (1978) looked at the factors that increase stability in the relationship between channel members and manufacturers and found that channel stability is increased when: (1) companies hold a clear view of the power and role structures in the channel, (2) there is increasing inflexibility over time in the allocation of channel roles until they form a rigid fabric of ethics, (3) companies have an unrealistically low estimate of their own power in a given relationship, and (4) when no member of the channel relationship has sufficient control to act as channel leader or captain. How distributors view distributor-supplier relationships was discussed by Joseph et al. (1995). Building good quality business relationships vital to successful channel management and overall business success must focus on meeting the needs of all parties in the value chain. These relationships can be arm's length, extremely close, or in between. It is important that all parties view the tasks and rewards of the relationship as being fairly allocated. Hutt and Speh (1983) provided insights into the problem of realigning channel structures to meet the dynamic needs of industrial customers. Any realignment (to new types of channel members or to simply new members) must analyze both the effectiveness and efficiency of the new versus old structure. Given the tremendous changes affecting industrial distributors (Michman, 1980), channel realignments and other modifications will become the norm rather than the exception. The increasing dynamic distributor environment provides both opportunities and challenges. Narus, Reddy, and Pinchak (1984) surveyed 461 industrial distributors and found five key problem areas: unstable economic conditions, intense competition among distributors, high sales call costs, low employee productivity, and manufacturer-distributor working relationships. Powers (1989) investigated the cost versus control tradeoff for six different channel structures (with various types and levels of channel members) and found the needs of the final customer are critical in selecting the appropriate channel setup.

One special type of industrial distributor is the manufacture's agent. Sibley and Teas (1979) profile manufacture's agents and their agencies and discuss the proper use of manufacture's agents as part of an overall distribution program. Another type of special concern for manufacturers is the growth of unauthorized distributors. Howell et al. (1986) found that traditional quantity discount pricing practices are a key contributor to gray markets. They found that most tactics that do not address the root quantity discount pricing structure are an ineffective means of eliminating unauthorized distributors. McDaniel, Ormsby, and Gresham (1992) reported on the effect that JIT philosophy is having on industrial distributors. A JIT system requires very close cooperation among channel members. JIT systems must be initiated by the channel leader and will result in fewer distributors remaining in the system as it is easier to coordinate a fewer number of members than a broad-based distribution system. The JIT trend is but one factor shaping the structure of distribution systems as we enter the twenty-first century. Herbig and O'Hara (1994) discuss several factors affecting distributor-manufacturer relationships and provide insights as to how astute manufacturers and distributors can benefit from these changes.

PRICING

Firms are in business to make a profit. When one considers the profit equation of revenues minus costs, it is noted that the only marketing variable to appear on the revenue side of the equation is price (price times quantity); all other marketing variables are reflected on the cost side of the equation (product development, advertising, selling, distribution, etc.) Because price is so important to the firm's success, one wonders why pricing has not received more attention in marketing journals. Fewer than 3% of the articles that have appeared in *Industrial Marketing Management* have dealt with the pricing issue. This is not much different for other marketing journals such as *Journal of Marketing, Journal of Marketing Research, Journal of Consumer Research*, or others. But exactly how important is price as a factor in industrial purchase decisions? Kelly and Coaker (1976) reviewed 360 bids received for 112 purchase decisions and found that the low bid was awarded the purchase 59% of the time. In 41% of the situations, the purchase was given to a non-low bidder due to other choice criteria.

Prices linked to perceived value is frequently mentioned as a means of maximizing transaction profitability. Kortge and Okonkwo (1993) show that traditional cost-based pricing models can reduce profitability. They develop a model of perceived-value pricing where the optimal price is within a range where the customer experiences satisfaction (suffering neither feeling of guilt nor unfair treatment). Kortge et al. (1994) calculate the customer's perceived value price range, using a combination of stage in the life cycle, experience cost curves, and learning curves. They calculate the lowest level of perceived value, using the prices of previous purchases and the slope of the experience and learning curves. Oxenfeldt (1977) reverses the normal sequence of using cost to determine price by showing that the way costs are calculated can vary according to the purpose for which they are collected. For example, cost calculations for a temporary promotional price may not include certain overhead factors. Likewise costs calculated in the early stage of the life cycle will differ from that calculated in later stages. Oxenfeldt illustrates these concepts with numerous examples. Jain and Laric (1979) develop a strategic matrix by looking at the relative strengths of buyers and sellers to come up with four general situations (see Figure 8): negotiated strategy (buyer and seller strong), defensive strategy (buyer strong, seller weak), gamesmanship strategy (both parties weak), and dictatorial strategy (seller strong and buyer weak.) Because the strategic quadrant can differ for the same seller with different buyers, multiple pricing strategies may evolve (see Figure 9). Morris (1987) emphasizes the strategic importance of charging different customers (or market segments) different prices but goes on to note that the great majority of

Figure 8 Pricing strategy quadrangle

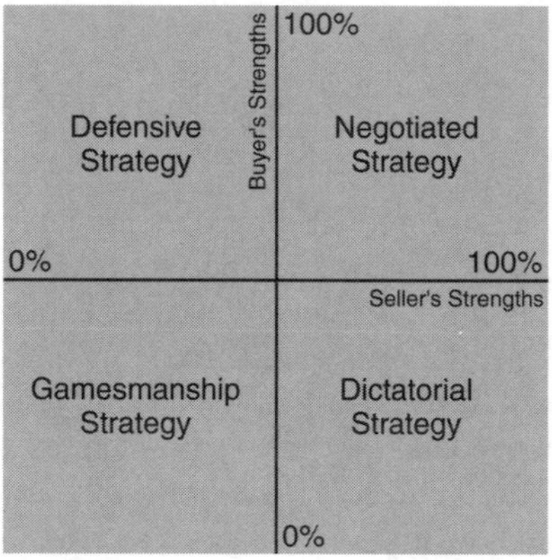

Adapted from Jain, Subhash, and Laric, Michael V., A Framework for Strategic Industrial Pricing. *IMM* 8(1) (1979): 78.

Figure 9 Pricing tactics matrix

SELLER	BUYER		
	Marginal Need	Moderate Need	Acute Need
Acute Need	Buyer is in complete control	Buyer has leeway	Neutral Ground
Moderate Need	Buyer has leeway	Neutral Ground	Seller has leeway
Marginal Need	Neutral Ground	Seller has leeway	Seller is in complete control

Adapted from Jain, Subhash, and Laric, Michael V., A Framework for Strategic Industrial Pricing. *IMM* 8(1) (1979): 78

marketing managers know little of the implications of this strategy with regard to the Robinson-Patman Act. Companies must make some changes in the product offering to avoid prosecution under this act. In a follow-up article, Morris and Joyce (1988) report on the ways in which marketing managers estimate sensitivity to price and demand price elasticity. The general methods used are: managerial judgment, informal customer feedback, analysis of past sales data, and formal customer surveys. Unfortunately they point out that the majority of firms do not make any attempts to calculate customer sensitivity to prices.

Day and Ryans (1988) show how a carefully designed price discount program offers opportunities for strengthening a company's long-run position. They develop price discount programs based on four key questions: (1) Who are the target customers? (2) What is included? (3) What is the discount schedule? and (4) What form does the discount take? They suggest that a combination of price and nonprice discounts are useful in building market share. Factors that affect the discount schedule are the bargaining power of customers and the likely reaction of competition. There is a high probability of fierce price competition in depressed markets where multiple suppliers are marketing relatively undifferentiated products such as situations commonly faced by distributors. Shipley and Bourdon (1990) found that under these conditions distributors offer substantial downward price flexibility and extensive discounting. Both of these methods reduce profitability, and distributors are encouraged to seek alternative, i.e., nonprice methods of competing. One such strategy espoused by Levy (1994) is the use of guaranteed pricing, especially in contractual relations. These guarantees take the forms of 'most favored customer' or 'meeting competition clauses.' Most favored customers enjoy the lowest price received by any of its buyers and meet competition clauses offer to meet the lowest cost offered by competitors. This kind of pricing deters competitors from stealing customers and thereby can lower selling costs and costs of retaining business. Price guarantees can be beneficial to both buyers and sellers. Caution should be raised about using predatory pricing tactics. Ursic and Helgeson (1994) discuss recent court rulings regarding predatory pricing. Whereas companies victimized by such tactics may have a difficult time collecting damages, firms using this tactic must exercise caution to avoid expensive legal battles.

It goes without saying that only one firm can be first into a market with a new product. What form of pricing strategy should the second, third, and subsequent entrants into a market utilize? Yoon (1991) presents a model for pricing new but imitative products. Using examples from the personal computer market, he describes three approaches (user-benefit consistency, competitive consistency, and strategic consistency) as possible mechanisms for establishing prices of imitative products.

PROMOTIONS AND ADVERTISING

Probably the greatest difference between consumer and industrial goods marketing is in the area of promotions. Not only do customer goods marketing managers rely more on promotions and advertising than their industrial counterparts, but published research on the use of advertising and promotions in industrial situations is much scarcer in all marketing journals. Only about 4% of the articles published in *Industrial Marketing Management* during its first 24 years were concerned with aspects of promotions or advertising. The low relative importance of promotions as part of the industrial marketing manager's overall strategy was documented by Parasuraman (1981). His study of 267 large industrial firms showed that managers perceive advertising to be the least important influencer of buyer decisions. Indeed one of the most important promotional tools that industrial marketers have is the proposal. Horowitz and Jolson (1980) described a method for improving the proposal preparation process and for incorporating more persuasive materials in the proposal itself.

In an early *IMM* issue, Brown and Brucker (1976) stated that rather than focusing on product features, effective industrial advertising should begin with a statement of the buyer's problem and how the advertiser's product will help the buyer solve the problem. Bellizzi and Hite (1986) also demonstrate how advertising copy that focuses on buyer needs is more effective than other forms of messages. They also present numerous suggestions for improving ad copy and layout for greater effectiveness. Although this can easily be incorporated into most industrial advertisements, ads should be pretested before their use. Zinkman (1984) presented a rating scale to be used when copytesting industrial ads.

Advertising that is part of a comprehensive ad campaign is more effective than randomly placed materials. But what constitutes a successful advertising campaign? Korgaonkar, Bellenger, and Smith (1986) looked at numerous ad campaigns and concluded that the content and structure of what is needed for successful ad campaigns depends on the objectives of the campaign. Campaigns that are designed to build awareness have different success factors from ads that are designed to increase sales or create favorable attitudes about the product. Park, Roth, and Jacques (1988) develop a four-stage development and evaluation model for industrial advertising and sales promotions. The model accounts for both direct and indirect communications effects. The stages are composed of an initial benchmark study, development of communications strategy, tracking effectiveness, and program analysis and modification, Lehman and Steckel (1985) also investigated different tactics for improving effectiveness of advertising in industrial supplier directories. They found that the size and number of ad placements can have a positive impact on effectiveness, whereas the use of photographs has a negative impact on effectiveness.

Stevenson and Swayne (1984) looked at the use of comparative ads by examining 2,100 full-page ads in trade publications and found that there was a decided reduction in the frequency of comparative advertising and that advertisers were using a more implied method as opposed to aggressive comparisons. Eleven years later these same two authors extended their study to the use of comparative advertising in business-to-business direct mail (Stevenson and Swayne, 1995). They found that comparative advertising is not as widely used in direct mail as in other forms of business-to-business advertising.

More industrial marketers do their advertising as an in-house function than do consumer goods companies, as was found in a study of 237 Canadian industrial companies by Ripley (1992). She found that the need for product knowledge is greater for industrial products, and this led companies to perform their own advertising functions. For those companies that do elect to find an outside agency, Harvey and Rupert (1988) recommend a five-step process: (1) preplanning the agency selection (what are you looking for), (2) agency visitations, (3) company visitations and discussions, (4) agency presentations, and (5) selection decision and control process.

CONCLUSION

Industrial Marketing Management was the first journal to be exclusively devoted to the field of marketing between businesses. Since 1971, it has published over 900 articles dealing with all aspects of industrial marketing. Our authors come from dozens of European, North American, Asian, and other countries.

What kinds of research are appropriate for publication consideration in *IMM*? Practicing marketers are well aware of the interactive nature of the marketing discipline. Research should focus on projects that approximate the many interactions found in the marketplace. For example, what are the most effective pricing strategies at different stages in the product life cycle, and does it matter if the product is a capital good, a raw material, a maintenance product, or a service? How does a type of sales organization (company sales force or manufacturer's reps) impact the firm's pricing strategy? How does the size of the firm and its structure family owned, partnership, corporation, division of a large or multinational corporation, etc.) affect the most effective ways of organizing for new product development? How do different stages of the technology cycle impact the effectiveness of alternative forms of organizing for new product development? We are also interested in the entire field of relationship marketing and how industrial marketers can utilize these developments, particularly in the areas of buyer-seller relationships, distribution partnerships, and strategic alliances. How do these and other types of relationships influence product development, pricing, promotions, sales strategies, marketing research, and other aspects of the marketing equation?

Another area of interest is case examples. *Industrial Marketing Management* is interested in publishing illustrative cases showing how companies have developed and implemented effective marketing strategies. In the past *IMM* has published numerous case histories, and we welcome the opportunity to consider more case stories in the future.

All manuscripts are subjected to a double blind review process. We welcome new contributions to the field of industrial or business-to-business marketing. Please submit four copies of your manuscripts to Peter LaPlaca, Editor, *Industrial Marketing Management*, 179 Middle Turnpike, Mansfield, CT 96268.

REFERENCES

Adler, Lee: How to Economize on Industrial Marketing Research. *Industrial Marketing Management* 4(5) (1975): 243–247.

Armstrong, J. Scott, and Yokum, J. Thomas: Effectiveness of Monetary Incentives. *Industrial Marketing Management* 23(2) (1994): 133–136.

Avlonitis, George J.: Industrial Product Elimination: Major Factors to Consider. *Industrial Marketing Management* 13(2) (1984): 77–86.

Barrett, John: Why Major Account Selling Works. *Industrial Marketing Management* 15(1) (1986): 63–74.

Bellizzi, Joseph A., and McVey, Phillip: How Valid Is the Buy-Grid Model? *Industrial Marketing Management* 12(1) (1983): 57–62.

Bellizzi, Joseph A., and Hite, Robert E.: Improving Industrial Advertising Copy. *Industrial Marketing Management* 15(2) (1986): 117–122.

Bellizzi, Joseph, and Walter, C.K.: Purchasing Agent's Influence in the Buying Process. *Industrial Marketing Management* 9(2) (1980): 137–141.

Bellizzi, Joseph, and Belonax, Joseph: Centralized and Decentralized Buying Influences. *Industrial Marketing Management* 11(2) (1982): 111–115.

Bellizzi, Joseph, and Cline, Paul: Technical or Nontechnical Salesmen? *Industrial Marketing Management* 14(2) (1985): 69–74.

Bello, Daniel, and Barksdale, Hiram, Jr.: Exporting at Industrial Trade Shows. *Industrial Marketing Management* 15(3) (1986): 197–206.

Blenkhorn, David, and Banting, Peter: Broadening the Concept of Industrial Purchasing. *Industrial Marketing Management* 7(6) (1978): 374–378.

Blois, K.J.: Matching New Manufacturing Technologies to Industrial Markets and Strategies. *Industrial Marketing Management* 14(1) (1985): 43–48.

Bonoma, Thomas, and Shapiro, Benson: Evaluating Market Segmentation Approaches. *Industrial Marketing Management* 13(4) (1984): 257–268.

Boyd, Harper W., and Headen, Robert: Definition and Management of the

Product-Market Portfolio. *Industrial Marketing Management* 7(5) (1978): 337–346.

Brasch, John J.: Sales Forecasting Difficulties in Developing Countries. *Industrial Marketing Management* 7(5) (1978): 354–360.

Briscoe, Geoffrey: Some Observations on New Industrial Product Failures. *Industrial Marketing Management* 2(2) (1973): 151–161.

Brown, Herbert E., and Brucker, Roger W.: The Buyer Problem Foundation of Industrial Advertising. *Industrial Marketing Management* 5(3) (1976): 163–167.

Calantone, Roger, and di Benedetto, Anthony: Defensive Industrial Marketing Strategies. *Industrial Marketing Management* 19(3) (1990): 267–278.

Cardozo, Richard, and Wind, Yoram: Industrial Market Segmentation. *Industrial Marketing Management* 3(3) (1974): 153–166.

Chawla, Sudhir, and Nataraajan, Rajan: Does the Name of the Sender Affect Industrial Mail Response? *Industrial Marketing Management* 23(2) (1994): 111–115.

Chawla, Sudhir, Balakrishnan, P.V., and Smith, Mary: Mail Response Rates from Distributors. *Industrial Marketing Management* 21(4) (1992): 307–310.

Choffray, Jean-Marie, and Lilien, Gary: Industrial Market Segmentation by the Structure of the Purchasing Process. *Industrial Marketing Management* 9(4) (1980): 331–342.

Cooper, Richard G., and de Brentani, Ulrike: Criteria for Screening New Industrial Products. *Industrial Marketing Management* 13(3) (1984): 149–156.

Cooper, Robert G.: Why New Industrial Products Fail. *Industrial Marketing Management* 4(6) (1975): 315–326.

Cooper, Robert G.: Identifying Industrial New Product Success: Project NEWPROD. *Industrial Marketing Management* 8(2) (1979): 124–135.

Cooper, Robert G.: New Product Success in Industrial Firms. *Industrial Marketing Management* 11(3) (1982): 215–223.

Cooper, Robert G., and Kleinschmidt, Elko J.: New Product Processes at Leading Industrial Firms. *Industrial Marketing Management* 20(2) (1991): 137–147.

Cooper, Robert G., and Kleinschmidt, Elko J.: Success Factors in Product Innovation. *Industrial Marketing Management* 16(3) (1987): 215–223.

Cox, James E., Jr.: Approaches for Improving Salespersons' Forecasts. *Industrial Marketing Management* 18(4) (1989): 307–311.

Cox, William E., Jr., and Dominguez, L.V.: The Key Issues and Procedures of Industrial Marketing Research. *Industrial Marketing Management* 8(1) (1979): 81–93.

Dalrymple, Douglas, Stephenson, Ronald, and Cron, William: Gross Martin Sales Compensation Plans. *Industrial Marketing Management* 10(3) (1981): 219–224.

Darmon, Rene. Y.: Compensation Plans That Link Management and Salesman's Objectives. *Industrial Marketing Management* 11(2) (1982): 151–163.

Dawson, Leslie: Transferring Industrial Technology to Less Developed Countries. *Industrial Marketing Management* 16(4) (1987): 265–271.

Day, George S., and Ryans, Adrian B.: Using Price Discounts for a Comprehensive Advantage. *Industrial Marketing Management* 17(1) (1988): 1–14.

Demirdjian, Z.S.: A Multidimensional Approach to Motivating Salespeople. *Industrial Marketing Management* 13(1) (1984): 25–32.

DeRose, Louis: Meet Today's Buying Influences with Value Selling. *Industrial Marketing Management* 20(2) (1991): 87–91.

Diamantopoulos, Adamantios, Schlegelmilch, Bodo, and Webb, Lori: Factors Affecting Industrial Mail Response Rates. *Industrial Marketing Management* 20(4) (1991): 327–339.

Dibb, Sally, and Simkin, Lyndon: Implementation Problems in Industrial Market Segmentation. *Industrial Marketing Management* 23(1) (1994): 55–63.

Dion, Paul, Easterling, Debbie, and Miller, Shirley J.: What is Really Necessary in Successful Buyer/Seller Relationships? *Industrial Marketing Management* 24(1) (1995): 1–9.

Dion, Paul, Banting, Peter, and Hasey, Loretta: The Impact of JIT on Industrial Marketers. *Industrial Marketing Management* 19(1) (1990): 41–46.

Doyle, Peter: Market Planning in the Multiproduct Firm. *Industrial Marketing Management* 4(4) (1975): 183–192.

Duhan, Dale, and Wilson, Dale: Prenotification and Industrial Survey Responses. *Industrial Marketing Management* 19(2) (1990): 95–105.

Eid, Nimr: Marketing in Undeveloped Countries. *Industrial Marketing Management* 1(13) (1972): 347–352.

Evans, Richard: Add Soft Data to Product Elimination Decisions. *Industrial Marketing Management* 6(2) (1977): 91–94.

Faria, A. J., and Dickinson, John R.: Mail Survey Response, Speed and Cost. *Industrial Marketing Management* 21(1) (1992): 51–60.

Farrer, Dean Grimes: The Military Market and the Product Life Cycle Concept. *Industrial Marketing Management* 1(1) (1971): 39–46.

Ferguson, Wade: A New Method for Routing Salespersons. *Industrial Marketing Management* 9(2) (1980): 171–178.

Ferguson, Wade: An Evaluation of the BUYGRID Analytical Framework. *Industrial Marketing Management* 8(1) (1979): 40–44.

Fluitman, Lourens P.: The Necessity of an Industrial Product Mix Analysis. *Industrial Marketing Management* 2(4) (1973a): 345–352.

Fluitman, Lourens P.: The Role of Industrial Marketing Research. *Industrial Marketing Management* 2(2) (1973b): 145–150.

Fogg, C. Davis: The New Business Planning Process. *Industrial Marketing Management* 4(6) (1975): 293–303.

Ford, I. David: Stability Factors in Industrial Marketing Channels. *Industrial Marketing Management* 4(6) (1978): 410–422.

Ford, Robert, McLaughlin, Frank, and Williamson, Steven: Using Certified Mail in Industrial Research. *Industrial Marketing Management* 21(4) (1992): 281–285.

Fox, Harold, and Rink, David: Purchasing's Role across the Product Life Cycle. *Industrial Marketing Management* 7(3) (1978): 186–192.

Gentry, Dwight W., and Hailey, William A.: Industrial Survey Sampling. *Industrial Marketing Management* 10(3) (1981): 183–189.

Giunipero, Larry, and O'Neal, Charles: Obstacles to JIT Procurement. *Industrial Marketing Management* 17(1) (1988): 35–41.

Grønhaug, Kjell: Autonomous vs. Joint Decisions in Organizational Buying. *Industrial Marketing Management* 4(5) (1975): 265–271.

Grønhaug, Kjell: Exploring a Complex Organizational Buying Decision. *Industrial Marketing Management* 6(6) (1977): 439–445.

Greer, Thomas, and Lohtia, Rita: Effects of Source and Color on Response Rates in Mail Surveys. *Industrial Marketing Management* 23(1) (1994): 47–54.

Gwin, John, and Perreault, William: Industrial Sales Call Planning. *Industrial Marketing Management* 10(3) (1981): 225–234.

Haggett, Sara, and Mitchell, Vincent-Wayne: Effect of Industrial Prenotification on Response Rate, Speed, Quality, Bias, and Cost. *Industrial Marketing Management* 23(2) (1994): 101–110.

Hall, William P.: Marketing Research for Industrial Products. *Industrial Marketing Management* 4(4) (1975): 209–212.

Hannaford, William: Systems Selling: Problems and Benefits for Buyers and Sellers. *Industrial Marketing Management* 5(2) (1976): 139–145.

Hansen, Robert A., Tinney, Cathie, and Rudelius, W.: Increase Response to Industrial Surveys. *Industrial Marketing Management*, 12(3) (1983): 165–169.

Harvey, Michael G., and Ruppert, J. Paul: Selecting an Industrial Advertising Agency. *Industrial Marketing Management* 17(2) (1988): 119–127.

Hempel, Donald, and LaPlaca, Peter: Strategic Planning in a Period of Transition. *Industrial Marketing Management* 4(6) (1975): 305–314.

Herbig, Paul, and O'Hara, Bradleu: Industrial Distributors in the Twenty-First Century. *Industrial Marketing Management* 23(3) (1994): 199–203.

Herbig, Paul, and Kramer, Hugh: Do's and Don'ts of Cross-Cultural Negotiations. *Industrial Marketing Management* 21(4) (1992): 287–298.

Herbig, Paul, and Golden, James: Innovation and Product Liability. *Industrial Marketing Management* 23(3) (1994): 245–255.

Hill, Roy W.: The Nature of Industrial Buying Decisions. *Industrial Marketing Management* 2(1) (1972): 45–56.

Hopkins, David S.: New Emphasis in Product Planning and Strategy Developments. *Industrial Marketing Management* 6(6) (1977): 410–419.

Horowitz, Harold M., and Jolson, Marvin A.: The Industrial Proposal as a Promotional Tool. *Industrial Marketing Management* 9(2) (1980): 101–109.

Howell, Roy, Britney, Robert, Kuzdrall, Paul, and Wilcox, James: Unauthorized Channels of Distribution: Gray Markets. *Industrial Marketing Management* 15(4) (1986): 257–263.

Hudson, Cyril L.: Buying-Selling: Greater Integration in the Seventies. *Industrial Marketing Management* 1(1) (1971): 59–80.

Hutt, Michael, and Speh, Thomas: Realigning Industrial Marketing Channels. *Industrial Marketing Management* 12(3) (1983): 171–177.

Ingram, Thomas, Schwepker, Charles, and Hutson, Don: Why Salespeople Fail. *Industrial Marketing Management* 21(3) (1992): 225–230.

Jackson, Ralph, and Cooper, Philip: Unique Aspects of Marketing Industrial Services. *Industrial Marketing Management* 17(2) (1988): 111–118.

Jain, Subhash, and Laric, Michael V.: A Framework for Strategic Industrial Pricing. *Industrial Marketing Management* 8(1) (1979): 75–80.

Jobber, David: Improving Response Rates in Industrial Mail Surveys. *Industrial Marketing Management* 15(3) (1986): 183–195.

Johnston, Wesley, and Cooper, Martha: Analyzing the Industrial Salesforce Selection Process. *Industrial Marketing Management* 10(2) (1981): 139–148.

Johnston, Wesley, and Shields, Michael: Evaluating the Newer Salesperson. *Industrial Marketing Management* 12(3) (1983): 193–200.

Joseph, W. Benoy, Gardner, John, Thach, Sharon, and Vernon, Francis: How Distributors View Distributor-Supplier Relationships. *Industrial Marketing Management* 24(1) (1995): 27–36.

Kallis, M. Jeffrey, and Giglierano, Joseph J.: Improving Mail Response Rates with Express Mail. *Industrial Marketing Management* 21(1) (1992): 1–4.

Kelly, J. Patrick, and Coaker, James W.: The Importance of Price as a Choice Criterion for Industrial Purchase Decisions. *Industrial Marketing Management* 5(5) (1976): 281–293.

Korgaonkar, Pradeep K., Bellenger, Danny N., and Smith, Allen E.: Successful Industrial Advertising Campaigns. *Industrial Marketing Management* 15(2) (1986): 123–128.

Kortge, G. Dean, and Okonkwo, Patrick A.: Perceived Value Approach to Pricing. *Industrial Marketing Management* 22(2) (1993): 133–140.

Kortge, G. Dean, and Okonkwo, Patrick A.: Simultaneous New Product Development: Reducing the New Product Failure Rate. *Industrial Marketing Management* 18(4) (1989): 301–306.

Kortge, G. Dean, Okonkwo, Patrick, Burley, James, and Kortge, Jeffrey: Linking Experience, Product Life Cycle, and Learning Curves. *Industrial Marketing Management* 23(3) (1994): 221–228.

Laughlin, Jan L., and Taylor, Charles: An Approach to Industrial Market Segmentation. *Industrial Marketing Management* 20(2) (1991): 127–136.

Lehman, Donald R., and Steckel, Joel H.: Effective Advertising in Industrial Supplier Directories. *Industrial Marketing Management* 14(2) (1985): 107–111.

Leisch, Peter: Government-Mandated Countertrade in Australia. *Industrial Marketing Management* 23(4) (1994): 299–305.

Levy, David T.: Guaranteed Pricing in Industrial Purchases. *Industrial Marketing Management* 23(4) (1994): 307–313.

Link, Peter L.: Keys to New Product Success and Failure. *Industrial Marketing Management* 16(2) (1987): 109–118.

Magrath, Allen, and Hardy, Kenneth: Gearing Manufacturer Support Programs to Distributions. *Industrial Marketing Management* 18(4) (1989): 239–244.

Mattson, Melvin R: How to Determine the Composition and Influence of a Buying Center. *Industrial Marketing Management* 17(3) (1988): 205–214.

Mattsson, Lars-Gunnar: Systems Selling as a Strategy on Industrial Markets. *Industrial Marketing Management* 3(2) (1973): 107–120.

McDaniel, Steve, Ormsby, Joseph, and Gresham, Alicia: The Effect of JIT on Distributors. *Industrial Marketing Management* 21(2) (1992): 145–149.

Mehr, Patrick: Identifying Independent Reps. *Industrial Marketing Management* 21(4) (1992): 319–322.

Meidan, Arthur: Optimizing the Number of Industrial Salespersons. *Industrial Marketing Management* 11(1) (1982): 63–74.

Merrifield, Bruce: Industrial Projects Selection and Management. *Industrial Marketing Management* 7(5) (1978): 324–330.

Miaoulis, George, and LaPlaca, Peter: A Systems Approach for Developing High Technology Products. *Industrial Marketing Management* 11(4) (1982): 253–262.

Michman, Ronald: Trends Affecting Industrial Distributors. *Industrial Marketing Management* 9(3) (1980): 213–216.

Mitchell, Paul, Quinn, Peter, and Percival, Edward: Marketing Strategics for Mature Products. *Industrial Marketing Management* 20(3) (1991): 201–206.

Morris, Michael H.: Separate Prices as a Marketing Tool. *Industrial Marketing Management* 16(2) (1987): 79–86.

Morris, Michael H., and Joyce, Mary L.: How Marketers Evaluate Price Sensitivity. *Industrial Marketing Management* 17(2) (1988): 169–176.

Murphy, Paul, Dalenberg, Douglas, and Daley, James: Improving Survey Responses with Postcards. *Industrial Marketing Management* 19(4) (1990): 349–355.

Narus, James, and Anderson, James: Industrial Distributor Selling: The Role of Outside and Inside Sales. *Industrial Marketing Management* 15(1) (1986): 55–62.

Narus, James, Reddy, Mohan, and Pinchak, George: Key Problems Facing

Industrial Distributors. *Industrial Marketing Management* 13(3) (1984): 139–147.

Nickolaus, Nickolas: Marketing New Products with Industrial Distributors. *Industrial Marketing Management* 19(4) (1990): 287–299.

Nicosia, Francesco, and Wind, Yoram: Emerging Models of Organizational Buying Processes. *Industrial Management* 6(5) (1977): 353–369.

O'Neal, Charles: JIT Procurement and Relationship Marketing. *Industrial Marketing Management* 18(1) (1989): 55–63.

Oxenfeldt, A. R.: The Computation of Costs for Price Decisions. *Industrial Marketing Management* 6(2) (1977): 83–90.

Pal, Sumit, and Bowonder, B.: Marketing Challenges of Technical Industries in Developing Countries. *Industrial Marketing Management* 8(1) (1979): 69–74.

Palia, Aspy: Countertrade Practices in Japan. *Industrial Marketing Management* 22(2) (1993): 125–132.

Palia, Aspy, and Shenkar, Oded: Countrade Practices in China. *Industrial Marketing Management* 20(1) (1991): 57–65.

Parasuraman, A.: The Relatve Importance of Industrial Promotion Tools. *Industrial Marketing Management* 10(4) (1981): 277–281.

Parasuraman, A.: Vendor Segmentation: An Additional Level of Market Segmentation. *Industrial Marketing Management* 9(1) (1980): 59–62.

Park, C.W., Roth, Martin S., and Jacques, Philip F.: Evaluating the Effects of Advertising and Sales Promotion Campaigns. *Industrial Marketing Management* 17(2) (1988): 129–140.

Penn, W.S.: Problem Foundation in Industrial Marketing Research. *Industrial Marketing Management* 7(6) (1978): 402–409.

Perrien, Jean, and Richard Line: The Meaning of a Marketing Relationship. *Industrial Marketing Management* 24(1) (1995). 37–44.

Phelps, Ernest D.: Improving the Product Development Process. *Industrial Marketing Management* 6(1) (1977): 47–52.

Plank, Richard E.: A Critical Review of Industrial Market Segmentation. *Industrial Marketing Management* 14(2) (1985): 79–91.

Plank, Richard, and Dempsey, William: A Framework for Personal Selling to Organizations. *Industrial Marketing Management* 9(2) (1980): 143–150.

Powers, Thomas: Industrial Distribution Options: Trade-Offs to Consider. *Industrial Marketing Management* 18(3) (1989): 155–161.

Powers, Thomas: Switching from Reps to Direct Salespeople. *Industrial Marketing Management* 16(3) (1987): 169–172.

Pressley, Milton M.: Improving Mail Survey Respones from Industrial Organizations. *Industrial Marketing Management* 9(3) (1980). 231–235.

Reisman, Arnold, Fuh, Duu-Cheng, and Li, Gang: Achieving an Advantage with Countertrade. *Industrial Marketing Management* 17(1) (1988): 55–63.

Reisman, Arnold, Aggarwal, Raj, and Fuh, Duu-Cheng: Seeking Out Profitable Countertrade Opportunities. *Industrial Marketing Management* 18(1) (1989): 65–72.

Rink, David R., and Dodge, H. Roberts: Industrial Sales Emphasis across the Life Cycle. *Industrial Marketing Management* 9(4) (1980): 305–310.

Ripley, M. Louise: Why Industrial Advertising is Often Done in House. *Industrial Marketing Management* 21(4) (1992): 331–334.

Robey, Daniel, and Johnston, Wesley. Lateral Influences and Vertical Authority in Organizational Buying. *Industrial Marketing Management* 6(6) (1977): 451–462.

Rochford, Linda: Generating and Screening New Product Ideas. *Industrial Marketing Management* 20(4) (1991): 287–296.

Roman, Dan: Technology, The Key to Market Expansion for Developing Countries. *Industrial Marketing Management* 3(3) (1974): 167–176.

Rosenbloom, Bert: Motivating Independent Distribution Channel Members. *Industrial Marketing Management* 7(4) (1978): 275–281.

Sager, Jeffrey: Recruiting and Training Committed Salespeople. *Industrial Marketing Management* 20(2) (1991): 99–103.

Seringhaus, F. H. Rolf: Using Trade Missions for Export Market Entry. *Industrial Marketing Management* 16(4) (1987): 249–255.

Shan, Kiran, and LaPlaca, Peter: Assessing Risk in Strategic Planning *Industrial Marketing Management* 10(2) (1981): 77–92.

Shipley, David, and Bourdon, Elizabeth: Distributor Pricing in Very Competitive Markets. *Industrial Marketing Management* 19(3) (1990): 215–224.

Shipley, David: Selection and Motivation of Distribution Intermediaries. *Industrial Marketing Management* 13(4) (1984): 249–256.

Shipley, David, and Neale, Bill: Industrial Barter and Countertrade. *Industrial Marketing Management* 16(1) (1987): 1–8.

Sibley, Stanley, and Teas, Kenneth: The Manufacturer's Agent in Industrial Distribution. *Industrial Marketing Management* 8(4) (1979): 286–292.

Skinner, Steven, Dubinsky, Alan, and Ingram. Thomas: Impact of Humor on Survey Responses. *Industrial Marketing Management* 12(2) (1983): 139–143.

Slatter, Stuart St. P.: The Salesman's Job in Competitive Bidding Situations. *Industrial Marketing Management* 16,3 (1987): 201–206.

Souder, William E.: Effectiveness of Product Development Methods. *Industrial Marketing Management* 7(5) (1978): 299–307.

Sousa de Vasconcell, Jorge A.: Key Factors in Marketing Mature Products. *Industrial Marketing Management* 20(4) (1991): 263–278.

Spitz, A Edward: Product Planning for Today and Tomorrow. *Industrial Marketing Management* 4(6) (1975): 327–334.

Stevenson, Thomas H., and Swayne, Linda: Comparative Industrial Advertising: The Content and Frequency. *Industrial Marketing Management* 13(2) (1984): 133–138.

Stevenson, Thomas H., and Swayne, Linda: The Use of Comparative Advertising in Business-to-Business Direct Mail. *Industrial Marketing Management* 24(1) (1995): 53–59.

Stiff, Ronald, and Khera, Inder: Industrial Product Positioning: Pragmatic Uses. *Industrial Marketing Management* 6(2) (1977): 119–124.

Thomas, Robert J.: Bases of Power in Organizational Buying Decisions. *Industrial Marketing Management* 13(4) (1984): 209–217.

Tyagi, Pradeep, and Block, Carl: Monetary Incentives and Salesmen Performance. *Industrial Marketing Management* 12(4) (1983): 263–269.

Ursic, Michael L., and Helgeson, James G.: Using Price as a Weapon. *Industrial Marketing Management* 23(2) (1994): 125–131.

van Dam, Andre: Marketing in Times of Global Scarcities. *Industrial Marketing Management* 5(5) (1976): 249–253.

Vesey, Joseph T.: Time-to-Market: Put Speed in Product Development. *Industrial Marketing Management* 21(2) (1992): 151–158.

Walker, Bruce J., Kirchmann, Wayne, and Conant, Jeffrey: A Method to Improve Response to Industrial Mail Surveys. *Industrial Marketing Management* 16(4) (1987): 305–314.

Wallace, Kathleen M.: The Use and Value of Qualitative Research Studies. *Industrial Marketing Management* 13(3) (1984): 181–185.

Wasson, Chester: The Importance of the Product Life Cycle to the Industrial Marketer. *Industrial Marketing Management* 5(6) (1976): 299–308.

Welch, Joe L.: Researching Marketing Problems and Opportunities with Focus Groups. *Industrial Marketing Management* 14(4) (1985): 245–253.

Williams, Alvin, and Smith, William: Involving Purchasing in Product Development. *Industrial Marketing Management* 19(4) (1990): 315–319.

Wind, Yoram, and Webster, Frederick: On The Study of Industrial Buying Behavior: Current Practices and Future Trends. *Industrial Marketing Management* 1(4) (1972): 411–416.

Wind, Yoram, Robertson, Thomas, and Fraser, Cynthia: Industrial Product Diffusion by Market Segment. *Industrial Marketing Management* 11(1) (1982): 1–8.

Winer, Leon: A Sales Compensation Plan for Maximum Motivation. *Industrial Marketing Management* 5(1) (1976): 29–36.

Woodside, Arch, and Samuel, David: Observations of Centralized Corporate Procurement. *Industrial Marketing Management* 10(3) (1981): 191–205.

Woodside, Arch, Sanderson, R. Hedley, and Brodie, Roderick: Testing Acceptance of a New Industrial Service. *Industrial Marketing Management* 18(1) (1988): 65–72.

Wotruba, Thomas, Macfie, John, and Colletti, Jerome: Effective Sales Force Recognition Programs. *Industrial Marketing Management* 20(1) (1991): 9–15.

Yoon, Eunsang: Pricing Imitative New Products. *Industrial Marketing Management* 20(2) (1991): 115–125.

Zaltman, Gerald, and Bonoma, Thomas: Organizational Buying Behavior: Hypotheses and Directions. *Industrial Marketing Management* 6(1) (1977): 53–60.

Zinkman, George M.: Rating Industrial Advertisements. *Industrial Marketing Management* 13(1) (1984): 43–48.

2 Purchasing management

Lars-Erik Gadde

THE IMPORTANCE OF PURCHASING

The role of purchasing has been changed in a very significant way during the decades after 1970. Traditionally purchasing has been considered almost a clerical function with the ultimate objective of buying as cheaply as possible. Today it is regarded as a function of major strategic importance. The main reason for the change is the increasing specialization that characterizes the industrial system as a whole. Companies have gradually concentrated their activities on more and more limited parts of the total value chain in order to enhance efficiency in operations. One consequence of this development is that manufacturing companies have become increasingly dependent on procurement of goods and components from other firms. External suppliers, therefore, have come to play an important role for most manufacturing companies. Purchased goods often account for more than half of the total costs of a company. This fact has put purchasing in focus, internally as well as externally.

Purchasing is a focus of internal interest because an increasing proportion of the resources of a company are handled within the purchasing function. If more than half of the costs of the company are determined by purchasing it must, by definition, be an important strategic function whose activities are decisive to the competitive power of the firm. Furthermore, owing to increasing specialization, technical resources are also made increasingly available to companies through their suppliers. The products and components purchased today are more technically sophisticated than before, which has increased complexity and raised the requirements on the purchasing staff. This has also been a reason for improving the status and strategic recognition of purchasing.

From an external point of view, one major consequence is that what goes on in the interface between individual companies has gained in importance. Concepts and techniques such as just-in-time deliveries, quality assurance and the zero-defect principle have more and more impact on company operations. All of this means bringing relations to suppliers into focus. It also means bringing purchasing into focus, as supplier relations are mainly handled and coordinated through the purchasing department. As a whole, therefore, purchasing is of major strategic importance to a company.

The changing view of purchasing is also reflected in the literature. Going back to the 'clerical' time, a representative title of a book within the profession might have been 'Handbook of Purchasing'. Such books were mainly concerned with questions regarding purchasing procedures – how much to buy, how to make inquiries, etc. The main objective of this literature was to improve purchasing efficiency. Around 1970 models of organizational buying behaviour were developed to increase the understanding of the decision-making process in the buying company and which factors determined the outcome of this process. One important contribution was the concept of a buying centre. The buying centre is an informal constellation of the members in the organization that are involved in the buying decision process. Knowledge of the behaviour and perceptions of buying centre members is an important input for the marketing strategies of selling firms. These models were thus primarily orientated at enhancing marketing effectiveness.

During the 1990s, however, titles like 'Handling Supplier Relationships' and 'Developing Partnerships' better reflect the prevailing attitudes and views of purchasing. This perspective takes the performance of both supplier and customer into consideration. The major reason behind the new perspective adopted in the literature is an alternative view of efficiency in purchasing, discussed in greater detail below.

THREE STRATEGIC ROLES OF PURCHASING

When analysing the strategic importance of purchasing three major roles can be distinguished: the rationalization role, the development role and the structural role. The role of rationalization covers the numerous day-to-day activities undertaken to affect the cost structure. Three types of rationalization may be identified. The first deals with specification of requirements of the item to be purchased. This is a major undertaking, requiring decisions including whether the item needed should be manufactured in-house or purchased from external suppliers (the make-or-buy decision) as well as the design of the item. Purchasing can contribute greatly to effectiveness in this process through cooperation with internal company functions such as R&D, design and production and a qualified awareness of the capacity and capability of different suppliers. Value analysis is a technique used in this respect, the objective of which is to reduce costs while maintaining the necessary levels of availability and product reliability.

The second type of rationalization is related to identifying the most cost-effective supplier, once the specifications have been decided. Traditionally this has been the same as finding the supplier offering the lowest price.

The third type of rationalization, finally, deals with affecting the various flows associated with a business transaction. During the 1980s substantial improvements of efficiency in material flows decreased the need for inventories, and increased profitability. Purchasing has played an important role in these operations as changing delivery frequencies and lot sizes were important prerequisites for gaining these benefits. Material flows are not the only potential source for rationalization. Information flows provide considerable opportunities for improvements. In many cases the magnitude of information exchange is substantial and major effects can be obtained by using modern information technology.

Suppliers are important potential resources for the technical development of the customer firm. Most often that potential is only used in a passive way (i.e. the buying company waits for the supplier to develop new solutions and then decides whether or not to purchase them). A more active strategy in this respect, however, can turn the purchasing function into a major catalyst for making better use of these resources. This is what can be identified as the development role of purchasing. One reason for activating this role is the increasing specialization of the industrial system. A purchasing firm that uses components from a number of suppliers needs to coordinate component development undertaken by different suppliers with their own R&D activities. The components may even represent different areas of technology, which makes it difficult for the customer firm to develop and maintain its own knowledge of each specialized technology. A customer relying on suppliers as a source of development has to involve them early in the R&D process. This provides another advantage. Early supplier involvement makes it possible to shorten lead times in product development, which is considered one of the major competitive factors in most industries today.

Purchasing also has a structural role in that the procurement activities will affect the structure of the supplier markets. A company might choose to concentrate its purchases of a certain item on one supplier. The competitiveness of that supplier is then strengthened as compared with the other potential suppliers. Another company might consider the

Figure 1 Three strategic roles of purchasing

availability of a number of alternative suppliers a major strategic aim. Such a company would probably divide its purchases among several suppliers to maintain an existing supplier structure. The actions undertaken by a firm – whether conscious or unconscious – thus, affect the structure of supplier markets in the long run, in terms of the number of location of potential suppliers. It is therefore important for a company to analyse the long-term consequences of its buying behaviour, as well as to identify and predict other trends affecting the supplier markets. A company activating the structural role of purchasing can orientate its own operations towards reinforcing tendencies beneficial to it and counteracting undesirable ones.

BASIC CONDITIONS AFFECTING PURCHASING MANAGEMENT

There are substantial disparities in the forms of purchasing management. Some of these differences are attributable to the fact that companies work under divergent basic conditions. The characteristics of supplier markets will pose certain opportunities for the procurement activities. The technology of the company will also have considerable effects. Purchasing strategies and behaviour have to be very different in mass-producing firms compared with firms manufacturing to customer specification. In this section, however, two other important conditions are discussed.

The first is external and related to the characteristics of the item being purchased. There are considerable differences between purchasing standardized raw materials and sophisticated complex machinery. The second factor is internal and deals with the way in which purchasing is organized in the buying company.

The impact of product characteristics

Some of the variability in purchasing management is explained by the characteristics of what is being procured. There are clearly significant differences between major equipment for a big turnkey project and industrial supplies for more or less immediate use. Procurement of major equipment is most often characterized by technical complexity, substantial financial investment and the fact that the products are going to be used for a long time. Therefore, negotiations proceding a purchasing decision will be extensive, including discussions of alternative designs and functions. One important issue is how the new equipment is related to the existing machinery and facilities. Availability of services, training and spare parts are other important matters. This type of procurement usually involves a large number of people and departments in the buying company. One of the major characteristics is that the choice of equipment may limit the freedom of the purchasing company for a long time. The equipment chosen will largely determine what raw materials and maintenance supplies will be bought.

Procurement of industrial supplies (for maintenance, repair and operations) is very different. Such purchases include a large number of products (fastenings, hand tools, glues and sealants etc.). They are purchased frequently, but not completely regularly, as the demand for them fluctuates. The absence of such products when they are needed can pose major problems for the purchasing company. Procurement of industrial supplies, therefore, is characterized by considerable administrative complexity. The major issue regarding these types of purchases, therefore, is to develop well-functioning order and delivery systems. Efficiency is obtained through establishing routines for purchasing as a whole, rather than carrying out each purchase in the most efficient way.

Between the extremes of major equipment and industrial supplies, there are other types of purchasing situations. One concerns raw materials and materials in different stages of processing, which are important input for many companies. Such items are often more or less standardized. They usually have a global market. Prices fluctuate in relation to the cycles of demand and supply. Expectations of changing prices, therefore, are important determinants of the timing of these purchases. Many companies buy components of various kinds for assembly operations. Procurement of components is characterized by recurring deliveries, which makes it important to take advantage of the repetitive feature to create efficiency. The need to adapt the components to each other and to the production context of the buying company is also an important determinant of these purchasing operations.

Thus, it is obvious that purchasing issues show considerable variation owing to their specific procurement characteristics. The differences can be related to technical, administrative or supplier market related reasons. Such variation is typical of purchasing in all companies, as every firm purchases various kinds of items. The major effect of this variation is that it is difficult for a company to find one best solution regarding organization and administrative routines.

Purchasing organization

There are two extremes of purchasing organization: centralization and decentralization. A centralized purchasing department provides three major advantages. One is economies of scale thanks to larger order quantities than would appear in a decentralized organization structure. The second is that it is possible to coordinate the combined activities from the purchasing company in relation to individual suppliers. The third is that centralization enhances effective allocation of resources. One example is that purchasing staff can specialize in procurement of specific items which promotes professionalism in purchasing. The major disadvantage of a centralized purchasing organization is problems with internal communication between purchasing staff and other departments (production, R&D, etc.). Especially in large companies there can be a substantial distance between them – both in physical terms and in attitudes. A sense of 'us-versus-them' between production and purchasing can easily arise.

These kinds of problem are better dealt with in a decentralized organization. Proponents of decentralized structures claim that purchasing should not be a specialized function, but rather an integral part of a larger context. During the last ten years the decentralized organization has gained in importance. One reason is that firms in general have turned towards decentralization. When company divisions and business units are made more and more responsible in economic terms for their operations, it is not possible to keep their major cost determinant – purchasing – under central control. The most obvious problem with a decentralized purchasing organization is the reduced professionalism of the purchasers. They become more generalists, needing competence and capability for purchasing across an extremely broad product range.

The choice between centralization and decentralization will always be a compromise. Settling for the benefits of one always means sacrificing the potential benefits of the other. For this reason purchasing will always have to put effort into eliminating the disadvantages of the organizational form that has been chosen. A decentralized organization may be supplemented with central purchasing staff, responsible for drawing up group agreements with the purpose of achieving economies of scale. A centralized purchasing organization can be supplemented with shop-floor purchasers who are responsible for acquisition of specific components. This makes it possible to work with a combined approach falling somewhere between the extremes. Such intermediate types showed to be the most common forms in a study of big Scandinavian companies (Figure 2).

Traditionally, the purchasing organization of a firm has been determined by internal factors. Over time, external factors have come to play an increasing role. When purchased goods account for almost two-thirds of total costs, it is very obvious that external factors have to be considered more. The purchasing company must be organized in such a way that the exchange with suppliers is facilitated as much as possible.

STRATEGIC ISSUES IN PURCHASING MANAGEMENT

There are two major strategic issues regarding supply management in a company. One of them is how much of the input resources needed by the manufacturing company should be directly controlled (i.e. the degree of vertical integration). The other regards the nature of customer-supplier relationships (i.e. the number of suppliers used and the characteristics of the relation to individual suppliers).

Figure 2 Combining centralized and decentralized purchasing organization

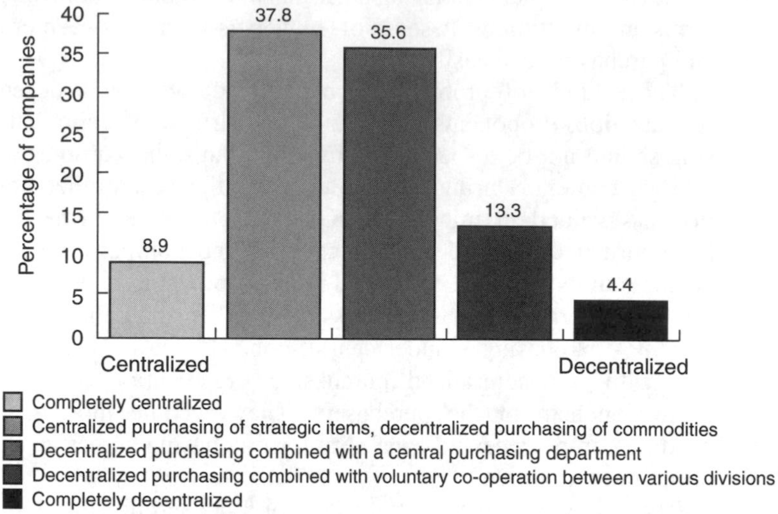

[Source: Gadde and Håkansson (1993: 129)]

The make-or-buy decision

The first issue relates to the make-or-buy decision. For every company the decision to produce in-house or to buy from external suppliers is a key strategic one. Vertical integration, historically, has been used as a strategy to secure availability of important resources. One example is automotive firms and ballbearing manufacturers that have been the owners of steelworks in order to guarantee the quality of the steel required. One main disadvantage of in-house production is that rapid changes in market demand might lead a company to be locked into obsolete technology. Another problem is that firms with a high degree of backward vertical integration might limit the prerequisites for and capability of creative thinking and development among their staff.

Over time there has been a substantial decrease in the degree of vertical integration in industry as a whole. As has already been mentioned, numerous manufacturing companies have become increasingly dependent on innovative subcontractors, who have proved able to contribute to making production as well as development work more effective. In make-or-buy analysis the loss of control has been considered a serious drawback when the degree of vertical integration has decreased. Over the years, however, manufacturing companies have identified other means for retaining control over their supply situations that do not require ownership of suppliers. There are a number of examples of more informal integration, such as strategic alliances, collaboration projects, joint investments in production tools, loans and credit guarantees. These examples of 'quasi-integration' can play the same role as vertical integration. They provide the buying company with some of the main advantages of ownership without the corresponding disadvantages.

The nature of customer-supplier relationships

The second, and more important, strategic issue is the nature of customer-supplier relationships. It is possible to identify two disparate views of what is an efficient way of managing supplier relationships. One is what can be regarded as an adversarial relationship. According to that view a customer-supplier relation is a zero-sum game (i.e. what one of the parties stands to gain, the other one stands to lose). One major issue in purchasing management, therefore, is that suppliers compete with one another. By switching from one supplier to the other, depending on the business conditions they offer, the customer will be guaranteed as low a price as possible. Using such a strategy requires the purchasing company to avoid being too dependent on individual suppliers, so that the customer always will be able to switch. Multiple sourcing, therefore, has been strongly advocated as an efficient purchasing strategy. Using a number of suppliers has also been considered an advantage in terms of handling risks (e.g. in relation to capacity problems of individual suppliers). Using this kind of procurement strategy, purchasing companies must maintain a deliberate distance in their relationship with their suppliers, which leads to an adversarial relation rather than a collaborative one. This can be called the traditional view of efficiency in purchasing.

During the 1980s a clear shift was observed in the view of what is an efficient number of suppliers. These tendencies were first observed in the automotive industry when American and European manufacturers were confronted with the supply strategies of their competitors in Japan, who relied on a more limited number of suppliers. Where Japanese firms were using 200–300 suppliers, the companies in the Western world were using 2–3,000 for a corresponding output of cars.

One example of a changing strategy is that Ford reduced its suppliers from 3,200 to 2,100 in 6 years. Changes of this type have not, however, been limited to the automotive industry. The most spectacular example is Rank Xerox which had more than 5,000 suppliers in 1981 and just over 300 five years later. Such a strategic change contrasts greatly with what was earlier regarded as efficient purchasing. The main reason for the change is that major advantages can be obtained through cooperation with individual suppliers. Price is only one of the costs that are dependent on the purchasing behaviour. A number of other (indirect) costs can be affected, due to the nature of the relationship (see Figure 3).

To affect the indirect costs and attain the potential benefits of close cooperation requires customer and supplier to adapt to one another.

Adaptations require deepened relationships, which makes it necessary
to reduce the number of counterparts. Doing so will make it possible to
improve considerably the efficiency of relationships. According to this
view a buyer-seller relationship is not a zero-sum game. Both parties
will attain benefits from mutual adaptations. In terms of the strategic
roles of purchasing as have been identified above, significant effects can
be obtained in terms of rationalization as well as in terms of development. The change also has definite structural consequences.

Networks of suppliers

Considerable economic effects can thus be attained through developing
relationships with individual suppliers. Even greater impact, however,
would be obtained if the activities of the individual suppliers could in
some way be coordinated. Sometimes the buying company would
increase its efficiency if the supplier's supplier could be persuaded to
make a certain change. Each relationship is embedded in a larger network of relationships, characterized by interdependencies of various
kinds. Therefore, the performance of every relationship is contingent on
a number of other relationships. Analysing and organizing suppliers and
supplier markets in terms of networks provides major advantages. The
best example again is the Japanese automotive industry and its reliance
on a more limited number of suppliers. These firms have organized their
suppliers in a hierarchical structure. Toyota, for instance, had direct
contacts with only a few suppliers (less than 200). These primary
suppliers are made responsible for structuring the rest of the supply network, which includes a very large number of firms (around 40,000). The

Figure 3   Costs affected by purchasing behaviour

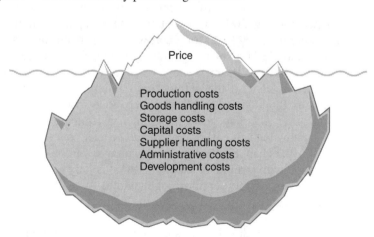

Price

Production costs
Goods handling costs
Storage costs
Capital costs
Supplier handling costs
Administrative costs
Development costs

[Source: Gadde and Håkansson (1993: 47)]

way that the supplier network is organized appears to have been deci-sive to the strong position established by Japanese automotive firms.

Purchasing companies relying on single sourcing increase the depen-dence on individual suppliers. The potential for playing off suppliers to achieve a price benefit is also severely restricted. Obviously the percep-tions of what is efficient purchasing behaviour must be based on differ-ent assumptions than the traditional view. We thus need to contrast that view with another way of looking at strategic efficiency, referred to as 'the alternative model'.

TRADITIONAL VIEW OF PURCHASING MANAGEMENT

Purchasing management deals with how to secure efficiency and effec-tiveness in purchasing operations. Therefore, an important determinant of purchasing strategy and management is which view of purchasing efficiency prevails in the buying company. The two contrasting views that have been identified are analysed below in terms of their impact on purchasing management.

According to the traditional model there is a very well-established view of how effective purchasing should be carried out (Figure 4). The first step in the decision-making process is to specify the needs to be satisfied. The next is to identify a number of potential suppliers. They are

Figure 4 A model of the buying decision-making process

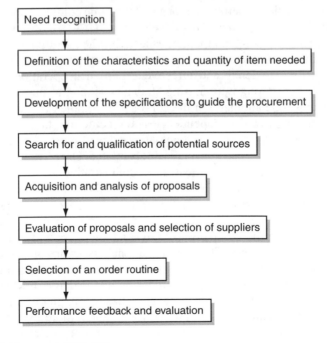

Need recognition

Definition of the characteristics and quantity of item needed

Development of the specifications to guide the procurement

Search for and qualification of potential sources

Acquisition and analysis of proposals

Evaluation of proposals and selection of suppliers

Selection of an order routine

Performance feedback and evaluation

[Source: Robinson *et al.* (1967: 14)]

requested to submit tenders, which are then compared on the basis of various criteria. According to this view efficiency in purchasing arises from the implementation of the decision-making process. The most important determinant of this procedure is enhancing competition among the suppliers. The struggle among suppliers forces them to make improvements that also benefit the purchasing company and affects its performance. To achieve such benefits, it is recommended that customers avoid being too dependent on individual suppliers. Keeping an arm's length relationship ensures that the buyer can easily switch to another supplier offering some kind of better conditions. The purchasing company will have contact with a number of potential suppliers for each item. By playing off these suppliers against each other it becomes possible to make an optimum choice. To promote competition among suppliers is thus the most important aspect of purchasing management. According to this perspective, efficiency in purchasing is attained if the price is minimized in each separate transaction. The underlying rationale is that price is the most significant cost and that other costs are not affected by a change from one supplier to another. On the contrary, there should be a great deal to be gained from such 'play-the-market' behaviour.

THE ALTERNATIVE VIEW OF PURCHASING MANAGEMENT

The alternative view is a consequence of the changing conditions described above. Today, due to increasing specialization, activities that were earlier undertaken in one and the same company are separated into different companies. This development has created a growing interdependence among companies, especially when dealing with products and components that are characterized by technological or logistical complexity. Efficiency and effectiveness in such operations can never be obtained through purchasing strategies aiming at playing off suppliers against one another. On the contrary, in complex relationships the customer has to create dependencies on specific suppliers to obtain gains in efficiency. To achieve the potential gains in performance, supplier and customer must become increasingly related. Only by mutual adaptations in technological, logistical and administrative terms can the indirect costs of the relationship be affected. This is the reason for the standpoint presented above, that purchasing organizations have to become more externally orientated. The most important organizational aspect is to relate the company to individual suppliers and to the whole network of suppliers. Thus, organizational issues are of major importance when discussing purchasing management from the alternative view. Rather than talking about purchasing organization, however, we go on to discuss various 'organizing' activities within purchasing, which leads to a more external than internal focus, and a more dynamic and developing view than the static one that often is associated with the word 'organization'.

The network approach to analysis of industrial markets is a relevant point of departure for discussing important organizing aspects of purchasing. According to this approach three important network dimensions are distinguished: activities, resources and actors. All three dimensions are essential in terms of organizing supplier relationships.

The activity structure of an industrial network is characterized by strong interdependence due to the specialization of firms. The performance of the network and the companies in the network is dependent on the efficiency of the activities *per se*, but also on the links connecting these activities. One important assignment for the customer, therefore, is to improve the coordination of its activities with those of the supplier. Linking of activities is thus an important organizing issue for improving purchasing efficiency. The development of coordinating mechanisms in transportation (just-in-time systems) and information exchange (integrated computer systems) have reduced the need for inventories and buffers.

Suppliers are providers of resources for a purchasing company. For example, a supplier can play an important role in the technical development of a customer firm. As said above, it is very difficult for a company to keep pace with rapid developments in different areas of technology. This is why a company should try to develop its resources in interaction with its suppliers, to be able to make use of their resources and competence. A second important organizing issue, therefore, is integrating customer-supplier resources. Various forms of technology transfer are relevant examples of such organizing activities. Most exchange of technology, however, takes place in the day-to-day contacts among individuals in the companies.

The third organizing issue is the need to connect the buying company to other actors, both in terms of single relationships and networks. One important prerequisite for quality in customer-supplier relationships is commitment. To attain the desired joint effects, a customer has to develop relationships of a long-term nature with an atmosphere of openness and trust. These characteristics do not evolve automatically. They have to be created, especially if previous conditions have been of an adversarial nature. Therefore, it is relevant to consider this a matter of organizing. Another important aspect is the nature of collaboration. Buyer–seller relationships relying on the alternative view of efficiency are characterized by a high degree of cooperation. For this cooperation to be successful, there is a need for a great degree of harmony in the relationship. In the same way there is a need for a certain degree of challenge. This is necessary to avoid stagnation and to secure a continuous development of the relationship. This challenge should partly be in terms of hostility and conflict since constructive conflicts promote dynamism. It is therefore an important organizing issue to create a balance between harmony and conflict in the relationship.

CURRENT ISSUES IN PURCHASING MANAGEMENT

In this final section we briefly discuss some of the major current issues in purchasing management.

The first issue is the degree of vertical integration. The question is whether the ongoing tendencies will continue or not. The basic argument for a continuing decrease in vertical integration is that the advantages provided by specialization will result in a decreasing proportion of in-house production. Design and R&D can also be expected, at an increasing rate, to be outsourced to suppliers. However, some things also speak in favour of an increasing degree of vertical integration. The argument advocating this view is that in industry today the companies in the final stages of the value chain (assemblers) are the ones that are most profitable, while those at the beginning (component producers) have financial problems, owing to heavy pressure from their customers. In the short run assembly firms have been able to improve returns thanks to disintegration. In the long run, however, it is very unlikely that independent component suppliers will be able to generate the funds needed for investments, in order to stay competitive. The only way to guarantee this is to increase the degree of vertical integration.

The divergent opinions about future integration can partly be explained by the fact that they concentrate on the formal degree of vertical integration. As discussed above, a number of forms of more informal integration, in fact, makes it possible to attain the major ownership advantages without its disadvantages. The most likely development, therefore, is continued specialization of activities, resulting in decreasing vertical integration, combined with various intermediate forms of quasi-integration based on extended supplier relationships.

The second issue deals with the nature of customer-supplier relationships. As has been argued, there are a number of good reasons for a company to develop extended supplier relationships according to the alternative view of efficiency. Most types of buyer-seller relations can be made more effective by attacking indirect costs through long-term cooperation and mutual adaptations. Sometimes, however, products from various suppliers are completely interchangeable from the perspective of the customer, sometimes the indirect costs are very small as compared to the direct costs. In such cases the purchasing firm can benefit from using the traditional view of efficiency and promoting supplier competition. It seems possible, therefore, to argue that a company aiming at purchasing efficiency should be able to behave according to both views, depending on the circumstances.

The characteristics of the business transaction determine whether the traditional or the alternative view is the most relevant one (Figure 5).

In case A in Figure 5, price accounts for most of the total cost. If switching to another supplier only causes minor problems, the best

Figure 5 Traditional versus alternative purchasing strategy

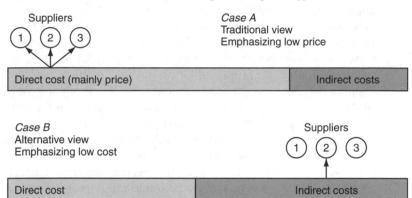

strategy seems to be to use a number of suppliers and promote competition among them to attain the lowest price possible.

Case B is a quite different situation. Suppose that the indirect costs related to purchasing are more substantial than in case A. There are always ways in which they can be influenced. In this case extensive cooperation with one of the suppliers should lead to lower costs as a whole. More extensive cooperation with a supplier might even affect the revenues of the buying company. Long-term relationships probably result in development of products and components better adapted to their functions in the products of the purchasing company. This, in turn, can be exploited in the market. Achieving these benefits requires adaptations and investments in the relationships, which creates dependencies on individual suppliers. According to the alternative model, therefore, dependency is a prerequisite for efficiency and effectiveness in purchasing.

However, using a dual approach to purchasing management is associated with major problems. Only in cases where the various supplier markets are completely unrelated to one another would it be possible for a company to behave as differently as is necessary to apply to the two different views of efficiency. Internally such a dualism would have organizational implications. It is almost impossible for individual purchasers to behave according to both views. Therefore, purchasing staff concerned with transactions and supplier markets characterized by the traditional view should be separated from those concerned with relationships of the alternative view.

On the whole, however, companies have a great deal to gain through working more in accordance with the alternative view. The traditional view, emphasizing independence and supplier competition, still has a very strong position. Most companies would therefore benefit from turning in the direction of deepened relationships. Many companies also state such ambitions in their purchasing policies. This leads to the third current issue – implementation of changes in purchasing strategy. Such changes are associated with major problems. Changing attitudes and behaviour will be required from the customer company. Purchasing staff need to act very differently and have to change completely their views of what is efficiency in purchasing behaviour. A lot of effort is required to affect prevailing attitudes. Another problem is to convince suppliers to undertake the necessary changes. If past relations have been of the adversarial type, there will be major communication problems as supplier attitudes and behaviour must also be affected.

This brings us to the fourth issue relating to organizing aspects. Traditionally, organizational structures of purchasing have mainly been determined by internal aspects. In purchasing situations characterized by the traditional view this might be a relevant point of departure. The alternative view of purchasing efficiency emphasizes the importance of individual suppliers and supplier networks. It has been shown that important determinants of effective purchasing are to link activities, to integrate resources and to connect actors. It is clear, therefore, that organizing the firm in a way that facilitates effective exchange with suppliers is the most important strategic issue. This means that purchasing management is mainly an organizing task.

REFERENCES

Gadde, L.-E. and Håkansson, H. (1993) *Professional Purchasing*, London: Routledge.
Robinson, P. J., Faris, C. W. and Wind, Y. (1967) *Industrial Buying and Creative Marketing*, Boston: Allyn & Bacon, Inc.

FURTHER READING

Axelsson, B. and Håkansson, H. (1984) *Inköp för konkurrenskraft,* Stockholm: Liber.
Blenkhorn, D. and Noori, H. (1990) 'What it takes to supply Japanese OEMs', *Industrial Marketing Management* 19: 21–30.
Blois, K. (1971) 'Vertical quasi-integration', *Journal of Industrial Economics* 20 (3): 33–41.
Burt, D. and Sukoup, W. (1985) 'Purchasing's role in new product development', *Harvest Business Review*, September–October: 90–97.
Frazier, G., Spekman, R. and O'Neal, C. (1988) 'Just-in-time exchange relationships in industrial markets', *Journal of Marketing* 52 (4): 11–27.
Gadde, L.-E. and Mattsson, L.-G. (1987) 'Stability and change in network relationships', *International Journal of Research on Marketing* 4: 29–41.
Håkansson, H. (ed.) (1982) *International Marketing and Purchasing of Industrial Goods – an Interaction Approach*, Chichester: John Wiley & Sons.

Håkansson, H. (1989) *Corporate Technological Behaviour – Co-operation and Networks*, London: Routledge.

Jansch, L. and Wilson, H. (1979) 'A strategic perspective for make or buy decisions', *Long Range Planning* 12: 56-61.

Kraljic, P. (1982) 'Purchasing must become supply management', *Harvard Business Review*, September–October: 109–17.

Kumpe, T. and Bolwijn, P. (1988) 'Manufacturing: the new case for vertical integration', *Harvard Business Review*, March–April: 75–81.

Lamming, R. (1993) *Beyond Partnership – Strategies for Innovation and Lean Supply*, Hemel Hempstead: Prentice Hall.

Miles, R. and Snow, C. (1986) 'Organizations: new concepts for new forms', *California Management Review*, XXVIII (3): 62–73.

Newman, R. (1988) 'Single source qualification', *Journal of Purchasing and Materials Management*, Summer: 10–17.

Sheth, J. (1973) 'A model of industrial buyer behaviour', *Journal of Marketing* 37 (4): 50–56.

Takeuchi, H. and Nonaka, I. (1986) 'The new new-product development game', *Harvard Business Review*, January–February: 137–46.

Webster, F. and Wind, Y. (1972) *Organizational Buying Behaviour*, Englewood Cliffs: Prentice Hall.

Westing, J., Fine, I. and Zens, G. (1969) *Purchasing Management, Materials in Motion*, New York: John Wiley and Sons.

3 Overhauling the new product process

Robert G. Cooper

The three cornerstones of successful product development are process, strategy, and resources, according to the benchmarking study reported in this article. Of the three, having a high quality new product process had the strongest impact on business's new product performance. A high quality new product process meant: an emphasis on up-front homework: sharp, early product definition; the voice of the customer evident throughout; tough go/kill decision points; a focus on quality of execution; and a thorough yet flexible process. The research results point strongly to a need to overhaul firms' new product processes – from idea to launch – to incorporate these and other key success drivers, such as the quest for real product superiority, and the need for true cross-functional teams. The goals of an effective new product process – that is, the specifications or key elements of a high quality process – are outlined, a vital starting point to any process reengineering exercise. The article ends with a quick look at a third generation stage-gate or new product process, together with some tips and hints on how to proceed to overhaul your company's new product process.

© Elsevier Science Inc., 1996

INTRODUCTION

The long-term survival of a business enterprise hinges upon its ability to successfully introduce new products into the marketplace. Rapidly

Address correspondence to Dr. Robert G. Cooper, Professor of Industrial Marketing and Technology Management, Michael G. DeGroote School of Business, McMaster University, 1280 Main Street West, Hamilton, Ontario L8S 4M4, Canada.

Industrial Marketing Management **25**, 465–482 (1996)
© Elsevier Science Inc., 1996
655 Avenue of the Americas, New York, NY 10010

THREE CORNERSTONES OF PERFORMANCE: RESOURCES, STRATEGY, AND HIGH QUALITY PROCESS

changing technologies, heightened competition, and dynamic customer needs and wants are rendering existing products obsolete at an ever increasing pace: product life cycles are becoming shorter. The message to senior management is simple: *either innovate or die!* Some of the 'innovations' required can be quite minor (such as modifying an existing polymer to yield enhanced performance characteristics), or they can involve the development of innovations based on entirely new technology platforms (such as the development of noninvasive methods for medical operations). Regardless of the nature of innovation required, the fact is that rapid and successful product development has become a *vital business endeavor*. The dilemma faced by managements in moderate to high technology industrial firms is that need for product development is stronger than ever, but the tools and methods to bring new products to market have not changed dramatically in the last decades.

There are new insights, however. The three cornerstones of successful product development are process, strategy, and resources, according to our recent benchmarking study [3]. *Strategy* is a well-known critical success factor: having a product innovation strategy for the business that ties product development to the corporate strategy and goals; that identifies areas of focus for product development; that has a longer term thrust; and that is clearly enunciated to all in the firm. *Adequate spending and resources* is yet another familiar success factor: having the necessary people and R&D spending in place. Of the three cornerstones, process – more specifically, *having a high quality new product process* to guide product innovations from idea to launch – is a less well-known critical success factor. Ironically, of the three, it is the new product process – its nature and quality – that has the strongest impact on the business's new product performance.

What then are the secrets to a *winning new product process*, one that consistently delivers a steady stream of successful and significant new products, and in a timely fashion? Our investigations have probed this vital question for some years. Here are the conclusions based on this

ROBERT G. COOPER is the Lawson Mardon Chaired Professor of Industrial Marketing and Technology Management at the M. G. deGroote School of Business. McMaster University, Hamilton, Ontario, Canada. He is a noted researcher in new product management, having published over 75 articles and books, and the developer of the *stage-gate* new product process and the *NewProd* diagnostic tool. His most recent book is *Winning at New Products* (Addison Wesley, Reading, MA). Cooper is also a lecturer and consultant to industry.

research: the specifications of successful new product development processes; insights into the latest product development processes from leading firms; and tips on implementing such a successful new product process in your firm. The topic is particularly relevant, as corporate managements have turned to process reengineering as a solution to what ails new product development in recent years. Often the results of these reengineering exercises are disappointing, largely because the 'reengineers' didn't understand the vital ingredients of a winning new product process; so they went about tweaking the current process, merely documenting current practices. By contrast, our research and this article conclude that a *total overhaul* of the new product process is necessary in order to realize real improvements in this critical function of the firm.

CORNERSTONES OF PERFORMANCE

Three critical success factors were found to be the drivers of new product performance at the business unit level (see Figure 1). This was the central finding of our most recent benchmarking study. This study of 161 business units considered 10 different measures of new product performance, including percentage of sales by new products, success rates, impact on the firm, and overall profitability of the business's total new product efforts (for more detail, see [3]), The top three drivers of performance, in order, were (see Figure 1 and Table 1):

1   A high quality new product process: (This process, either explicit or implicit, includes those steps and activities in a new product project from idea to launch). Here, the better performers had quality processes where:

- there was an emphasis on up-front homework (on predevelopment work);
- the process included sharp, early product definition (before development work began);
- the voice of the customer was evident throughout – there was a strong focus on the customer/user and marketplace;
- there were tough go/kill decision points in the process, where projects really did get killed;
- there was a focus on quality of execution (where every activity was carried out in a quality fashion);
- the process was complete or thorough (where every activity was carried out – no hasty short-cuts); and yet
- the process was flexible, where stages and decision points could be skipped or combined, as dictated by the nature and risk of the project.

A clear and well-communicated new product strategy for the business unit, that is:

Figure 1 The new product performance triangle and the three cornerstones of performance [3]

- there were goals or objectives for the business unit's total new product effort; i.e., what sales, profits, etc., new products would contribute to the corporate goal;
- the role of new products in achieving the business's goals was clearly communicated to all;
- there were clearly defined arenas – specified areas of strategic focus, such as products, markets, or technologies – to give direction to the business's total new product effort; and
- the new product effort had a long-term thrust and focus, including some long-term projects (as opposed to short-term, incremental projects).

Adequate resources for new products, that is:

- senior management had devoted the necessary resources to achieve the business unit's new product objectives;
- R&D budgets were adequate; and
- the necessary people were in place and had their time freed up for new products.

Note that R&D spending devoted to new products (as a percentage of sales) was the strongest single driver of new product impact on the business (see Table 1).

#1 CRITICAL SUCCESS FACTOR: A QUALITY NEW PRODUCT PROCESS

A *high quality* new product process was the strongest common denominator among high performance businesses – more powerful than having

Table 1 Major drivers of new product performance at the business unit level

Major Drivers and Ingredients	Effect on Profitability*	Effect on Impact	Rating (0–100)†
High quality new product process	0.416	0.226	59.4
Solid up-front homework	0.198	0.235	57.5
Sharp, early product definition	0.236	0.201	66.8
Strong market orientation (voice of customer)	0.254	–	61.0
Tough go/kill decision points	0.364	–	49.0
Quality of execution throughout	0.434	0.220	64.5
A complete, thorough NP process	0.292	–	54.3
A flexible process	0.205	–	63.0
A clear new product strategy	0.228	0.211	58.7
Goals defined for total new product effort	–	0.213	58.8
Role defined for new products re. business goals	–	0.223	51.5
Clearly defined areas (areas of focus)	0.264	–	68.0
A long-term thrust	0.213	0.186	56.5
Adequate resource for new products	0.244	0.197	56.5
Resources in place to achieve NP objectives	0.200	0.232	60.3
R&D budgets adquate	–	–	58.8
Necessary people in place, time freed up	0.257	–	50.3
R&D spending on new products (% of sales)	–	0.395	2.91%
High quality project teams	0.196	0.208	48.1
Dedicated leader (to one project at a time)	–	0.220	34.8
Team interactions (good team communication)	–	0.243	57.3
Handle outside decisions well	0.323	–	52.3
True cross-functional teams	0.230	–	67.2
Projects have assigned team	0.189	–	65.3
Team is cross-functional	0.208	–	72.8
Team has defined and accountable leader	–	–	75.5
Accountable from beginning to end of project	–	0.220	55.3

* Profitability refers to the profitability of the business's total new product efforts. Impact refers to whether or not product development had a major positive impact on the business unit. Both effects were measured via Pearson product-moment correlations. All correlations are significant at the 0.01 level.

† Ratings: how well business units fared on each ingredient, on average. These rating scores were measured on a 1–5 scale, then converted to 0–100 points. Here 100 = excellent and 0 = very poor.

a new product strategy for the business or even having the right resources in place (although the three critical success factors were intimately connected, and the symbionic effect of all three acting together yielded the most positive results – see Figure 1).

A word of caution here. The mere existence of a *formal* product development process had absolutely *no effect* on performance, according to the benchmarking study: there was no correlation at all between merely having a formal process and performance results. The message is this: those companies who mistakenly believe they can 'go through the motions' and reengineer their new product processes (usually amounting to documenting what they're already doing!) are in for a big disappointment.

Having a process didn't seem to matter; rather it was *the quality and nature of that process* – building in best practices – which really drove performance.

In highlighting these results, several of our studies are frequently cited:

- The first is the benchmarking study of 161 business units, mentioned above; the 10 performance metrics were reduced to two key dimensions: profitability and impact, shown in Table 1. Henceforth, refer to this study as 'the benchmarking study' [3].
- The second includes two studies that looked specifically at new product projects instead of business units: 203 new North American industrial new product projects consisting of 123 successes and 80 failures; and 103 North American and European new products from the chemical industry (68 commercial successes and 35 failures). These are called 'the projects study' – see Table 2 [1].

Note that two sets of results are referred to: first, there is the profile or rating of the typical company or project on each dimension – for example, for the first ingredient below, do companies typically undertake solid up-front homework in projects? And second, there is the impact that this dimension has on performance – for example, does solid homework really have a significant positive payoff?

Consider now the *ingredients* of such a quality new product process, and the message to managers:

- *First, there is an emphasis on up-front homework in the process – both market and technical assessments – before projects move into the development phase.*

Too many projects move from the idea stage right into development with little or no assessment or up-front homework. Homework includes those many activities that occur before development begins: initial screening; market, user and competitive studies: technical and manufacturing appraisals; and financial analysis – Exhibit 1.

Table 2 Practical success factors at the project level

Project Success Factors*	How Much Each Factor Drove Up Success Rates: 203 Industrial Products†	Quality of Execution (0–10 Rating) 203 Industrial Products‡	Correlation with Success Rates 103 Chemical Products§	Quality of Execution (0–10 Rating) 103 Chemical Products‡
Product superiority:				
Differentiated product				
Unique customer benefits				
Superior value for the customer	79.6 percentage points	Not applic.	0.510	Not applic.
Sharp, early product definition:				
Target market	59.2 percentage points	Not applic.	0.373	Not applic.
Product concept and benefits				
Requirements and specs				
Solid, up-front homework				
Before development begins	43.2 percentage points	5.93	0.37*	5.35
High quality marketing activities				
Assessment, research, testing with customers, and launch	38.6 percentage points	6.22	0.448	5.61
High quality technological activities:				
Assessment, development, testing, preproduction and production start-up	45.9 percentage points	6.66	0.260	7.06
Cross-functional teams:				
Cross-functional; dedicated; accountable: strong leader	Not measured	Not measured	0.304	Not applic.

* Multiple performance metrics were gauged: all were intercorrelated. The success factors cited here are based on success rates, measured by financial performance.

† The effect of each success factor is gauged in terms of the difference in success rates for projects 'high' on the success factor versus those 'low' on that success factor (the top 20% versus the bottom 20%). Similar strong effects were detected for the other measures of performance. All differences cited above are significant 0.001 level.

‡ Quality of execution: how proficiently certain activities were undertaken in projects: a 0–10 rating where 10 = excellent and 0 = very poor.

§ Pearson product-moment correlations with success rates: all significant at the 0.001 level; correlations with other performance metrics were also strong.

EXHIBIT 1

Solid Up-Front Homework

Up-front homework, an often-missing ingredient in new product projects, means building in a 'first cut' or preliminary investigation stage, involving:

1. A preliminary market assessment: a quick scoping of the marketplace to assess market existence, probable market size, and expected product definition; this is largely *detective work*: desk research; assessing available public and commercial databases, reports, articles, etc.; utilizing in-house information and people; contacting a few lead users.

2. A preliminary technical assessment: a quick technical appraisal to propose a technical solution, map out a probable route, and assess technical costs, times, and risks; this work is a largely conceptual: technical literature search; utilizing in-house technical expertise; brainstorming and creative problem-solving sessions; reviewing competitive product solutions; drawing on technical gurus outside the firm.

3. A preliminary business assessment: a quick financial assessment (e.g., payback period) based on very rough estimates of sales, costs, and investment required; a cursory legal assessment; and a quick risk assessment.

For larger and more complex projects, many firms build in a *second and more detailed* homework phase, namely a detailed investigation stage, prior to development.

This second stage often includes:

1. Detailed market studies and market research, such as:
   - user needs-and-wants studies: entails personal interviews with prospective customers and users to determine customer needs, wants, and preferences; product performance requirements; and a definition of the customer's wish list.
   - value-in-use studies; assessment of the customer's economics – what economic value the product will bring to the customer (this often involves an in-depth look at the customer's use system, the current solution, and various cost drivers).
   - competitive analysis: a detailed look at competitors' products, pricing, bases of competing, and performance (e.g., share and profitability).
   - concept tests: a testing of the proposed product (in concept or *protocept* form) to gauge interest, liking, and purchase intent (and an estimate of expected sales); also price sensitivity.

2. Detailed technical assessment: a more thorough technical activity to prove technical feasibility, identify the likely technical solution, deal with technical risks, assess manufacturability (route, costs, and probable capital requirements), and deal with safety, health, legal, and regulatory issues. This usually involves some physical technical work, such as lab work, modeling, or the development of a crude working model or protocept.

3. Building the business case: this defines the business proposition and product, provides the justification for the project (the economic and business rationale for the new product), and maps out the action plan through to launch. Tasks here include detailed financial analysis and business risk assessment.

The results of this 'ready, fire, aim' approach are usually disastrous. In the projects study, inadequate up-front homework was a major failure reason [1]. By contrast, solid up-front homework drove up new product success rates by 43.2 percentage points and was strongly correlated with performance – see Table 2; and projects that boasted solid up-front homework achieved 2.4 times the success rate and 2.2 times the market share as those with poor homework. More evidence: the benchmarking study revealed that homework is a key ingredient in a high quality new product process and was significantly and positively correlated with the two performance dimensions, namely *profitability* as well as *impact* of the firm's total new product efforts – see Table 1.

A lack of homework seems to be the rule in product development, however. Indeed, the benchmarking study gauged the mean quality score on this ingredient to be a mediocre 57.5 points out of 100. (Note: in the benchmarking study, firms rated their proficiencies on each of the performance drivers on a 0- to 100-point scale; here 100 was 'excellent' and 0 meant 'very poor'). Similarly, in the projects study, quality of execution was rated (0–10) for each of 13 key tasks. The results:

- quality of execution across homework or predevelopment tasks was mediocre at best (ratings of 5.35 and 5.93 out of 10 for the two projects studies – see Table 2); and
- successful teams undertook superior up-front homework (more time, money, and effort; also better quality work) and executed the early-stage marketing actions much better than did failure teams.

Message: Build a detailed homework stage (or two) into your new product process – a homework phase that results in a business case based on fact rather than speculation. Insist that solid up-front homework be undertaken and ensure that no significant project enters development missing this vital homework – see Exhibit 1 for an insight into what the top performers do.

■ *A high quality new product process includes sharp, early product definition, before development work begins.*

A failure to *define the product* – its target market; the concept, benefits, and positioning; and its requirements, features, and specs – before development begins is a major cause of both new product failure and serious delays in time to market [1]. In spite of the fact that *early product definition is consistently cited as a key to success*, firms continue to perform poorly here: the benchmarking study revealed a modest mean score for the product definition step of 66.8 points out of 100 – hardly stellar performance (Table 2). More importantly, this same study found that sharp, early product definition was significantly correlated with both the profitability and the impact of the firm's total new product efforts. In a similar vein, the projects study discovered a very strong impact of product definition on performance; sharp, early product definition enhanced project success rates by 59.2 percentage points; such well-defined projects had 3.7 times the success rate and 1.6 times the market share as those which lacked definition; and product definition was significantly and strongly correlated with performance (Table 1) [1].

Message: Sharp, early product definition follows from solid homework (above). This definition includes:

■ the target market;
■ the product concept, benefits to be delivered, and positioning strategy; and
■ the product's requirements and high level specifications.

Make it a rule: no project enters development without a product definition, agreed to by the project team and signed off by senior management.

■ *The new product process emphasizes a strong market orientation and builds in the voice of the customer throughout.*

Successful business units, and teams that drive winning new product projects, pay special attention to the voice of the customer. New product projects that featured high quality marketing actions – preliminary and detailed market studies, customer tests, field trials, and test markets, as well as launch – were blessed with more than double the success rate and 70% higher market shares than those projects with poor marketing actions; further, a strong market orientation increased success rates by 38.6 percentage points and was strongly correlated with new product performance (projects study [1]). In the benchmarking study, a process

HAVING A FORMAL PROCESS HAD NO IMPACT AT ALL

that emphasized the customer and marketplace via market studies, market research, concept tests, competitive analysis, customer field trials etc., was significantly correlated with profitability of the business unit's total new product efforts.

A market orientation and customer focus were noticebly lacking in many firm's new product projects. The marketing actions were among the most weakly executed in the entire new product process, according to both the projects study and benchmarking study. The mean quality-of-execution rating for marketing tasks was a dismal 5.61 out of 10 in the chemical projects study and 6.22 out of 10 for all industrial products. Further, building in the voice of the customer was rated a mediocre 61 points out of 100 in the benchmarking study.

Message: Spare no effort in building the customer or user into your new product process. This means right from the beginning of the process, namely *ideation*: 75% of all successful new products saw the idea come from the marketplace. So focus on the customer to identify needs and wants and to solicit new product ideas. Next, the customer must be *an input into product design*, and not just an after-the-fact check that the design is satisfactory. Some companies use QFD (quality function deployment) as a method of building the customer's voice into the product design. The customer is also an integral facet of the project during the development phase: use multiple iterations of rapid prototype and tests, so that by the end of development, there are no surprises. Finally, as the project moves toward commercialization, ensure that rigorous customer tests (perhaps even test markets or trial sells) are built into your process, along with a properly resourced, well-planned launch phase.

■ *There are tough go/kill decision points in the process, where projects really do get killed.*

Projects tend to get a life of their own! In too many companies investigated, projects moved too far down the process without serious scrutiny: once a project began, there was very little chance that it would ever be killed – the process was more like a *tunnel* rather than a *funnel*. The lack of tough go/kill decision points meant: too many product failures; resources wasted on the wrong projects; and a lack of focus. The result was many marginal projects underway, whereas the truly meritorious projects were starved.

A new product process that features tough go/kill decisions is a critical but often missing success ingredient. Having tough go/kill decisions was strongly correlated with business units' profitabilities of their new

TOUGH GO/KILL DECISION POINTS WERE THE WEAKEST PART OF THE PROCESS

product efforts (benchmarking study). Sadly, this ingredient – tough go/kill decision points – was *the weakest ingredient* of all process ingredients studies, with a poor score of 49.0 points of out 100 across all firms. Further, in the projects study, for 88% of projects studied, the initial screen was judged as deficient; 37% of projects did not undergo a predevelopment business or financial analysis; and 65% did not include a precommercialization business analysis [1]. The fact is that most of the critical evaluation points – from initial screening through to precommercialization business analysis – are characterized by serious weaknesses: decisions not made, little or no real prioritization, poor information inputs, no criteria for decisions, and inconsistent or capricious decision-making [1].

Message: A gating mechanism, featuring a series of rigorous go/kill decision points or 'gates' throughout the process, is essential. The goal is to move from a *tunneling process* – where projects are rarely killed – to a *funneling process* – where mediocre projects are culled out at each gate and resources are focused on the truly meritorious projects.

■ *There is a focus on quality of execution, where activities in new product projects are carried out in a quality fashion.*

Quality of execution of key tasks and activities throughout the new product process is emphasized in top performing firms. This was one of the most important ingredients of a quality process, with strong correlations to profitability of the business unit's total new product efforts, as well as significant correlations with impact, according to the benchmarking study. Similarly, in the projects study, quality of execution of key tasks stands out as the major driver of performance – note the high correlations and effect on success rates in Table 2 [1]. Sadly, quality of execution is mediocre on average – a quality rating of 6.08 out of 10 across the 103 chemical projects and 6.34 across all industrial products. Similarly, the benchmarking study found the mean score for quality of execution to be a modest 64.5 out of 100 across all firms.

Message: When overhauling your new product process, make every effort to build in best practices at every stage; focus on quality of execution throughout; and set high standards at gate reviews, where deliverables are scrutinized, with gates becoming the quality control check points in the innovation process.

Some managements become concerned that emphasizing quality of execution *adds time to projects*. The research shows this is *not true*: indeed, quality of execution is one of the key drivers of cycle time reduction [1]. Remember: no one is advocating postponing decisions or leaving projects in a queue awaiting perfect information; the message is that taking the time to do a quality job saves time later. Make 'doing it right the first time' a rule in your new product projects!

■ *The new product process is complete or thorough, where every needed activity is carried out – no hasty corner cutting.*

This ingredient follows closely on the one above. Many companies had discovered that not only was the quality of work lacking, but in some cases, the *work was lacking altogether*. In the benchmarking study, the mean score here was a very mediocre 54.3 points out of 100. That is, key tasks, such as market analysis, business assessment, and customer or user research, were simply not done (or left until far too late in the process).

A thorough and complete process is critical to success, however. Completeness was correlated significantly with profitability of firms' new product efforts, whereas a plot of activities undertaken versus success rate across the 203 projects revealed a dramatic negative impact of deleting activities and steps in the process (projects study; plot not shown):

Message: When designing your new product process, error on the side of thoroughness. Flexibility and shortcuts can be built in, especially for lower risk projects and when the risks of omission are understood. But for significant and higher risk projects, adopt and adhere to a disciplined, thorough new product process.

■ *The new product process is flexible – where stages and decision points can be skipped or combined, as dictated by the nature and risk of the project.*

One pitfall some firms encounter when they do reengineer their product development process is the failure to build in flexibility. Instead of being a template or roadmap, the 'formal process' becomes a straightjacket beset with bureaucracy (the benchmarking study revealed some problems here: a mean 'flexibility score' of 63.0 points out of 100). Note that process flexibility was significantly correlated with positive profits (see Table 1), whereas yet another study of firms' new product processes revealed flexibility to be a key yet often-missed success ingredient [1].

Message: When overhauling your new product process, be sure to provide for flexibility. Remember, the new product process is a *risk management model*: it is simply a series of steps designed to gather information to reduce uncertainty and thereby manage risk. Thus, strict adherence to every stage, step, activity, and gate in the 'formal process' depends on the risk level of the project.

In a flexible process, stages can be collapsed, gates combined, and long lead-time activities moved ahead. The point is that these decisions to *streamline the process* are made consciously, ahead of time, and at gate decision points, rather than on an ad hoc, spur-of-the-moment

> ## PRODUCT SUPERIORITY IS THE NUMBER ONE SUCCESS FACTOR BUT IS RARELY HIGHLIGHTED IN FIRMS' NEW PRODUCT PROCESSES

basis. And they are made for the right reasons, where the risks of streamlining (e.g., omitting a stage or activity) are weighed against the costs. Some examples of streamlining:

Consider the case of a straightforward and low cost development project. The decision may be to omit detailed market and technical assessments prior to the development phase. Here, at the preceding gate or decision point, management weighs the costs and time of including these detailed studies versus the costs and risks of moving ahead without the desired information. For lower risk, simple projects, often the decision is to collapse the homework stages.

Another example: Acquisition of capital equipment is usually left to the end of the project, after the development phase is completed and the product tested in the field. Sometimes, however, capital expenditures involve very long lead-time items. In flexible processes, management may opt to move this capital expenditure decision forward. Here, the costs of delaying the decision are weighed against the cost and risk of acquiring equipment, when there is still a reasonable likelihood that the project might yet be canceled.

A high quality new product process clearly pays off. Business units that boasted proficient new product processes – ones that incorporated the seven ingredients listed above – were rewarded with superior performance: they outscored the other firms on 10 performance metrics, ranging from success rates to profitability of the total new product effort, according to the benchmarking study [3]. In particular, these businesses' total new product efforts met sales and profit objectives more so and had a strong positive impact on business unit profits. Additionally, new product projects that featured the first six ingredients of a positive new product process (above) were far more successful: typically more than double the success rates, and close to double the market shares [1].

OTHER SUCCESS FACTORS THAT IMPINGE ON A WINNING PROCESS

How projects are organized, strictly speaking, is an organizational design concern, not a process design issue. But project organization is so closely connected to process that it cannot be ignored in a process overhaul exercise. The way projects are organized boils down to two distinct factors, according to the benchmarking study. The first captures the *quality* of the project team; the second, whether the project team is a *true cross-functional* team or not (see Table 1).

BUILD IN THE LESSONS FROM NEW PRODUCT SUCCESS INTO YOUR ROAD-MAP

1   *Having a high quality project team* means:

- The team leader *is dedicated to one project* at a time (as opposed to trying to lead many projects, or having myriad other assignments). This was a particularly weak ingredient of team quality, scoring a dismal 34.8 points out of 100. Simply stated, team leaders were *spread too thinly* across too many projects or had too many other duties to run projects effectively!
- High quality teams interact and communicate well and often, with *frequent project update meetings*, progress reviews, and problem resolution sessions. The best teams had short but weekly meetings to ensure that the entire team was up-to-speed. Teams received mediocre ratings here, on average (57.3 points out of 100).
- *Decisions made by outsider* groups or people (outside the team) are handled *quickly and efficiently*. This was usually the result of proficient team actions: for example, the team was able do whatever internal marketing, communication and persuasion that was necessary to get outsiders on-board and to deliver quick, efficient decisions. Here the mean team scores were also mediocre (52.3 points out of 100).

Business units that boasted good quality project teams, as defined above, had positive results in a number of areas: higher new product success rates, a higher impact total new product effort, higher profitability versus competitors, met sales new product objectives, and were rated more successful overall [3].

2   *Employing true cross-functional teams means*:

- All projects have an *assigned team of players*. That is, people are specifically assigned as team members. Here businesses fared modestly well, with a mean score of 67.2 points out of 100. Many firms have heeded the call for formally designating project team members, but in others, it wasn't clear just who was on the project team and who wasn't!
- These assigned players are *a cross-functional team* – from R&D, marketing, manufacturing, engineering, etc. Businesses scored quite positively here (72.8 points out of 100).
- All significant projects have a *defined and accountable team leader* – a person who is responsible for progressing the project. Businesses also did well on this success ingredient, scoring a positive 75.5 points out of 100.
- Projects leaders are *responsible* for the project *from beginning to end* (as opposed to being responsible for only *one phase* of a project; or having project leadership change hands many times during a project's life).

> ## NEXT GENERATION STAGE-GATE SYSTEMS ARE BLUEPRINTS, DRIVING NEW PRODUCTS TO MARKET QUICKLY AND EFFECTIVELY

Here business units received a mediocre score on average: 55.3 points out of 100.

Message: When overhauling your new product process, don't forget the team! Even the best designed process or game plan proves futile if there's no team, captain, or players on the field, or if they don't function as a true team. Ensure that every significant project has a defined and accountable team leader, accountable from beginning of project to end; don't spread the leader too thin – make him/her a *dedicated* leader. Every team should have assigned players from various essential functions, with agreed release times for the project. And the team members should be in constant contact with each other – frequent (weekly) but short project updates.

LAST BUT NOT LEAST – PRODUCT SUPERIORITY

The one vital success ingredient that plays a pivotal role in the process and, coincidentally, that most firms failed to address is the *product itself*. One of the top success factors is delivering a *differentiated product* with *unique customer benefits* and *superior value for the user*. Countless success/failure studies reveal this to be the overriding success factor; for example, the projects study cited above reveals that such superior products had five times the success rate, over four times the market share, and four times the profitability as products lacking this ingredient [1].

Surprisingly, very few firms can point to specific facets of their new product processes that emphasize this one vital success ingredient. Often 'product superiority' or 'sustainable competitive advantage gained via the product' are noticeably absent as screening or project selection criteria; whereas rarely are steps deliberately built into the process that encourage the design and delivery of such superior products (indeed, quite the reverse is true: the preoccupation with cycle time reduction and the tendency to favor simple, inexpensive projects actually penalizes projects that lead to product superiority).

Message: Product superiority – delivering differentiated products that promise unique benefits and superior value to customers – must be emphasized throughout the new product process. This can be done by using elements of product superiority as key screening criteria at go/kill decision points, and also by demanding that certain actions be included in the process – actions such as *user needs and wants studies*, constant *iterations with users* during development, and *user preference tests* – to ensure that product superiority becomes a goal of the project team.

ONE SOLUTION: STAGE-GATE SYSTEMS

An overhaul of the product innovation process is one solution to what ails so many firm's new product efforts. Facing increased pressure to reduce the cycle time yet improve their new product success rates, companies are redesigning their new product processes and increasingly looking to 'stage-gate systems' to manage, direct, and control their product innovation efforts. That is, they have developed a systematic process – a blueprint or road-map – for moving a new product project through the various stages and steps from idea to launch. But most important, they have built into their road-map *the many lessons for new product success* – including the key points highlighted above – in order to heighten the effectiveness of their projects.

GOALS OF AN OVERHAULED NEW PRODUCT PROCESS

Goal #1: Quality of execution

A quality-of-execution crisis exists in the product innovation process. This deficiency was evident in the benchmarking study as well as the two projects studies: key activities were poorly done or not done at all; too many projects omitted too many vital actions; and both quality of execution and thoroughness of the process received mediocre scores. There was also clear evidence that the activities of the new product process – the quality of execution and whether these activities are carried out at all – have a dramatic impact on performance.

This quality-of-execution crisis provides strong evidence in support of the need for a more *systematic and quality approach* to the way firms conceive, develop, and launch new products. The way to deal with the quality problem is to visualize product innovation as a process and to apply *process management* and *quality management techniques* to this process. Note that any process in business can be managed, and managed with a view to quality. Get the details of your processes right, and the result will be a high quality output.

Quality of execution is the goal of the new product process. More specifically, the ideal game plan should:

1 *focus on completeness*: ensure that the key activities that are central to the success of a new product project are indeed carried out – no gaps, no omissions, a 'complete' process.
2 *focus on quality*: ensure that the execution of these activities is proficient – that is, treat innovation as a process, emphasize DIRTFooT (doing it right the first time), and build in quality controls and checks.

EFFECTIVE ROLL-OUT OF A STAGE-GATE PROCESS IS THE MOST CHALLENGING TASK

---

3 *focus on the important*: devote attention and resources to the pivotal and particularly weak steps in the new product process, notably the upfront and market oriented activities.

The new product process or stage-gate system is simply a *process management tool*. One builds into this process *quality of execution* in much the same way that quality programs have been successfully implemented on the factory floor.

Goal #2: Sharper focus, better project prioritization

Most firms' new product efforts suffer from a lack of focus: too many projects and not enough resources. Earlier, adequate resources were identified as a principal driver of firms' new product performance, but a lack of resources plagued too many firms' development efforts. Sometimes this lack is simply that management hadn't devoted the needed people and money to the firms' new product effort. But often this resource problem stemmed from a lack of focus, the result of inadequate project evaluations – the failure to set priorities and make tough go/kill decisions. In short, the 'gates' are weak.

The need is for a *new product funnel*, rather than *tunnel*. A new product funnel builds in tough go/kill decision points (or bail out points throughout the process); the poor projects are weeded out; scarce resources are directed toward the truly meritorious projects; and more focus is the result. One funneling method is to build the new product process or game plan around a set of gates or go/kill decision points. These gates are the bail out points where we ask, 'Are we still in the game?' They are the *quality control check points* in the new product process and check the quality, merit, and progress of the project.

Each gate has its own set of *metrics and criteria* for passing, much like a quality control check in production. These criteria and questions capture various facets of the project including:

- Quality of execution of tasks in the preceding stage: have the tasks in the previous stage been executed in a quality fashion? And are the deliverables to the gate of high quality? Unless the answers are 'yes', the project is sent for 'rework.'
- Economic and business rationale for the project: a list of qualitative and quantitative criteria, both 'must meet' and 'should meet'; these include strategic alignment; unique product benefits and superior value for the customer; technical feasibility; market attractiveness; the existence of synergies (ability to leverage core competencies); competitive

advantage; and financial attractiveness (risk versus return). These criteria are used to make both the go/kill and prioritization decisions.
- Appropriateness of the action plan through to launch: action items, time line, resources requested, and resource availability.

Goal #3: A strong market orientation

A market orientation is the missing ingredient in most industrial new product projects. A lack of a market orientation and inadequate market assessment are consistently cited as reasons for new product failure. Moreover, the market-related activities tend to be the weakest in the new product process, yet are strongly linked to success. Whereas many managers profess a market orientation, the evidence – where the time and money are spent on projects – proves otherwise [1].

If positive new product performance is the goal, then a market orientation – executing the key marketing activities in a quality fashion – must be built into the new product process as a matter of routine rather than by exception. Marketing inputs must play a decisive role from beginning to end of the project. The following actions are *integral and mandatory plays* in the new product game plan (but they rarely are):

- *Preliminary market assessment*: a relatively inexpensive step very early in the life of a project, designed to assess market attractiveness and to test market acceptance for the proposed new product.
- *Market research to determine user needs and wants*: in-depth surveys or face-to-face interviews with customers to determine customer needs, wants, preferences, likes, dislikes, buying criteria, etc., as an input to the design of the new product.
- *Competitive analysis*: an assessment of competitors – their products and product deficiencies, prices, costs, technologies, production capacities, and marketing strategies.
- *Concept testing*: testing the proposed product in concept form to determine likely market acceptance. Note that the product is not yet developed, but a model or representation of the product is displayed to prospective users to gauge reaction and purchase intent.
- *Customer reaction during development*: continuing concept and product testing throughout the development phase, using rapid prototypes, models, and partially completed products to gauge customer reaction and seek feedback.
- *User tests*: field trials using the finished product (or prototype) with users to verify the performance of the product under customer conditions, and to confirm purchase intent and market acceptance.
- *Test market or trial sell*: a mini-launch of the product in a limited geographic area or single sales territory. This is a test of all elements of the marketing mix, including the product itself.

- *Market launch*: a proficient launch, based on a solid marketing plan, and backed by sufficient resources.

Goal #4: Better up-front homework and sharp, early product definition

New product success or failure is largely decided in the first few plays of the game – in those crucial steps and tasks that precede the actual development of the product. Solid up-front homework and sharp early product definition are key ingredients in a successful new product process, according to the benchmarking study; and result in higher success rates and profitability in the projects study. The up-front homework helps to define the product and to build the business case for development. Ironically, most of the money and time spent on projects is devoted to the middle and back-end stages of the process, whereas the up-front actions suffer from errors of omission, poor quality of execution, and under-resourcing [1].

The ideal new product process ensures that these early stages are carried out and that the product is fully defined before the project is allowed to proceed – before the project is allowed to become a full-fledged development project. These essential up-front activities in a well-designed game plan are outlined in Exhibit 1.

Goal #5: A *true* cross-functional team approach

The new product process is multifunctional; it requires the inputs and active participation of players from many different functions in the organization. The multifunctional nature of innovation coupled with the desire for parallel processing means that a *cross-functional team approach* is mandatory. Essential characteristics of this team are:

- The team is cross-functional, with committed team players from the various functions and departments – marketing, engineering, R&D, manufacturing. Release time for the project is provided to team members.
- Every significant project team has a clearly defined team captain or leader. This leader is dedicated to the project (not spread across numerous other duties or projects) and is accountable from beginning to end of the project – not just for one phase.
- The leader has formal authority: this means co-opting authority from the functional heads. When the senior management approve the team's action plan at gate meetings, they also commit the resources – money, people, and release time – to the project leader and team; at the same time, senior management *transfers decision-making power* to the team. Expectations and the scope of this authority are made very clear to the team at the gate.

- The team structure is fluid, with new members joining the team (or leaving it) as work requirements demand. But *a small core group of responsible, committed, and accountable team players should be present from beginning to end of project.*

Goal #6: The process must deliver products with competitive advantage – differentiated products, unique benefits, superior value for the customer

Don't forget to build in product superiority at every opportunity. This is one key to new product success, yet all too often, when redesigning their new product processes, firms fall into the trap of repeating current, often faulty, practices: there's no attempt to seek truly superior products. And so the results are predictable – more ho hum, tired products. Here's how to drive the quest for product advantage:

- Ensure that at least some of the criteria at every gate focus on product superiority. Questions such as 'Does the product have at least one element of competitive advantage.' 'Does it offer the user new or different benefits,' and 'Is it excellent value for money for the user' become vital questions to rate and rank would-be projects.
- Require that certain key actions designed to deliver product superiority be included in each stage of the process. Some of these have been mentioned above (goal #3) and include: customer-focused ideation; user needs-and-wants market research studies; competitive product analysis; concept and protocept tests, preference tests and trial sells; and constant iterations with customers during development via rapid prototype and tests.
- Demand that project teams deliver evidence of product superiority to project go/kill reviews: make product superiority an important deliverable and issue at such meetings (rather than just dwelling on the financial calculations).

Goal #7: A fast-paced and flexible process

The new product process must be built for speed. This means eliminating all the time-wasters and work that adds no value in your current new product process. It also means designing a flexible process, one that accommodates the risks and nature of different projects. Some firms are moving towards a *third generation process* [2], which features three Fs:

- *Flexible*: the process is not a straightjacket or a hard-and-fast set of rules; rather, each project can be routed through the process according to its risk level and needs: stages can be omitted and gates combined, provided the decision is made consciously, at gates, and with a full understanding of the risks involved.

- *Fuzzy gates*: Go decisions can be conditional: the decision can be made in the absence of perfect information, conditional on positive results delivered later.
- *Fluidity*: the process is fluid and adaptable. For example, stages can be overlapped – a project can be in two stages at the same time: and activities are done concurrently within stages, much like a rugby approach (rather than a series or relay race scheme).

STRUCTURE OF THE STAGE-GATE SYSTEM

These seven key goals have been fashioned into a next (or third) generation stage-gate[1] new product game plan – a *conceptual and operational model* for moving a new product project from idea to launch [1]. This stage-gate system is a blueprint for managing the new product process to improve effectiveness and efficiency.

Stage-gate systems break the innovation process into a predetermined set of stages, each stage consisting of a set of prescribed, cross-functional and parallel activities (see Figure 2). The entrance to each stage is a gate: these gates control the process and serve as the quality control and go/kill check points.

Stages

The stage-gate system breaks the new product project into discrete and identifiable stages, typically four, five or six in number. Each stage is designed to gather information needed to progress the project to the next gate or decision point. Each stage is multi- or cross-functional. There is no 'R&D stage' or 'Marketing Stage'. Rather, each stage consists of a set of parallel activities undertaken by people from different functional areas within the firm, but working together as a team, and led by a project team leader.

In order to manage risk via a stage-gate scheme, the parallel activities within a stage must be designed to gather vital information – technical, market, financial, etc. – in order to drive down technical and business uncertainties. Each stage costs more than the preceding one, so that the game plan is an incremental commitment one. As uncertainties decrease, expenditures are allowed to mount.

Finally, flexibility is built in to promote acceleration of projects. In order to speed products to market, stages can overlap each other; long lead time activities can be brought forward from one stage to an earlier one; projects can proceed into the next stage, even though the previous stage has not been totally completed; and stages can be collapsed and combined.

The general flow of the typical or a *generic* stage-gate process is shown pictorially in Figure 2. Here the five key and overlapping stages are:

- **Stage 1**. Preliminary Investigation: a quick investigation and scoping of the project. Typically, this stage is undertaken by a very small core team of technical and marketing people; it includes the 'first cut' homework, such as preliminary market assessment, preliminary technical assessment, and preliminary business assessment (see 'preliminary investigation' in Exhibit 1).
- **Stage 2**. Detailed Investigation: the detailed homework leading to a *business case*. Stage 2 includes market research (a user needs and wants study to identify requirements for the ideal product; competitive analysis; and a concept test to confirm purchase intent); detailed technical and manufacturing assessment; and a detailed financial and business analysis. This stage should be undertaken by a core team of marketing, technical, and manufacturing people – the beginnings of the ultimate project team in stage 3. The deliverables from stage 2 include a defined product (on paper: target market, product concept and benefits, and product requirements): a business justification (economic and business rationale); and a detailed plan of action for the next stages (including resource requirements and timing).
- **Stage 3**. Development: the actual design and development of the new product. Here the development plan is implemented; a prototype or sample product is developed; and the product undergoes in-house testing along with limited customer testing (e.g., rapid prototype and tests with potential users). Additionally, the manufacturing process and requirements are mapped out; the marketing launch plan is developed; and the test plans for the next stage are defined. Stage 3 sees the project gain momentum, with a marked increase in resource commitment; here the full cross-functional project team – marketing, technical, manufacturing, and perhaps quality assurance, purchasing, sales, and finance people – is in place.

Figure 2 A funneling approach, with five overlapping stages and gates.

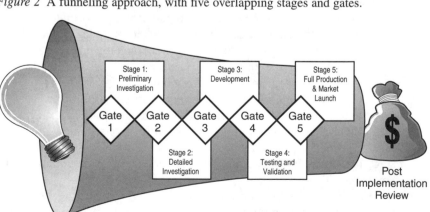

The Third Generation Stage-Gate New Product Process

- **Stage 4**. Testing and Validation: the verification and validation of the proposed new product, its marketing and production. This stage witnesses extensive in-house product testing; customer field trials or trials in the marketplace; pilot or pre-production trials in the plant; and even test marketing or a trial sell. The deliverable is a fully tested product and production process, ready for commercialization. The project team and leader from Stage 3 remain accountable for actions and deliverables in Stage 4.
- **Stage 5**. Full Production and Market Launch: full commercialization of the product. Stage 5 marks the beginning of full production and commercial selling. This stage sees the implementation of the marketing launch plan, the production plan, and the postlaunch activities, including monitoring and adjustment. Although new members may be added to this 'commercialization team' (e.g., from the sales force and from operations), the core project team from Stages 4 and 5 remains in place and accountable for commercialization and beyond. There are no hand-offs in this game!

Note that there are two homework stages in this process: stage 1, a quick homework phase done on a number of projects; and Stage 2, which provides for a more detailed investigation, but on fewer projects. The result is superb up-front homework and sharp, early product definition (goal #4). Additionally, constant customer contact and a market orientation are evident throughout all five stages; the actions outlined in goal #3 above are heavily featured in the process. These actions heighten the odds of delivering a superior product with real value to the customer (goal #6). Finally, a cross-functional team approach is mandatory in order to successfully execute each stage (goal #5).

Gates

Preceding each stage is an entry gate or a go/kill decision point, shown as diamonds in Figure 2. Effective gates are central to the success of a fast-paced new product process:

- Gates serve as quality control check points, where quality of execution is the focus: is this project being executed in a quality fashion (goal #1)?
- Gates also serve as go/kill and prioritization decisions points (goal #2): Gates provide for the funneling of projects, where mediocre projects are culled out at each successive gate (hence the funnel shape of the process in Figure 2).
- Finally, gates are the points where the path forward for the next play or stage of the process is decided, along with resource commitments. Once again, quality of execution becomes a central issue.

Gate meetings are usually staffed by senior managers from different functions, who own the resources required by the project leader and team for the next stage.

Gates have a common format:

- *Inputs*: these are the *deliverables* to a gate review – what the project leader and team deliver to the meeting; they are the results of the actions of the previous stage and are based on a standard menu of deliverables for each gate.
- *Criteria*: these are questions or metrics on which the project is judged in order to make the go/kill and prioritization decision. they include both qualitative (e.g., strategic fit; product superiority; market attractiveness) and quantitative criteria (financial return; risk via sensitivity analysis), and can include must meet (mandatory) as well as should meet^2 (desirable) criteria.
- *Outputs*: these are the results of the gate review – a decision (go/kill/hold/recycle); a prioritization level; resource commitments and action plan approved; and date and deliverables for next gate agreed.

In the fastest stage-gate processes, gates decisions are made with incomplete information; this means that the project team is given a 'go' decision, conditional on positive results occurring early in the next stage. In this way, the project is not held up, awaiting the completion of one or two tasks from the previous stage.

IMPLEMENTING THE STAGE-GATE APPROACH

Designing an effective new product process, such as the stage-gate model outlined above, is the first and easiest phase. Typically a task force is assigned; their actions include:

- a process audit to identify strengths and weaknesses of the current process;
- a retrospective analysis of past new product projects, again seeking areas needing improvement;
- benchmarking other firms and their processes;
- a review of the literature (much has been written on what shape the new product process should take – see [1, 2] as examples);
- establishing specs and requirements for the new process – what the process will be and do;
- the design of a skeleton of the process, much like the model in Figure 2;
- seeking feedback from potential users in the company;
- the detailed design for the process, spelling out stages, activities, gates, deliverables, criteria, methods, and procedures (with constant feedback from in-company users); and
- the design of a roll-out plan.

This first phase is relatively easy. The next phase – effective roll-out and implementation within your company – is much more challenging, however. Here are some implementation tips based on experiences with dozens of firms, and also on another benchmarking session held with leading firms [1]:

1   *Don't underestimate the difficulty, costs, and time of implementing any new system*, including a stage-gate approach. For every dollar or hour you spend on the design of the process, count on up to 10 times that amount for its effective implementation!

2   *It takes time!* A stage-gate approach is not a flavor of the month nor a quick fix. Properly implemented, it will change dramatically how your firm goes about conceiving, developing, and launching new products, as well as the management approaches dealing with resource allocation, budgeting, and prioritization decisions. Most companies required in excess of 2 years to achieve operational effectiveness here. So be prepared to *hold the course*!

3   *Implementation begins the minute you commit to designing a new product process.* The task force should treat the design of a stage-gate process very much like the introduction of a new product. From day one, there must be constant user involvement. This begins with understanding the current process, and why it doesn't work: a retrospective analysis of past projects with the project teams along with a diagnosis of the current process (for example using the ProBE method[3]). As your new process takes shape, there must be constant *information-and-feedback sessions* with various user groups within the organization – seeking their reaction, suggestions, and of course, their buy in.

4   *Training is critical.* People will not use what they don't understand. Many firms underestimated training requirements when they introduced new product processes and paid the price [1]. Users need to be trained on the details and use of the process, as well as on skills required to use the process (for example, the use of project management software). Count on about a 2-day intensive training program for team leaders, team members, and critical resource providers; and 1 day for the senior management, who will be the gatekeepers.

5   *Internal marketing is essential.* Implementing a new method in the company is analogous to rolling out a new product. Develop an implementation plan, much like a marketing plan, complete with communication, promotion, and personal selling elements. Key groups and individuals may require face-to-face or personal selling to ensure that they buy into the new process; communication pieces (below) must be carefully crafted: training (above) is yet another internal marketing tool.

6   *Documentation is a key facet of internal marketing.* Most firms investigated confessed to having to redo the documentation shortly

after initial implementation. The first time, instead of writing a user-friendly guide to the process, they produced a detailed manual – more like a voluminous textbook, complete with detailed appendices: it overwhelmed even the most dedicated adherent. Produce a relatively short (20–25 pages) guide along with an even shorter (2–3 page) quickie guide. Appendices or drill-down software, provided later, can be used to fill in the needed information, details, forms, etc.

7 *Bring products into the process almost immediately.* Once the process is ready for implementation, don't wait for totally new projects as initial feedstock. Shoe-horn in ongoing projects, even though they might be halfway through development. Give the project leaders 1 month to determine exactly where they are in the 'new' scheme, and to declare the next gate and a date for that gate. Better yet, as the process is being designed, start piloting a few projects through the process, both to test the process and also to start moving projects into the process.

8 *Designate a process owner.* There has not been one successful implementation of a new product process, to my knowledge, where there hasn't been a *process owner* or 'keymaster' in place. Task forces are fine to design the process; but task forces do not implement systems well. One person – the keymaster – must be charged with making it happen: s/he ensures that projects are really 'in the process'; that gate meetings are held, in a timely fashion, with decisions based on the stated gate criteria; that projects are on time and the deliverables in place; that projects are tracked and metrics kept; and that training on the process is provided and process documentation is in place.

9 *Get expert help.* The design and implementation of a new product process looks like an easy task, at first glance. But there are many problems and pitfalls along the way. To heighten the odds of success, and to improve the time efficiency of the task force, hire an expert – someone who has been through this exercise before.

New product development is a vital endeavor for the modern corporation. Indeed it is the critical challenge as business prepares for the next millennium. Companies must learn how to innovate effectively, or they will wither. Understanding the critical success factors – what separates high performing business units and winning new products from the rest – is the first step toward improving one's own performance. Overhauling your new product process, and incorporating these success factors into this *stage-gate process*, is the way many companies are now *winning at new products*.

NOTES

1 'Stage-gate' is a term coined by the author: some of this section is taken from [1]. Second generation processes are what many companies began to implement toward the end of the 1980s; the third generation processes of the mid 1990s have improved time efficiencies [2].

2 Often, should meet criteria are scored (1–5 or 0–10) and added to yield an overall project score; this project score becomes useful for project ranking and prioritization.

3 ProBE is a diagnostic methodology developed for use by industry. It is based on the benchmarking study cited in the article [3] and enables your firm to compare your new product performances and practices with other firms and with the best firms.

REFERENCES

This article reported results from research studies, in which the author was a principal investigator. Not all have been cited here. More detail can be found in:

Cooper, R. G. *Winning at New Products: Accelerating the Process from Idea to Launch*. Addison-Wesley, Reading, MA, 1993.

Cooper, R. G. Third-Generation New Product Processes. *Journal of Product Innovation Management* **11**, 3–14, 1994.

Cooper, R. G. and Kleinschmidt, E. J., Benchmarking Firms' New Product Performance and Practices. *Engineering Management Review* **23**, 112–18, 1995.

4 An Interaction Approach

The IMP Group

INTRODUCTION

In a joint research project with several researchers with different backgrounds there are always problems in developing a common theoretical framework. This was further complicated in this project by differences in language, approach and emphasis between the researchers. We were however fortunate in having similar *basic* approaches to the analysis of Industrial Marketing and Purchasing.[1] Extensive discussion within the project group led to the discovery of important concepts and assumptions which were shared by all. It is on this theoretical basis that the design and the methodology are built. These concepts and basic assumptions are now presented in this chapter.

RELATIONS TO PREVIOUS RESEARCH

Our theoretical framework can be traced back to two major theoretical models from outside the marketing literature. These are Inter-organizational Theory and the New Institutional Economic Theory. At the same time it is possible to relate our approach to earlier thinking in marketing and purchasing as well as some emerging trends in the marketing and purchasing literature.

Inter-organizational theory and marketing literature

Much of the work in Inter-organizational Theory involves attempts to apply theory and concepts from intra-organizational studies to problems where several organizational units are involved. Here the focus of attention is on relationships between those organizations rather than within each individual organization. Works in this area can be classified into three groups, based upon differences in the relation between

Reprinted by permission of John Wiley & Sons Limited. An Interaction Approach by the IMP Group from *International Marketing and Purchasing of Industrial Goods* 471279870 pp. 10–27.

the organization and its environment as proposed by Van de Ven *et al.* (1975). It is also possible to classify marketing literature along similar lines, again depending on the perspective of researchers when dealing with organization–environmental relationships. Such a categorization of the marketing literature has been presented by Sweeney (1972). We will consider the categorization of the inter-organizational literature and the marketing literature in parallel:

(a) Organization based studies. The environment is seen as an external limitation for the organization in this group of studies. Inter-organizational studies which can be included in this group are those which examine the internal organization based on an open systems approach. Here, the organization is seen as being dependent on its environment, for example in obtaining access to certain inputs. At the same time the organization seeks to manipulate or control parts of its environment. Because of this, the characteristics of the environment will influence the shape of the internal organization structure. This organization –environment connection is central and is analysed in many studies.[2]

The predominant current viewpoint in marketing shares this perspective. It is characterized by Sweeney as the 'organizational system perspective', and is exemplified in the so-called 'managerial approach' to the study of marketing. In this, marketing researchers are concerned with techniques for the development and management of product, price, distribution, and promotional strategies to optimize desired market response. The boundaries of marketing are defined as those 'publics' which have a ' . . . potential impact on the resource converting efficiency of the organization' (Kotler and Levy, 1969). It is implicit in this approach that buyers are passive and only react to the stimuli of the seller by buying or not buying. The selling firm is the active partner in the buyer–seller relationship. Further, this relationship is largely seen to be between the seller, and some generic 'market', rather than with individual customers.[3]

It is worth noting at this stage that a side effect of this approach to the study of marketing has been that the study of buyers has developed along somewhat separate lines from the study of sellers. Here, researchers have analysed the factors which affect both the individual and company buying processes, e.g. previous purchase experience, the importance of 'task' and 'non-task' variables, the effect of different organizational forms and the degree of formality in hypothesized decision-making processes. These analyses have concentrated on the stages in a *discrete* purchase. Thus, there has been an emphasis in the industrial buyer behaviour literature on single rather than continuing purchases from a particular supplier. Additionally, the study of the buying process has taken place with relatively scant regard to the influence of the selling firm in that process.[4]

Thus, the first group of studies includes two distinct and *separate* approaches to the study of what occurs in industrial markets. On the one hand, there is an analysis of the manipulation of marketing variables by the seller to achieve a desired market response. On the other hand, there is the separate analysis of a single buying process and the factors which affect that process, from which lessons can be drawn for marketing.

(b) Studies based on several organizations. In this second group of inter-organization studies, the organization is seen as part of a group of interacting units. Studies within this category are often based on the dependence between the particular organization and its environment as defined by studies from category (a). In order to obtain necessary resources, the organization is seen to develop relations with a number of other organizational units and thus it enters into a network of relationships.

Two aspects of this network have mainly been studied. Firstly, the characteristics of the different organizations have been investigated as they relate to the other organizations within the same network. Secondly, the links between the units have been analysed in terms of, for example, formalization, intensity, and standardization.[5]

The parallel to these studies in the marketing area are those from a 'distribution system perspective'. In this, the field is viewed as a system of interconnected institutions performing the economic functions required to bring about exchange of goods or services. This perspective is, of course, broader than the organizational system perspective. The boundaries of marketing at this level of aggregation include those institutions involved in the distribution of goods within the society. The focus is on the nature of the functions being performed by the system and on the structure, performance and inter-relationships of the institutions which comprise the system. Aspects of these areas which have received study are the division of roles and responsibilities between different members of a manufacturing–distribution channel, the conflicts between different levels and within levels in the channel as well as the patterns of power and communication which exist between them.[6] During recent years, a number of works on more general aspects of marketing and purchasing have appeared which fit within this group.[7]

(c) Studies of the organization in a societal context. In this third category, the organization is seen as an integrated part in a larger social system. In order to describe and understand how a certain organization functions it is necessary, according to this approach, to see the organization in relation to the larger system. The organization is part of what some authors call 'inter-organization collectives' and these groups influence to a large extent the actions of the organization.[8] The view of marketing from a 'social system perspective' sees it as a social process which evolves to facilitate the society's needs for efficient and effective exchange of values. There is a clear distinction between this approach and its emphasis on analysis of the exchange

process, and the organizational system approach which is concerned with the technology employed to execute that exchange process.

The view of marketing from a social system perspective is little developed. The majority of the marketing literature can be classified into group (a) above, while our approach belongs to group (b). There are also some minor attempts in our study to go in the direction of the works in group (c). However, the major focus of our attention is on the units (the buying and selling firms) and the link between them (the process of interaction).

The new institutionalists

The second theoretical area outside the marketing literature that we have built upon has been characterized by Williamson (1975) as 'the New institutionalists'. This line of thought within micro-economic theory is based on a criticism of certain aspects of traditional economic theory. Williamson discerns two alternative ways in which the exchange (transaction) may be handled between technologically separable units in a production or transformation process. Firstly, the transaction can take place within a market setting. On the other hand it can be internalized in one organizational unit (a hierarchy), i.e. two successive stages in the production process are vertically integrated in a hierarchically built organization. There are certain deficiencies in markets that favour the internalization of transactions. Similarly, there are also deficiencies in the way organizations function that operate in favour of keeping the transactions in the market, i.e. keeping the successive production stages under separate control and reaching agreements on buying and selling, through, for example, negotiated contracts.

Williamson argues that many transactions which are internalized in one organization could be carried out by separate organizations, from the point of view of technological separability. However, the co-ordination of these units by means of market relations involves disadvantages. Markets may be considered to operate inefficiently in certain instances, due to human and environmental factors. When the environment is characterized by complexity and uncertainty, then the bounded rationality of man makes it very costly to design and negotiate viable contracts. An example would be between two subsequent stages in a steel mill. Furthermore, the parties to such transaction may become very dependent on each other. This evolves into a small-numbers bargaining relation. Although the parties in a formal sense retain the option of selecting partners in the market, this is not a viable alternative due to transaction costs. Thus it will be very costly to design and negotiate contracts with new partners. This is because it is often difficult for one party to achieve information parity with the other party, which is necessary for a 'fair' deal. Man is not just characterized by bounded rationality but also by opportunism ('self-seeking interest with guile'), and this makes markets operate inefficiently when there is an imbalanced dependence between the parties.

The high transaction costs that would be associated with operations in markets of the atomistic kind provide incentives for the internalization of such expensive transactions in vertically integrated units. Conflicts are considered to be settled in a more efficient and less costly way within an organization (by fiat rather than by haggling), and sequential, adaptive decision-making is facilitated. Opportunism is checked by control and audit.

However, there are also conditions counteracting the internalization of transactions. Firstly markets often do not operate as rigidly, and organizations do not operate as smoothly as depicted in the idealized extreme models (internal control is made more difficult as organizations grow in size), and thus transaction costs increase. Also there are checks on the opportunism in markets, e.g. courtesy, the interest in establishing conditions for future business and the effects of the firm's reputation on business deals with others. Imbalances are not always exploited in the short term in a way that increases transaction costs. Secondly, transactions do not take place in an attitudinally neutral setting. The establishment of satisfying exchange relations (an 'atmosphere') modifies and is modified by the transactions.

Thus there are several factors that influence transaction costs and there are also intermediary settings for the exchange relations. Many industrial markets can be seen as such intermediary forms. Here we find such market characteristics as established small-numbers bargaining relations and lack of information parity. There are also organizational characteristics such as checks on opportunism due to established social relationships. Often a specific atmosphere has evolved that is characterized both by environmental and human factors.

Our theoretical framework is closely related to both 'inter-organizational theory' and the 'new institutionalists'. At the same time it is directly related to evolutions in the literature of marketing, and particularly to the emphasis on inter-company relationships. This has emerged from those studies having a distribution system perspective and more recently from those empirically based studies which have emphasized the importance of inter-company relations.

OUTLINE OF THE MODEL

Our approach to industrial markets – *The Interaction Approach* – is based on the theoretical idea described earlier. It is also built on a number of factors which our earlier empirical studies indicate are important in industrial markets and which appear to have been largely neglected in previous research:

Firstly, that both buyer and seller are active participants in the market. Each may engage in search to find a suitable buyer or seller, to prepare specifications of requirements or offerings and to manipulate or attempt to control the transaction process.

Secondly, the relationship between buyer and seller is frequently long term, close and involving a complex pattern of interaction between and within each company. The marketers' and buyers' task in this case may have more to do with maintaining these relationships than with making a straightforward sale or purchase.

Thirdly, the links between buyer and seller often become institutionalized into a set of roles that each party expects the other to perform, for example the division of product development responsibility, or the decision as to who should carry inventory and test products. These processes may require significant adaptations in organization or operation by either or both companies. Clearly, these relationships can involve both conflict as well as co-operation.

Fourthly, close relationships are often considered in the context of continuous raw material or component supply. However, we would emphasize the importance of previous purchases, mutual evaluation and the associated relationship between the companies in the case of infrequently purchased products. Further, we are concerned in this research with the nature of the relationship between a buying and selling company which may be built up during the course of a single major transaction.

Our focus is generally on a two party relationship, but the approach can be applied also to a several party relationship. This, indeed, may be necessary to accommodate the study of the simultaneous interactions between several buying and selling companies in a particular industry. The main components of our approach are illustrated in Fig. 1.

In the figure we identify four groups of variables that describe and influence the interaction between buying and selling companies:

Fig. 1 Main elements of the interaction model

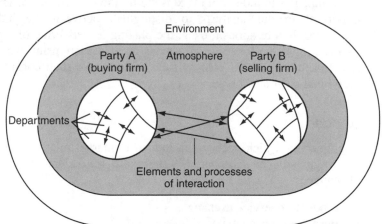

1   Variables describing the *parties* involved, both as organizations and as individuals.
2   Variables describing the *elements and process of interaction*.
3   Variables describing the *environment* within which the interaction takes place.
4   Variables describing the *atmosphere* affecting and affected by the interaction.

The approach does not only involve an analysis of these groups of variables but it also includes the relations between them.

THE INTERACTION MODEL

The marketing and purchasing of industrial goods is seen as an interaction process between two parties within a certain environment. Our way of analysing industrial marketing and purchasing has four basic elements which in turn are sub-divided. These are:

1   The interaction process.
2   The participants in the interaction process.
3   The environment within which interaction takes place.
4   The atmosphere affecting and affected by the interaction.

In this section we will describe each of these four basic elements more extensively. The major focus here is on *description* of buyer–seller relationships and interactions. Only secondary emphasis is placed here on the interplay between the separate elements which we discuss. These interrelationships are developed later in the book.

The interaction process

We have already noted that the relationships between buying and selling companies in industrial markets are frequently long term. Thus, it is important in our analysis to distinguish between the individual 'Episodes' in a relationship, e.g. the placing or delivering of a particular order, and the longer-term aspects of that relationship which both affects and may be affected by each episode. We shall consider these individual episodes, first.

(a) Episodes

The episodes which occur in an industrial market relationship involve exchange between two parties. There are four elements which are exchanged:

i   Product or service exchange;
ii   Information exchange;

iii Financial exchange;
iv Social exchange.

(i) Product or service exchange. The exchange of product or service is often the core of the exchange. As a result, the characteristics of the product or service involved are likely to have a significant effect on the relationship as a whole. For example, one major aspect of the product or service which seems important is the uncertainty with which they are associated. The exchange process will be quite different depending on whether or not the product is able to fulfil a buyer need that is easy to identify, and for which the characteristics of an appropriate product are easy to specify. It will also be important whether either buyer or seller is uncertain as to the requirements or resources of their opposite number.[9]

(ii) Information exchange. Several aspects of information exchange are of interest. The content of information is, of course, important. This can, for example, be characterized by the degree to which technical, economic, or organizational questions dominate the exchange. Furthermore, the width and depth of the information for each of these groups of questions should also be of importance. Information can be transferred between the parties by either personal or impersonal means. Impersonal communication is often used to transfer basic technical and/or commercial data. Personal channels are more likely to be used for the transfer of 'soft data' concerning, for example, the use of a product, the conditions of an agreement between the parties, or supportive or general information about either party. Finally, the formality of the information exchange is important. The degree of formality may depend on wider organizational characteristics which can affect the nature of the interaction process and the relationship between the companies as a whole.

(iii) Financial exchange. Money is the third element. The quantity of money exchange is an indicator of the economic importance of the relationship. Another important aspect is connected with the need to exchange money from one currency to another and the uncertainties in these exchanges over time.

(iv) Social exchange. Social exchange has an important function in reducing uncertainties between the two parties (Håkansson and Östberg, 1975). This is particularly significant when there exists spatial or cultural distance between the two parties or where the experience of the two parties is limited. Social exchange episodes may be important in themselves in avoiding short term difficulties between the two parties and in maintaining a relationship in the periods between transactions. However, perhaps the most important function of social

exchange is in the long term process by which successive social exchange episodes gradually interlock the two firms with each other. Many aspects of the agreements between the buying and selling firms are not fully formalized nor based on legal criteria. Instead the relationship is based on mutual trust.[10] Building up this trust is a social process which takes time and must be based on personal experience, and on the successful execution of the three other elements of exchange. Furthermore, the need for mutual trust and the requirement of social exchange varies with differences in the elements exchanged in different relationships. Examples are variations in the amount of money exchanged, in the need for large amounts of informational exchange or in the complexity of the product exchanged. However, the development of trust is also dependent upon experience in exchange of the other three elements.

(b) Relationships

Social exchange episodes are, as has been described above, critical in the build up of long-term relationships. Exchanges of product and service (which can be in both directions) and of the other elements of money and information can also lead to the build up of long-term relations. The routinization of these exchange episodes over a period of time leads to clear expectations in both parties of the roles or responsibilities of their opposite numbers. Eventually these expectations become *institutionalized* to such an extent that they may not be questioned by either party and may have more in common with the traditions of an industry or a market than rational decision-making by either of the parties (Ford, 1978).

The communication or exchange of information in the episodes successively builds up inter-organizational contact patterns and role relationships. These *contact patterns* can consist of individuals and groups of people filling different roles, operating in different functional departments and transmitting different messages of a technical, commercial, or reputational nature. These patterns can interlock the two parties to a greater or lesser extent and they are therefore an important variable to consider in analysing buyer–seller relationships. It is important to note that information and social exchange between parties can continue for a considerable time without there being an exchange of product or money. Thus, literature, specification development, and visits between companies can occur before the first order is placed or between widely spaced individual orders.

Another important aspect of the relationship is the *adaptations* which one or other party may make in either the elements exchanged or the process of exchange. Examples of this are adaptations in product, in financial arrangements, in information routines or social relations. These adaptations can occur during the process of a single, major transaction or over the time of a relationship involving many individual transactions. The benefits of these adaptations can be in cost reduction, increased revenue, or differential control over the exchange. Adaptations in specific episodes may also be made in order to modify the overall relationship. Thus one party may make a decision not to offer special products to a customer out of a wish to be more distantly involved with that customer, rather than being closely involved and or heavily dependent on it.

The manipulation of different aspects of adaptation is of course a critical marketing and purchasing issue. Although adaptations by either party can occur in an unconscious manner as a relationship develops, it is important to emphasize the conscious strategy which is involved in many of these adaptations. Thus, modifications to product, delivery, pricing, information routines and even the organization itself are part of the seller's marketing strategy. Similarly, the buying organization will consider adaptations in its own product requirements, its production methods, the price it is prepared to accept, its information needs and the modification of its own delivery or stocking policies in order to accommodate the selling organization.

The interacting parties

The process of interaction and the relationship between the organizations will depend not only on the elements of the interaction but also on the characteristics of the parties involved. This includes both the characteristics of the two organizations and the individuals who represent them. The organization factors include the companies' position in the market as manufacturer, wholesaler, etc. It also includes the products which the selling company offers, the production and application technologies of the two parties and their relative expertise in these areas. Below, we will discuss some of the major factors in more detail:

(a) Technology. Technical issues are often critical in buyer–seller interaction in industrial markets. The aims of the interaction process can be interpreted as tying the production technology of the seller to the application technology of the buyer. Thus the characteristics of the two technological systems and the differences between them give the basic conditions for the interaction. These basic conditions influence all the dimensions of the interaction processes: for example, the requirements for adaptations, mutual trust and contact patterns. Similarly, if the two organizations are separated by a wide gulf of technical expertise then the relationship between them can be expected to be quite different from a situation where the two companies are close in their level of expertise. Technology will be one of the variables which are in focus in the rest of this book. It will be further discussed in the methodological chapter, then in relation to the company cases and finally as a separate theme.

(b) Organizational size, structure, and strategy. The size and the power of the parties give them basic positions from which to interact. In general, a large firm with considerable resources has a greater possibility of dominating its customers or suppliers than has a small firm. The structure of each organization and the extent of centralization, specialization and formalization influence the interaction process in several ways: this influence is seen in the number and categories of persons who are involved. It also affects the procedure of the exchange, the communications media used, the formalization of the interaction and substance of what is exchanged – the nature of product or service and the finance which is involved. In the short term, organizational structures can be considered as the frameworks within which interaction takes place. In the longer term, it is possible that these organizational structures may be modified *by* the emerging interaction process or indeed by individual episodes.

The strategies of the parties are, of course, important influencing variables on the relationships. Later on we will describe how strategies can be formulated and analysed in relation to our theoretical approach.

(c) Organizational experience. A further factor is the company's experience not only in the relationship but also its experience and activities outside it. This experience may be the result of many other similar relationships and will equip the company with knowledge about the management of these kinds of relationships. It may also affect the level of importance attached to any one relationship, and hence the company's commitment to that relationship.

The variables which we will discuss in the next section under the title of The Interaction Environment will be mediated by the experience of specific individuals in a company as well as by the more generalized 'experience' of a company. Thus the company's experience in particular markets will enable it to be more or less fitted for dealing in that market. Similarly, its experience of international operations will affect its willingness and ability to establish international relationships.

(d) Individuals. At least two individuals, one from each organization, are involved in a relationship. These are usually a buyer and a salesman. More commonly, several individuals from different functional areas, at different levels in the hierarchy and fulfilling different roles become involved in inter-company personal interactions. They exchange information, develop relationships and build up strong social bonds which influence the decisions of each company in the business relationship.

The varied personalities, experience, and motivations of each company's representatives will mean that they will take part in the social exchange differently. Their reactions in individual episodes could condition the ways in which the overall relationship builds up. Further, the role, level, and function of central persons in the interaction affect the chances of future development occurring in the relationship.

Individual experience may result in preconceptions concerning certain suppliers or customers, for example those in a certain country. These will affect attitudes and behaviour towards those buyers or suppliers. The process of learning from experience on both an individual and corporate level is communicated to and affects detailed 'Episodes' in interaction. Additionally, the experience gained in individual episodes aggregates to a total experience. Indeed, the experience of a single episode can radically change attitudes which may then be held over a long period of time.

The interaction environment

The interaction between a buying and selling firm cannot be analysed in isolation, but must be considered in a wider context. This wider context has several aspects:

(a) *Market structure*. Firstly, a relationship must be considered as one of a number of similar relationships existing either nationally or internationally within the same market. The structure of this market depends in part on the concentration of both buyers and sellers and the stability or rate of change of the market and its constituent members. It also consists of the extent to which the market can be viewed as strictly national or needs to be thought of in wider international terms. The extent of buyer or seller concentration determines the number of alternatives available to any firm. This has a clear bearing on the pressure to interact with a certain counterpart within the market.

(b) *Dynamism*. The degree of dynamism within a relationship and in the wider market affects the relationship in two ways that are opposite to each other. Firstly, a close relationship increases the knowledge of one party of the likely actions of the other party and hence its ability to make forecasts based on this inside information. Secondly, and conversely, in a dynamic environment the opportunity cost of reliance on a single or small number of relationships can be very high when expressed in terms of the developments of other market members.

(c) *Internationalization*. The internationalization of the buying or selling market is of interest as it affects either firm's motivations in developing international relationships. This in turn may affect the company's organization, in needing sales subsidiaries or overseas buying units, the special knowledge it may require, e.g. in languages and international trade and its more general attitudes.

(d) *Position in the manufacturing channel*. A further aspect of the environment which must be brought into consideration is the position of an individual relationship in an extended 'channel' stretching from primary producer to final consumer. Thus, for example, manufacturer A may sell electric components to manufacturer B, who then incorporates these components into actuators that are sold to manufacturer C, who adds them to valves. These valves, with many other products, may form the stock of distributor D and so on. The marketing strategy of A may thus be influenced by and directed at several markets at different stages in the channel. Clearly his relationship with buying company B will be affected by both A's and B's relationship with C and other subsequent organizations.

(e) The social system. As well as the effects of both horizontal market and vertical channel influences on a relationship, we must also consider the characteristics of the wider environment surrounding a particular relationship – the social system. This is particularly relevant in the international context where attitudes and perceptions on a generalized level can be important obstacles when trying to establish an exchange process with a certain counterpart. An example of this is nationalistic buying practices or generalized attitudes to the reliability of buyers or customers from a particular country. Other aspects of these general influences concern regulations and constraints on business, for example exchange rates and trade regulations. There are other, more narrow social system variables which will surround a particular industry or market. For example, a supplier who has not previously delivered to a certain type of customer, e.g. in the automobile industry, has to learn both the 'language' and the rules before it will be accepted in that industry.

The atmosphere

The relationships between buying and selling firms are dynamic in being affected by the individual episodes which take place within them. At the same time they have the stability which derives from the length of the relationship, its routinization and the clear expectations which become held by both parties. The relationship is influenced by the characteristics of the parties involved and the nature of the interaction itself. This in turn is a function of the technology involved and the environment within which the interaction takes place. Organizational strategy can also affect both the short-term episodes and the long-term relationships between the parties. One of the main aspects of the relationship which may be affected by conscious planning is the overall atmosphere of the relationship. This atmosphere can be described in terms of the power–dependence relationship which exists between the companies, the state of conflict or co-operation and overall closeness or distance of the relationship as well as by the companies' mutual expectations. These variables are not measured in a direct way in this study. Instead the atmosphere is considered as a group of intervening variables, defined by various combinations of environmental, company specific, and interaction process characteristics. The atmosphere is a product of the relationship, and it also mediates the influence of the groups of variables. There are reasons for the buying and selling firm to both develop a high degree of closeness with their counterpart as well as to avoid such closeness. There are both advantages and disadvantages connected with different atmospheres. We can analyse the reasons involved with regard to an economic (cost-benefit) dimension and a control dimension.

(a) The economic dimension. There are several types of cost that can be reduced for a firm by a closer interaction with a buying or selling firm. One of these costs is that which Williamson (1975) describes as the transaction cost. A closer connection means that it may be possible to handle distribution, negotiations, and administration more efficiently. Another type of cost which may be reduced is the production cost. A close relationship gives opportunities to find a more optimal division of the production process between the supplier and the customer. The supplier and buyer may reallocate some production processes between each other or co-operate in the design so as to make the product easier to produce or for the customer to develop further. There are also increased revenues which can be gained by a closer interaction. Both sides may achieve positive gains by better use of the other's competence, facilities, and other resources. New products can be developed together or old products may be redesigned. Furthermore, the parties can also often give each other valuable technical and commercial information.

(b) The control dimension. Another important reason for closer connection with a counterpart can be to reduce the uncertainty associated with that input or output by increasing its control over the other company. Such an increase in control improves the firm's chances of forecasting and determining that part of its environment. The ability to control a relationship is related to the *perceived* power of the two parties. Perceptions of power are likely to be unclear in the early stages of a relationship and one of the key functions of initial exchange episodes will be to enable each party to come to an understanding of each other's power. Even so, perceptions of power may change over the life of a relationship. They will, in turn, be related to the resources perceived to be possessed by each party as well as to their relative dependence on this individual relationship. Inter-organizational power will depend on the ability of either party to reward or coerce each other through exchange, or their relative expertise and access to information, as well as on their referent power, i.e. the value which one party places on association with another because of its wish to learn from and act similarly to the other.

The power of organization A over B is directly related to the dependence of B on A. The dependence on any one relationship by an organization is a major element in the wish to restrict interaction. Investment of time and resources in one relationship has an opportunity cost related to the value of those investments in another relationship. Also, the level of dependence on one relationship affects the vulnerability of an organization to the exercise of power by its opposite number. In everyday terms this is exemplified by a selling company which has a large proportion of its sales to one single buying company. It is the management of the closeness of the relationship, with its associated power and dependence, which is perhaps a crucial aspect of many industrial marketing and purchasing strategies.

Summing up this discussion of the reasons for a close interaction, we can conclude that relationships are established and used in order to gain economic benefits, lower costs, higher profits, and/or improving the organization's control of some part of its environment. A critical aspect of the management of these relationships is the extent to which the firm can balance its inter-dependence with others. The firm must seek to balance the advantages of a close relationship, perhaps in terms of cost reduction and ease and speed of interaction against the opportunity costs of that single relationship and the dependence which it involves.

SUMMARY

In Fig. 2 we have tried to illustrate the different variables which have been presented here. The model shows the short-term and long-term aspects of the 'Interaction Process' between buying and selling companies A and B. The short-term 'Exchange Episodes' involve product–service, financial, information, and social exchange. These are separated from the longer term processes of 'Adaptations' and 'Institutionalization'.

Both the short- and long-term aspects of the interaction are considered as being influenced by the characteristics of the organizations and individuals involved (circles A and B). Additionally, we see the interaction taking place within an 'Environment' consisting of the vertical and horizontal market structure and general social influences.

Finally, we include 'Atmosphere'. As the company's relationship develops so the parties' views of their relative power may change. Previous research has shown quite clearly that the interaction between buying and selling companies is conditioned by a clear and commonly held view of the relative power of the parties to the interaction and the areas to which this power extends. At the same time we have noted that conflict can characterize these relationships as well as co-operation. Thus it is quite possible for a company to have one relationship with a particular buyer–seller which is characterized by co-operation. It is also possible for the company to have a relationship with another company which

Fig. 2 An illustration of the interaction model

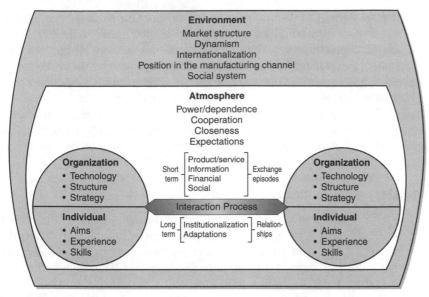

is characterized by co-operation on the *minimum* level, in order for transactions to take place but thereafter is marked by frequent conflict over means and allocations of resources. Thus the detailed interaction process is subject to the perceptions of both parties of the overall state of relations between them – power–dependence and conflict–co-operation.

The figure shows that it is possible to identify and study connections between the variables on different levels. Firstly, at the most general level, one variable group can be related to another, for example it is possible to relate the parties in the exchange process to the interaction environment. Secondly, it is possible to investigate the linkage between variables in one variable group, for example between the elements of exchange and the process of exchange. Thirdly, it can be valuable to explore the relation between the variables within a sub-group. An example of this is the connection between the characteristics of the product and the characteristics of the information which is exchanged. Some of the relationships between the variables mentioned above are more obvious and are documented in other studies. Others are more hypothetical and have never been studied systematically. Furthermore, the whole picture has never been studied as a totality. Our approach is to select combinations of variables from the environment, company, and interaction categories. This provides a number of 'interaction atmospheres', within which different linkages are studied as well as systematic comparisons made.

IMPLICATIONS FOR MANAGEMENT

Before starting to discuss how our theoretical model has been used in this project we would like to briefly indicate the kind of help this model can give practitioners. The practical use of a theoretical model is, of course, that it helps to structure the 'world' and thereby the problems. A new model can as a consequence give new opportunities because problems which were neglected earlier may be identified and solved. We shall now give some examples of problems that can be identified for managers of marketing or purchasing departments in firms working in certain industrial markets. We shall start with the marketing side.

Marketing management

The key problems in marketing according to the marketing mix model are (1) allocation of resources and (2) design of individual competitive means.[11] In the same way we can use the interactive model and identify two groups of important problems. These groups have been named (1) limitation and (2) handling problems.[12]

Two different kinds of limitation problems can be specified. The first problem concerns the marketing firm's overall limitation of its activities in certain types of relationships. This must be achieved because the demands on its technology, organization and knowledge, etc., are closely related to the type of relationships. For example, it is very difficult for a seller to have customers with very high demands on the quality and performance of the product *and* customers which just want a standard quality as cheaply as possible. The marketing firm, thus, has to limit itself to be an efficient counterpart in a certain type of relationship and to design its technology, organization, and knowledge in accordance with this.

The second type of limitation problems for the marketing firm are concerned with its individual counterparts. The question is, should customers be treated in a uniform way, or should some customers get special treatment? Normally there is a very clear difference between how those 'special' customers – often those who buy most – get special services, extra attention and so on. The customers are in other words often dealt with quite differently and it is therefore necessary for the marketing firm to develop a policy on these questions.

The handling problem concerns both the long-term aspects of the relationships as well as the short-term exchanges of different elements. The long-term problems concern handling the power–dependence and the co-operation–conflict aspects of the relationships. The aim is to have a controlled development of the relationships. This can sometimes mean closer co-operation and sometimes the opposite. The short-term problems are primarily related to attaining an efficient way of handling the elements (the different exchange processes) with individuals as well as groups of customers. One problem area, is, for example, to design one's own adaptations and to influence the counterpart's adaptations in order to make exchange processes easier. The way of solving the short-term handling problems affect, of course, the long-term problems. Adaptation is an example of one aspect of the power–dependence relationship. This means that the long- and short-term problems in a relationship cannot be divided; they can better be seen as short- and long-term effects of all of the activities which constitute the relationship.

Purchasing management

The key problem in purchasing that can be identified using the interaction model are (1) to develop an appropriate structure of suppliers and (2) to handle each relationship in an efficient way. The second group of problems are the same as the handling problems for the marketing side and we, therefore, can leave them aside and concentrate on the first group.

A supplier can be seen as an external resource by the buying firm. The buyer's aim in relationships is to use these external resources in an efficient way. But in order to be attractive as a counterpart, the purchasing firm has to have some internal resources. One strategic purchasing question, therefore, is to find and maintain a balance between the external and internal resources. The problem in the short term can be formulated as using these external resources as much as possible given the internal resources of the buying firm.

Another problem is that suppliers can be used in different ways. In some situations the purchasing firm may want to use a supplier's ability to develop and design a special product, while in other situations it may just want to use the supplier's ability to produce a standardized product at low cost. The counterparts are used in different ways and a problem is then to find the right combination of suppliers, i.e. to develop an appropriate external resources structure.

NOTES

1   The background of the research teams can be seen in the following references: Cunningham and White (1974), Cunningham and White (1973/6), Cunningham and Kettlewood (1976), Cunningham and Roberts (1974), Ford (1976), (1978), Håkansson and Wootz (1975a), (1975b), (1975c), (1975d), (1979), Håkansson, Johanson, and Wootz (1977), Håkansson et al. (1979), Håkansson and Östberg (1975), Johanson and Vahlne (1977), Johanson and Wiedersheim-Paul (1975), Kutschker (1975), Kutschker and Roth (1975), Kirsch, Lutschewitz, Kutschker (1977), Lutschewitz and Kutschker (1977), Kirsch and Kutschker (1978), Kutschker and Kirsch (1978), and Valla (1978a), (1978b), (1978c), (1978d), and (1978e).

2 Important works within this category: Dill (1958), Burns and Stalker (1961), Thompson (1967), Emery and Trist (1968), Aiken and Hage (1968), and Hall (1972).

3 Important works within this area are textbooks such as Kotler (1976) and McCarthy (1978). These deal mainly with consumer marketing but these and similar works have formed a basis for the development of literature in the industrial marketing field. Examples within industrial marketing which share this approach are Corey (1976), Hill *et al.* (1975), Hill (1972), and Wilson (1972) and (1973).

4 Important works regarding purchasing using this approach are textbooks such as England (1970), Lee and Dobler (1971) and Westing, Fine, and Zenz (1976) and research oriented book like Buckner (1966). Robinson and Faris (1967), and Webster and Wind (1972a). The two most well-known models of purchasing are Webster and Wind (1972b) and Sheth (1973).

5 Important works within this category: Levine and White (1961), Litwak and Hylton (1962), Evan (1966), Warren (1967), Marrett (1971), and Aldrich (1972).

6 See for example Rosenberg and Stern (1970), Little (1970), Heskett, Stern, and Beier (1970), El-Ansary and Stern (1972), Hunt and Nevin (1974), Angelmar (1976), and Reve and Stern (1979).

7 Examples are Blois (1975), Guillet de Monthoux (1975), Mattsson (1975), Jarvis and Wilcox (1977), Melin (1977), Webster (1979), and Arndt (1979).

8 Important works are: Levine and White (1972), Warren (1973), Van de Ven *et al.* (1975), Zeitz (1975), and Aldrich (1979).

9 Need uncertainty has for example been used as a variable by Håkansson, Johanson, and Wootz (1977) in order to describe this aspect.

10 See for example Macaulay (1963).

11 See IMP Group (1982).

12 This section builds on Håkansson, Johanson, and Wootz (1977), and Håkansson and Wootz (1979).

REFERENCES

Aiken, M. and Hage, J. Organizational interdependence and intra-organizational structure. *American Sociological Review* **33:6**, 912–30 (1968).

Aldrich, H. E. Cooperation and conflict between organizations in the manpower training system: an organization–environment perspective. In Negandhi, A. R. (ed) *Conflict and Power in Complex Organizations: An Inter-Institutional Perspective*. Kent State University Press, Kent, Ohio (1972).

Aldrich, H. E. *Organizations and Environments*. Prentice-Hall, Englewood Cliffs, New Jersey (1979).

Angelmar, R. Structure and determinants of bargaining behaviour in a distribution channel simulation: A content analytic approach. *Unpublished Ph.D. Dissertation*. Northwestern University, New York (1976).

Arndt, J. Toward a concept of domesticated markets. *Journal of Marketing*, **43**, (4), 69–76, (1979).

Blois, K. J. Supply contracts in the Galbraithian planning system. *Journal of Industrial Economics*, **24**, (1), 29–39 (1975).

Buckner, H. *How British Industry Buys*. Hutchinson, London (1966).

Burns, T. and Stalker, G. M. *The Management of Innovation*. Tavistock Publications, London (1961).

Corey, E. R. *Industrial Marketing: Cases and Concepts*. 2nd ed., Prentice-Hall, Englewood Cliffs, New Jersey (1976).

Cunningham, M. T. and Kettlewood, K. Source loyalty in freight transport buying. *European Journal of Marketing*, **10**, (1), 60–79 (1976).

Cunningham, M. T. and Roberts, D. A. The role of customer service in industrial marketing. *European Journal of Marketing*, **8**, (1), 15–28 (1974).

Cunningham, M. T. and White, J. G. The determinants of choice of supplier. *European Journal of Marketing*, **7**, (3), 189–202 (1973).

Cunningham, M. T. and White, J. G. The behaviour of industrial buyers in their search for suppliers of machine tools. *Journal and Management Studies*, **1**, (2), 115–128 (1974).

Dill, W. R. Environment as an influence on managerial autonomy. *Administrative Science Quarterly*, **2**, (4), 409–443 (1958).

El-Ansary, A. I. and Stern, L. W. Power measurement in the distribution channel. *Journal of Marketing Research*, **9**, 47–52 (1972).

Emery, F. G. and Twist, E. L. The causal texture of organizational environments. *17th International Congress of Psychology*, Washington, DC (1968).

England, W. *Modern Procurement Management: Principles and Cases*. 5th ed., Irwin, Homewood, Illinois (1970).

Evan, W. M. The organization-set: toward a theory of interorganizational relation, in Thompson, J. (ed) *Approaches to Organizational Design*. University of Pittsburgh Press. Pittsburgh, Philadelphia (1966).

Ford, D. I. An analysis of some aspects of the relationships between companies in channels of distribution. *Unpublished Ph.D. thesis*. University of Manchester, Manchester (1976).

Ford, D. I. Stability factors in industrial marketing channels. *Industrial Marketing Management*, **7**, 410–422 (1978).

Guillet de Monthoux, P. Organizational mating and industrial marketing conservation – some reasons why industrial marketing managers resist marketing theory. *Industrial Marketing Management*, **4**, (1), 25–36 (1975).

Håkansson, H., Johanson, J. and Wootz, B. Influence tactics in buyer–seller processes. *Industrial Marketing Management*, **5**, 319–332 (1977).

Håkansson, H. and Wootz, B. Supplier selection in an international environment – an experimental study. *Journal of Marketing Research*, **12**, (February), 46–51 (1975a).

Håkansson, H. and Wootz, B. *Företags inköpsbeteende* (Buying Behaviour of the Firm). Studentlitteratur, Lund (1975b).

Håkansson, H. and Wootz, B. Risk reduction and the industrial purchaser. *European Journal of Marketing*, **9**, (1), 35–51 (1975c).

Håkansson, H. and Wootz, B. *Changes in the Propensity to Import – An Interaction Model on the Firm Level*. Department of Business Studies, University of Uppsala (1975d).

Håkansson, H. and Wootz, B. A framework of industrial buying and selling. *Industrial Marketing Management*, **8**, 28–39 (1979).

Håkansson, H., Wootz, B., Andersson, O. and Hangård, P. Industrial marketing as an organizational problem. A case study. *European Journal of Marketing*, **13**, 81–93 (1979).

Håkansson, H. and Östberg, C. Industrial marketing – An organizational problem? *Industrial Marketing Management*, **4**, 113–123 (1975).

Hall, R. H. *Organization, Structure, and Process*. Prentice-Hall, Englewood Cliffs, New Jersey (1972).

Heskett, J. L., Stern, L. W. and Beijer, F. J. Bases and uses of power in interorganizational relations. In Bucklin, L. P. (ed) *Vertical Marketing Systems*. Scott, Foresman, and Company, London (1970).

Hill, R. M., Alexander, R. S. and Cross, J. S. *Industrial Marketing*. 4th ed., Homewood, Irwin, Illinois (1975).

Hill, R. W. *Marketing Technological Products to Industry*, Oxford, UK (1972).

Hunt, S. D. and Nevin, J. R. Power in a channel of distribution: sources and consequences. *Journal of Marketing Research*, **11**, 186–193 (1974).

Jarvis, L. P. and Wilcox, J. P. True vendor loyalty or simply repeat purchase behavior? *Industrial Marketing Management*, **6**, 9–14 (1977).

Johanson, J., and Vahlne, J.-E. The internationalization process of the firm – a model of knowledge development and increasing foreign market commitments. *Journal of International Business*, **8**, (1), 23–32 (1977).

Johanson, J. and Wiedersheim-Paul, F. The internationalization of the firm – four Swedish case studies. *Journal of Management Studies*, **2**, (3), 305–322 (1975).

Kirsch, W. and Kutschker, M. *Das Marketing von Investitionsgütern – Theoretische und empirische Perspektiven eines Interaktionsansatzes*. Verlag Gablers, Wiesbaden (1978).

Kirsch, W., Lutschewitz, H. and Kutschler, M. *Ansätze und Entwicklungstendenzen im Investitionsgütermarketing – Auf dem Wege 3^u einem Interaktionsansatz*. C. E. Poeschel Verlag, Stuttgart (1977).

Kotler, P. *Marketing Management, Analysis, Planning, and Control*. 3rd ed. Prentice-Hall, Englewood Cliffs, New Jersey (1976).

Kutschker, M. *Rationalität und Entscheidungskriterien komplexer Investitionsentschridungen – ein empirischer Bericht*. Aus dem Sonderforschungsbereich 24 Der Universität Mannheim, Mannheim (1975).

Kutschker, M. and Kirsch, W. *Verhandlungen auf dem Markt für Investitionsgüter*. Plannungs – und Organisationswissenschaffliche Schriften, München (1978).

Kutschker, M. and Roth, K. Das Informationsverhalten vor industriellen Beschaffung-sentscheidungen. *Veröffentlichung aus dem SFB 24 der Universität Mannheim*. (1975).

Lasswell, H. D. and Kaplan, A. *Power and Society*, Routledge, London (1952).

Lee, Jr. L. and Dobler, D. W. *Purchasing and Materials Management: Text and Cases*. 2nd ed. McGraw-Hill, New York (1971).

Levine, S. and White, P. Exchange as a conceptual framework for the study of interorganizational relationships. *Administrative Science Quarterly*, **5**, (4), 583–601 (1961).

Levine, S. and White, P. The community of health organizations. In Freeman, H. E., Levine, S. and Reader, L. (eds) *Handbook of Medical Sociology*, Prentice-Hall, Englewood Cliffs, New Jersey (1972).

Little, R. W. The marketing channel; who should lead this extra-corporate organization. *Journal of Marketing*, **34**, 31–38 (1970).

Litwak, E. and Hylton, L. F. Interorganizational analysis: A hypothesis on coordinating agencies. *Administrative Science Quarterly*, **6**, (4), 395–420 (1962).

Lutschewitz, H. and Kutschker, M. *Die Diffusion innovativer Investitionsgüter – Theoretische Konzeption und empirische Befunde*. Verlag Kurt Desch, München (1977).

Macaulay, S. Non-contractual relations in business: a preliminary study. *American Sociological Review*, **28**, (1), 55–67 (1963).

Marrett, C. B. On the specification of interorganization dimensions. *Sociology and Social Research*, **61**, 83–99 (1971).

Mattson, L.-G. System interdependencies – A key concept in industrial marketing? *Proceedings from the Second Research Seminar in Marketing as Senanque*. Fondation Nationale pour l'Enseignement de la Gestion des Entreprises (1975).

McCarthy, E. J. *Basic Marketing*. 6th ed. Irwin, Homewood (1978).

Melin, L. *Strategisk inköpsverksamhet – organisation och interaktion*. (Strategic Purchasing Actions – Organization and Interaction) (with summary in English). University of Linköping, Linköping (1977).

Reve, T. and Stern, L. W. Interorganizational relations in marketing channels. *Academy of Management Review*, **4**, (3), 405–416 (1979).

Robinson, P. J. and Faris, C. W. *Industrial Buying and Creative Marketing*. Allyn and Bacon Inc. and the Harbeling Science Institute, Boston, Massachusetts (1967).

Rosenberg, L. J. and Stern, L. W. Toward the analysis of conflict in distribution channels; a descriptive model. *Journal of Marketing*, **34**, 40–46 (1970).

Sheth, J. N. A model of industrial buyer behavior. *Journal of Marketing*, **37**, 50–56 (1973).

Thompson, J. *Organizations in Action*. McGraw-Hill, New York (1967).

Valla, J.-P. Basic concepts in industrial marketing: Specificities and implications. *Institut de Recherche de l'Entreprise*, Editions Verve, Lyon (1978a).

Valla, J.-P. Strategies in Industrial Marketing. *Institut de Recherche de l'Entreprise*. Editions Verve, Lyon (1978b).

Valla, J.-P. Organization and Structure in Industrial Marketing. *Institut de Recherche de l'Entreprise*. Editions Verve, Lyon (1978c).

Valla, J.-P. Information and Communication Systems in Industrial Marketing. *Institut de Recherche de l'Entreprise*. Editions Verve, Lyon (1978d).

Valla, J.-P. Implementing the marketing concept in the industrial firm: problems and possible solutions. *Institut de Recherche de l'Enterprise*. Editions Verve, Lyon (1978e).

Van de Ven, A. H., Emmit, D. C. and Koenig, R. Frameworks for interorganizational analysis. In Negandhi, A. R. (ed) *Interorganizational Theory*. Kent State University Press, Kent, Ohio (1975).

Warren, R. The interorganizational field as a focus for investigation. *Administrative Science Quarterly*, **12**, 396–419 (1967).

Warren, R. The interactions of community decision organizations: some conceptual considerations and empirical findings. In Negandhi, A. R. (ed) *Modern Organization Theory*. Kent State University Press, Kent, Ohio (1973).

Webster, Jr., F. E. *Industrial Marketing Strategy*. John Wiley and Sons, New York (1979).

Webster, Jr., F. E. and Wind, Y. *Organizational Buying Behavior*. Prentice-Hall, Englewood Cliffs (1972a).

Webster, Jr., F. E. and Wind, Y. A general model for understanding organizational buyer behavior. *Journal of Marketing*, **36**, 12–19 (1972b).

Westing, J. H., Fine, I. V. and Zenz, G. J. *Purchasing Management: Materials in Motion*. John Wiley and Sons, New York (1976).

Wilson, A. *The Marketing of Professional Services*, Publications Service, New York (1972).

Wilson, A. *The Assessment of Industrial Markets*. International Publications Service, New York (1973).

Zeitz, G. Interorganizational relationships and social structure: A critique of some aspects of the literature. In Negandhi, A. R. (ed) *Interorganization Theory*. Kent State University Press, Kent, Ohio (1975).

—PART III
Cases

Introduction

The cases below have been chosen to help put the discussion and readings of Parts I and II into the context of organizational marketing practice. Most of the cases are drawn from the author's personal experience and empirical research into marketing and competitive strategies in technology-intensive sectors, especially the automotive and IT sectors. This focus on IT markets and on the motor manufacturing industry is intended to provide a rich, integrated network of cases which can deliver, collectively, greater understanding than might have been achieved through a wider range of relatively unrelated cases.

The cases form two groups – two longer cases (addressing supplier–customer relationships and product development issues) and 13 mini-cases (illustrating a variety of issues indicated in the matrix below).

Longer cases

1 Marketing IT systems to supermarket retailers
2 Product development in reality

Mini-cases

1 Professionalism in purchasing: two examples
2 Just some of the issues in new-task buying faced by a car manufacturer
3 Energy purchasing at the Big Building Society
4 Adapting and compromising over product specification
5 Goods receiving and payment systems in a UK car manufacturer
6 A report on windscreen problems by a quality inspector
7a The problems of cost-based pricing . . .
7b . . . and of market-based pricing
8 Uncooperative supplier–customer relationships in the US automobile industry
9 *Mielbon Vite* – telesales staff replace field sales representatives
10 The MCI case: sales force management
11 How IBM and Dove Computers won major hospital contracts
12 Internal marketing: top-down or bottom-up?
13 Purchasing and inventory management at Jimmy's

The first long case deals with customer–supplier relationships in the context of supermarket IT systems. The case provides sub-cases looking at the marketing relationship between specific UK supermarket operators and their respective suppliers of IT systems. By comparing and contrasting the strategies and management practices involved, extensive insights can be derived. Since readers, in their capacity as consumers, are themselves the driving force behind supermarket retailing and therefore the ultimate reason for investing in retail CBS (an illustration of derived demand), they can readily use their personal experience to contextualize and assess the strategies involved.

The product development case (long case 2) is itself in two parts. The first part deals with the memories and reflections of some of the pioneers of computing technology and this puts the theory and recommended practices of product development (see the third reading by Cooper) into a sharp and critical focus. The second part illustrates some of the problems of finding suitable organizational markets for two innovative IT products supplied by an organization which clearly had much to learn about innovation management, market research, and strategic business planning in a competitive environment. So this case as a whole contrasts the perspectives and motivating factors of the individual with those of the organization in developing radical new technology-intensive offerings. Readers should ask themselves how things might have been different if the theory of product development had been used to guide the management of the processes described, assuming this would indeed have been practicable – and whether the theory should be adjusted to accommodate the very personal and idiosyncratic behaviour described in the case. To what extent are such individual processes 'manageable' at all? And does that mean that we should treat all product development situations in the same way? Comparing these insights to how IT systems were eventually marketed to the organizational customers in the first two cases will provide further lessons.

Finally, the 13 mini-cases are designed to illustrate situations discussed in Part I (where they are cross-referenced) and they also provide 'snapshot' insights to some of the rich complexities of managing organizational marketing. The matrix indicates how the mini-cases might be used, for example in seminars, to stimulate discussion on particular issues of theory and practice.

Matrix of mini-cases and organizational marketing issues (● indicates a match between mini-case and issue)

Mini-case no.	Product issues	Service issues	Packaging issues	Pricing issues	Logistics issues	Communications and sales issues	Marketing research issues	Marketing planning issues	Internal marketing issues	Purchasing professionalism issues	Relationship management issues	Mini-case no.
1	●			●			●		●	●	●	1
2	●			●			●	●		●	●	2
3	●	●		●	●					●	●	3
4	●	●	●				●	●			●	4
5	●	●		●	●				●	●		5
6	●		●	●	●				●	●	●	6
7a	●	●		●		●	●	●				7a
7b	●	●	●	●		●	●	●				7b
8	●			●		●				●	●	8
9		●		●	●	●	●	●	●		●	9
10		●			●	●			●		●	10
11		●		●		●				●	●	11
12	●								●		●	12
13	●		●	●	●	●	●	●	●	●	●	13

Index of Mini-cases

1	Professionalism in purchasing: two examples
2	Just some of the issues in new-task buying faced by a car manufacturer
3	Energy purchasing at the Big Building Society
4	Adapting and compromising over product specification
5	Goods receiving and payment systems in a UK car manufacturer
6	A report on windscreen problems by a quality inspector
7a	The problems of cost-based pricing . . .
7b	. . . and of market-based pricing
8	Uncooperative supplier–customer relationships in the US automobile industry
9	Mielbon Vite – telesales staff replace field sales representatives
10	The MCI case: sales force management
11	How IBM and Dove Computers won major hospital contracts
12	Internal marketing: top-down or bottom-up?
13	Purchasing and inventory management at Jimmy's

1 *Marketing IT systems to supermarket retailers*

This case is derived from empirical research (Wilson, 1994) involving extensive interviews with senior IT purchasing managers in superstore retailing organizations and with senior marketing managers in their suppliers of computerized business systems (CBS). Names and sources have been masked to preserve confidentiality. Occasional quotations are taken from interview records to illustrate the issues under discussion.

INTRODUCTION

Close relationships have developed between the four leading UK superstore retailers of the early 1990s (referred to below as Hawk, Parrot, Robin and Sparrow) and their principal suppliers of CBS (referred to as QED, PES and MTB). These relationships reflect not only the technical intricacies of customizing the complex systems and the very large scale of retail activities involved, but also the competitive importance of these systems to the retailers in terms of the effects on their operations and on their customers.

The installation of retail CBS to a superstore is not only a matter of installing and commissioning scanners at the checkout counters to read barcodes, and EPOS (electronic point of sale) systems to match these codes to price information and to update stock replenishment data; these systems also have to be integrated with whatever coordinating and administrative systems are used in the 'back office' of the superstore and at the regional distribution centres, all of which have to be integrated with the mainframe systems in operation at the corporate head office. In addition, most leading retailers have invested in EDI (electronic data interchange) and other forms of computerized logistics systems which facilitate rapid ordering and delivery of stock from suppliers. Each of these particular computer systems will be running software packages which may have been fine-tuned over time to the unique circumstances of specific stores and in line with the different skill levels and preferences of individual operators. Since these various CBS elements (possibly from different suppliers) may well have been introduced to the overall system at different times they will be at different stages of technological sophistication and reliability with respect to both the hardware and the software. To compensate for these differences, all these elements are integrated through a communications network which itself will depend on additional minicomputer controllers and terminals, with their own operating software and internal communications software. The problems of making sure that the entire system works efficiently, predictably and reliably – and that staff can work with the systems – are such that intensive trials of up to six months are often necessary for the introduction of major system changes.

For the CBS suppliers, a close relationship with a leading supermarket retailer is also competitively necessary for credibility in UK retail markets and for developing insights to the future needs of customers in the retail sector. For the more successful UK CBS suppliers there is the additional prospect of enhanced competitive opportunities in Commonwealth, European and even global retail markets.

Two of these relationships between a leading retailer and its CBS supplier are described below in the context of how retail CBS were developed and of how the benefits arising were thought to have affected the competitiveness of the customer and supplier involved.

A THE HAWK GROUP AND QED

At the time of this case, the Hawk Group had over 250 superstores and had been consistently profitable for several years. In the early 1980s a major acquisition had significantly expanded the number of superstores operated by the Hawk Group and this prompted a complete reassessment of the strategic and operational role of retail CBS in Hawk superstores.

Development of retail CBS

In 1982 the Hawk Group's retail CBS were limited to a minor role in financial management. Hawk decided to develop its competitive strategy around the improvement of logistics supported by a rapid expansion of retail CBS in order to catch up with the current market leaders in retailing. It was recognized from the start that 'the business strategy was to be delivered by the CBS strategy'.

This strategy was developed in detail in an eight-week period of concentrated analysis and discussion in 1984. First Hawk's retailing business in general was analyzed, using the value chain concept developed by Michael Porter (Porter 1980, 1985), and Hawk's own processes and practices were compared against this analysis. Then 20 key managers, in consultation with newly recruited senior IT staff, drew up a list of 275 business problems, focusing on the generation of sales rather than on the reduction of costs. For example, it became obvious that Hawk did not have a clear idea of customers' preferences and purchasing patterns, a problem which it was thought could be addressed through the installation of checkout scanning systems.

Hawk decided that their CBS would be designed around a single architecture, that of QED. QED's architecture was thought to provide the widest range of offerings based on a single architecture and also seemed to guarantee the level of support and commitment necessary to an organization which expected to base much of its competitive advantage on CBS. The decision to source from QED (or reliable QED-compatible suppliers) was also influenced by Hawk's own experience with QED systems, by the familiarity of many key managers with QED systems and service, and by the switching costs that these factors imposed on any decision to re-orientate around a different supplier.

A major part of the emerging Hawk CBS strategy was the decision to invest in *relational database technology* (RDT), an innovative approach to database management which seemed to have great potential for rapid, flexible and sophisticated statistical analysis but which was not yet well established in mainframe systems and was both costly and unreliable at the time with few other retailing or food processing businesses having any experience or active interest in this largely unproven technology. Hawk's decision was also based on the assumptions that in the long run RDT would be superior to the more traditional *hierarchical database technology* (HDT); that Hawk could adopt RDT more easily than rivals because Hawk had so few existing CBS installations at the time; and that rivals with more sophisticated CBS were already committed to HDT and would therefore face significant switching costs and operational disruption if and when they eventually migrated to RDT.[1]

As Hawk grew rapidly (turnover increased approximately tenfold over the period 1984–1990) and the competitive environment of food retailing became more intense and complex, the advantages of RDT over HDT became increasingly apparent. RDT is now firmly established as the standard approach to database management and, because of its flexibility, those with most experience of how to use RDT have a significant (though probably temporary) advantage in getting most benefit from the vast quantities of data generated by CBS in retailing.

The decision to commit Hawk to RDT when it was still unreliable and ineffective was indicative of the strength of Hawk's relationship with QED, Hawk's long-standing supplier of CBS. QED was convinced of the long-term advantages of RDT over HDT and was investing heavily in the development of its first commercial RDT package – the *DB2* database management system. When Hawk decided to place *DB2* at the heart of its data systems, QED collaborated extensively with Hawk to develop customized versions of *DB2* for retail applications. For Hawk, this meant that complex management reports could be replaced with headline reports while individual managers could use QED's proprietary *systematic interrogation language* (SIL) to access the *DB2* data-

bases directly for more specific analysis. Following investment in training, most of Hawk's senior managers soon became proficient in the use
of SIL, thereby relieving the DP staff of having to produce elaborate
regular management reports, a task which had previously dominated DP
work schedules.

From QED's perspective, the collaboration with Hawk was an important step towards QED's objective of establishing RDT, and *DB2* in
particular, as the industry standard for database management. QED also
saw the relationship as important to developing a more competitive
position in UK and European retailing markets where QED was much
weaker than in US retailing markets. Significantly, QED's success in
US retail markets was not found to be especially advantageous in competing in UK and Europe because of the important cultural and operational differences between the two markets. In the USA food retailing
profit margins are very low (typically around 1 per cent) and competition is much more intense and price oriented than in UK or even in
Europe. US food stores also remain open longer (sometimes per-
manently) than in UK or Europe where up to half of all purchases are
made on Friday and Saturday. These differences are reflected in the
design of retail CBS for each market with US systems being typically
more sophisticated in data capture, in reporting detail (both to customers and to management), and in flexibility with respect to pricing
and promotions while UK systems tend to be more flexible in terms of
coping with varying checkout congestion levels (e.g. in operator
ergonomics and technical reliability under pressure).

Hawk is now QED's largest food retailing customer and is regarded
by QED as a strategic customer. Since 1989 senior QED executives
have discussed mutual corporate strategies with Hawk executives three
times per year and Hawk is used by QED as a world-wide reference
centre. QED has set the 'benchmark' for Hawk's relationships with
CBS suppliers – for example, Hawk observed that PES's practice of
using junior sales staff in its dealings with Hawk compared most
unfavourably with the level of respect and professionalism evident in
dealings with QED (always represented at an appropriately senior
level).

Benefits of retail CBS

The benefits of adopting QED's retail CBS were seen by Hawk as not
specifically technological, since QED technology tends to be available
from imitators quite soon after launch by QED, but more to do with the
complete integration of QED systems and the level of service and commitment that QED provided. For example, QED generally consult key
users during the latter stages of product development with respect to the
priorities and formats of the various product functions and features. So
when QED adapted its US EPOS till for Hawk's UK markets, QED

re-prioritized the cheque processing functions – at Hawk's suggestion – so that it took two seconds rather than 20 seconds (cheque payment is unusual in US retail markets).

Hawk considered that the major disadvantage of using QED systems used to be their high price relative to rivals but as QED has become more flexible in pricing, this problem has diminished. For the smaller elements of retail CBS it is also possible to use a wide range of reliable and inexpensive QED-compatible offerings from reputable sources. A more important limitation was the necessity for non-QED elements in Hawk's retail CBS network to be compatible with the QED infrastructure, even though alternative technologies were sometimes superior. For example, Hawk judged the proprietary scanning systems offered by an alternative source to be superior in technology and operation to QED-compatible alternatives, but the QED-compatible alternatives had to be purchased.

EDI forms a particularly important part of Hawk's retail CBS strategy. Hawk is linked to several of its major suppliers through an EDI system sourced from QED in deliberate preference to what was at the time the established standard EDI network in UK retail markets, because of Hawk's concern that the supplier of this EDI network was taking advantage of its dominant position in EDI markets to charge unrealistic prices. The QED system was still undergoing trials at the time and Hawk (together with its own upstream suppliers) played a significant role in collaboratively developing the new system as a faster and more responsive system than the more established alternative. For Hawk, expertise in EDI was seen as crucial to competitive prospects not only in UK retailing markets but also in Europe where Hawk jointly established a collaborative venture with major French and Dutch retailers in anticipation of retailing opportunities arising from deregulation and harmonization of European markets.

Hawk assessed the benefits of EPOS/EFTPOS systems with much the same findings as did other leading retailers; for example, Hawk estimated its EFTPOS systems reduced checkout time by around 40 seconds. Hawk was also attracted by the prospect of using tills as cash dispensers to expand the range of customer services despite the competition this would imply with banks and building societies (a service later offered by rivals also). Hawk and QED have continued to research collaboratively a number of novel retail CBS applications such as screen-based teleshopping and electronic trolleys which automatically scan items as they are loaded by customers. Some of these new applications have proved competitively successful while others, such as teleshopping, while technologically proven, have not (yet) become as accepted as they are in some other cultures.

Conclusion

The Hawk Group Chairman summed the importance of CBS:

'[Hawk] survives and prospers on the efficiency and effectiveness of IT. It has enabled us to cut working capital, to manage our mix more intensively, and to test the evolving structure of the business. We depend on it for our everyday operations and our future development . . . IT and the business are one.'

Not surprisingly perhaps, Hawk consider that CBS suppliers do not, and probably cannot, fully understand the application of CBS in retailing, though, of course, some do better than others. This may explain the irritation felt by many retailers when CBS suppliers promote their retail systems too insistently – one of the reasons, Hawk concludes, why QED failed to win a hugely important contract to provide retail CBS to the market-leading retailer. QED now fully accepts the importance of learning from customer expertise in retail CBS markets, and of becoming 'less patronizing' and 'more collaborative'.

B   THE SPARROW GROUP AND MTB

The Sparrow Group pioneered the development of large store retailing in the 1960s with a range of products extending from groceries to clothing and household goods. By 1989 Sparrow had over 200 stores, most of which were large superstores. During the 1970s and 1980s Sparrow positioned itself at the cheaper end of the superstore market compared to the market leaders and was dominant in this sector where its stores were much larger and its range far wider than those of rivals with similar low-cost, high-quality strategies. However, this sector soon came under competitive pressure from the emergence of specialist discount operators (e.g. Discount Giant, PoundStretcher, Low-Cost) and the development of inexpensive, low-margin 'own-brand' lines by the more quality-oriented upmarket superstore retailers. This pressure became more severe with the entry to UK markets of successful North European discounters (e.g. Netto, Aldi), the prospect of imminent entry by North American 'warehouse' retailers (e.g. Costco), and the growth of catalogue mail order suppliers of clothing unencumbered with the overheads of retail premises. The profitability of the Sparrow Group was further eroded by intense competition in the household goods and furniture markets where the Group owned two specialist retailing chains, and by Sparrow's costly expansion into new retailing sectors (e.g. estate agency).

Development of retail CBS

The use of CBS at Sparrow dates from 1968 when a mainframe system was installed at the Group head office for accounting and general administration functions. There was little further investment and Sparrow was still 'largely uncomputerized' in terms of retailing systems by the early 1980s when 'management complacency' and an 'inability to respond promptly' to the competitive changes sketched above triggered a sequence of financial crises.

Sparrow responded to these crises with a wide-ranging turnaround strategy which included a new livery, an extensive store refurbishment programme, expanded product ranges, acceleration of the new store opening schedule, an emphasis on staff training, the development of a centralized distribution system through Sparrow's own warehouses, and – crucially – a radical review of future CBS requirements. The review concluded in 1984 that to meet Sparrow's needs for the foreseeable future, a comprehensive MTB 'solution' should be adopted which would include general-purpose computing systems, EPOS and scanning systems, stock replenishment systems, and also systems to support Sparrow's plans for a new strategic distribution network.

Sparrow's Board of Directors felt that the use of CBS for operational efficiency would, more than any other single issue, distinguish successful superstore retailers from unsuccessful ones. Perhaps preoccupied at the time with the urgency of cost control, and in the wake of Sparrow's strategic review and investment programme, the Sparrow Board nevertheless perceived the role of CBS very much in terms of operational efficiency, rather than, for example, as a basis for generating data for marketing purposes, or more generally as an investment in future strategic flexibility. Sparrow's Director for IT commented that the use of EPOS data for marketing purposes was a trivial issue and it was the use of this data for logistics management that was important.

The apparent low priority given to longer-term strategic marketing issues in Sparrow's emerging competitive strategy may help to explain Sparrow's difficulty in regaining competitive levels of profitability, notwithstanding the improvements in its operating efficiency following the sale of its furniture-selling subsidiaries. A more telling reason was probably the culture of Sparrow at director level where, according to the IT Director, there was an innate 'conservatism' especially among the many rather 'elderly' directors, which resulted in a lack of familiarity with IT issues and an apparent 'nervousness' at the prospect of investing in CBS, despite its acknowledged urgency. Because of the need for swift progress towards at least a basic level of retail CBS, Sparrow realized it would have to rely very heavily on the service, support and experience of whichever supplier was chosen across a wide range of systems and applications – all factors thought to favour MTB. In fact Sparrow was so impressed with MTB's recommended 'solution' supported by the IT Director, an ex-MTB salesman) that competitive tenders were not even sought: 'there was no real alternative'.

Several specific reasons were given for selecting MTB as Sparrow's preferred CBS supplier:

- the breadth and depth of MTB's product range (implying future commitment to retailing CBS offerings at a time when rival suppliers seemed significantly less committed),
- the quality of MTB's engineering (implying reliability),
- the high level of service and support provided by MTB,
- the option of reliable, low-cost MTB-compatible systems (implying economical system development),
- MTB's extensive experience in retail CBS (though this experience had been gained mostly in overseas markets and UK retailing was widely recognized as having significant cultural and operational differences),
- MTB's claimed reputation for passing on the benefits of productivity gains to customers in terms of reduced upgrade costs.[2]

Apparently, while the Sparrow Board was very impressed by MTB's proposed solution to Sparrow's competitive situation, it was equally concerned at the high costs involved which, given Sparrow's cash-flow problems at the time, seemed prohibitive. However, the Sparrow Board endorsed the deal after MTB, fearing the account was slipping away, offered to arrange flexible finance with staged payments.

Despite this appearance of uniform enthusiasm for investment in CBS, the Sparrow Board was divided on the issue of the considerable costs involved. Sparrow's proud traditions of frugal management, tight cost control and minimal investment in corporate overheads remained influential amongst the more conservative and long-serving members of the Sparrow Board, leading them to recommend only a minimal level of CBS investment. Other Board members recalled a previous occasion when Sparrow had installed cheap till receipt printers in all its stores which then had to be replaced because they could not cope with the surge of weekend transactions. This experience persuaded many Sparrow Board members that price should not be a prime criterion in CBS purchasing decisions. A compromise was eventually agreed whereby CBS would be adopted in two phases: first the proposed MTB systems would be purchased to establish a fundamental platform for Sparrow's CBS requirements and then, after sufficient time to identify Sparrow's specific interests and requirements, a fully competitive review of IT systems would be undertaken with a view to inviting tenders for EPOS/EFTPOS systems.

The second phase of this process was initiated in 1986/87 when invitations to tender were issued to five of the leading suppliers of retail CBS. The Sparrow contract was for systems combining scanning and EFTPOS facilities which could cope with the typically large size of Sparrow superstores and the volatile shopping patterns of consumers, but Sparrow did not require the systems to be particularly sophisticated with respect to the detail of data recorded by the scanning systems since the priority was on stock replacement rather than marketing information. The preference for unsophisticated systems, reinforced by the sensitivity of Sparrow's Directors to the cost of CBS, resulted in Sparrow specifying a much less expensive EFTPOS system than was favoured by rivals (at about one-third of the cost of the market leader's tills).

Of the five suppliers invited to tender, one declined the invitation because it considered its systems to be inadequate to cope with the unusually large size of many of Sparrow's superstores. Two further suppliers were eliminated in the preliminary analyses for technical and cost reasons. Of the remaining two – MTB and PES – MTB had a record of satisfactory performance at Sparrow, a wider range of products and services, and more reassuring prospects for long-term survival. Against this PES had to cope with the costs of ensuring full connectivity with MTB back-office systems, and had a difficult task in marketing a relatively unfamiliar system against MTB – not only a global CBS supplier (PES operated on a more modest scale) but also Sparrow's established supplier of CBS. MTB also had important design advantages over PES's system in terms of its tolerance for variation in electricity supply, its smaller size, its staffing requirements and its ease of maintenance. Notwithstanding these technical and operational disadvantages, Sparrow's frugal Directors concluded that PES's bid of £150,000 per store was convincingly lower than MTB's bid of £180,000.

On the point of awarding the contract to PES, Sparrow's Board was suddenly informed that a new MTB range had just been announced and that this would fortuitously reduce the MTB bid to £120,000, a figure which PES promptly matched. However, the apparent 'flexibility' of PES's profit margins and the implication that the Sparrow Board had been about to incur inflated costs persuaded the Board that PES had not had Sparrow's best interests at heart and the contract was awarded instead to MTB.

So by the end of the 1980s Sparrow had an extensive network of relatively new CBS extending from checkouts to back-office systems to central mainframes to regional warehouses and back to the inventory systems feeding the shelves of each superstore – virtually all of which was supplied by MTB (or MTB-compatible suppliers).

Benefits of retail CBS

Sparrow considered that its extensive investment in retail CBS had provided important competitive advantages especially in the areas of distribution, networks, EFTPOS and teleshopping, each of which is discussed briefly below.

Distribution benefits

Sparrow estimates that it invested about £180 million in its new distribution system, which was expected to be probably the single most important element of Sparrow's future competitive advantage. In effect, the previous paper-based distribution system had allowed external suppliers considerable latitude in delivering whatever and whenever they wished. Some suppliers occasionally took advantage of the system to 'dump' sub-standard, damaged or outdated stock hidden in the general flow of deliveries and invoiced at normal rates. With an average of 60 deliveries per day to each store, coupled with Sparrow's vast range of individual lines, pack sizes, short-term promotional variants and frequent competitive price adjustments, even keeping track of the paperwork was very difficult and controlling it was a 'practical impossibility'. In addition, while the costs of managing the delivery and stock systems were rising, especially with respect to manual and clerical labour, further problems were emerging in terms of variable stock quality, high wastage, and increasing customer complaints about product availability and quality.

The new system used scanning data to give almost real-time stock levels which allowed dramatic inventory reductions while improving the freshness, variety and availability of products. External suppliers now deliver in bulk to Sparrow's purpose-built regional warehouses rather than piecemeal to individual stores, incidentally allowing Sparrow to negotiate lower wholesale prices. Store delivery schedules are now governed by the sales patterns of each superstore and co-ordinated through the regional warehouses, rather than being determined by the convenience of suppliers' delivery schedules and the intuition and guesstimates of inventory managers. Other benefits arising from the new system include a reduced need for storage space in existing stores (creating additional sales space) and lower costs of future stores, profits from the disposal of superseded distribution facilities, lower labour costs (in warehouses, picking, transport and administration), increased transportation efficiencies (in lower maintenance and running costs), and the option for individual stores to use local competitive suppliers which would be unable to tender for national contracts.

Sparrow has also developed a new fleet of innovatively designed trailers with five independently controllable temperature zones, allowing more efficient use of space in trailers and in stores, and greatly reducing the number of store deliveries. The combination of new trailers and new CBS provides a good illustration of the highly profitable synergies available from investment in a fully integrated and co-ordinated system of logistics management, and helps to explain why Sparrow believes this distribution system is so important to its competitive future.

Nevertheless, and in marked contrast to the experience of other leading retailers, Sparrow found that the vastly improved efficiency of its inventory management systems arose not so much from the availability of scanning data, as from improvements in physical distribution systems. In practice, suppliers delivered goods to Sparrow's regional warehouses (as they delivered to other retailers) in a wide variety of different formats and with widely differing quantity numbering systems (packaged by the dozen, gross, score, pound, kilo, litre, pint, EC units ...) due to frequent changes in pack size, style, promotions, labelling, materials, cartons, units of delivery and so on. Suppliers also sometimes changed the advised order at the last moment (due to stock-out or because they wanted to pass on fading stock rather than a fresh batch), substituting different pack sizes or promotion variations to make up the order. It then became practically impossible, in Sparrow's experience, to match the outflow of goods through the checkouts precisely with a replacement inflow of deliveries to the regional warehouses.

Other retailers resolved this complexity with increasingly sophisticated real-time data capture systems at the checkout. Although Sparrow's checkout systems were less sophisticated, this situation presented fewer problems than might have been expected because Sparrow's highly centralized control of distribution kept store inventory at a low level, allowing full manual stock counts in as little as three hours (assisted by specially adapted hand-held computers).

The difference between Sparrow's strategy and that of other leading retailers over investment in EPOS/EFTPOS probably reflects Sparrow's much wider range of products (extending well beyond groceries) and Sparrow's frugal culture making it reluctant to invest in sophisticated CBS. Yet the necessity to undertake frequent three-hour manual stock counts could not be regarded as cost-free, and more significantly, rivals' access to comprehensive proprietary scanning data would prove to be an increasingly valuable strategic competitive resource as the market leaders developed greater insight to customers' purchasing patterns, prompting ever more elaborately packaged offerings. With its subtly different customer profiles, Sparrow could not even rely on imitating rivals' novel customer offerings, making it increasingly difficult for Sparrow to break into the typically more affluent and lucrative markets enjoyed by the leading retailers.

Network benefits

In order to link Sparrow's existing mainframe system with the new MTB EPOS and back-office systems, Sparrow installed a sophisticated communications network which was subsequently extended to link all stores, distribution centres and management units. The system also provided Group-wide electronic mail services and was deliberately designed to be flexible and open-ended in line with Sparrow's conviction that the network would eventually become an important strategic asset. This has proved to be so in three ways: the increased operational efficiency of on-line EDI ordering and invoicing; the economies generated by Sparrow's decision to develop its own low-cost EDI system for local suppliers rather than buying access to the much more expensive proprietary national retail EDI service used by most rivals; and the lucrative possibility of selling real-time EPOS data to grocery manufacturers through controlled access to Sparrow's communications network. There is also a possibility of leasing access to Sparrow's network not only for EDI but also for electronic mail, facsimile transmissions, EFTPOS, bureau mainframe services, and general telecommunications – a possibility which could attract organizations not able to invest independently in such facilities.

Interestingly, Sparrow's Board seems to have been relatively comfortable with the prospect of investing in sophisticated internal CBS networks delivering administrative and managerial benefits, yet relatively uncomfortable at the prospect of investing in sophisticated scanning systems delivering data about customers but with no immediate indications of how to use such data. Perhaps this preference may also have something to do with the Board's cultural reluctance to invest in an external proprietary communications network used by London-based rivals (Sparrow is proud of its Northern origins and values), and its long-standing enthusiasm for frugality and efficiency in internal 'housekeeping' systems.

EFTPOS benefits

Sparrow has developed its own software to manage the relationship between its EFTPOS systems and the banking institutions. Sparrow's system is adapted from the Connex banking software package and illustrates Sparrow's strategy of maintaining proprietary control over its software systems wherever practicable (reflecting Sparrow's belief that CBS are at the core of its competitive advantage). By using the independent Connex system rather than the proprietary software packages offered by individual banks, Sparrow can negotiate for the most favourable system charges and switch from bank to bank as it pleases, generating considerable savings.

In common with other retailers, Sparrow has found additional important benefits of EPOS/EFTPOS to be: greater customer convenience; faster and more accurate checkout procedures; reduced pilfering and wastage; more accurate information on sales trends; reduced need for manual pricing (through shelf-edge pricing rather than item pricing) and so increased pricing flexibility; and more rapid cash flow (especially with fewer cheques).

Teleshopping benefits

In 1989 Sparrow believed it had an important potential competitive advantage in teleshopping – a market which other leading retailers abandoned, or avoided after initial consideration, but which attracted Sparrow based on the personal enthusiasm of Sparrow's IT Director at the time (now replaced) reinforced by the success of teleshopping in North American markets. With demographic changes in the UK population increasing the proportion of the elderly, Sparrow estimated the market for teleshopping to be worth well over £1 billion in the 1990s. Sparrow also estimated that it had a clear competitive advantage in teleshopping because the space liberated within Sparrow stores and warehouses by centralized distribution would provide more than enough room for the necessary teleordering, picking and packing facilities, whereas rivals would have to develop this space on existing store sites at an estimated cost of around £100 per square foot. Oddly, Sparrow seems not to have appreciated that similar efficiencies (and liberated space) were also being achieved in the physical distribution systems of its leading rivals, if on a more evolutionary and so perhaps less obvious scale.

In 1989 Sparrow pursued these anticipated competitive benefits by conducting two sets of teleshopping trials in the London area. Neither trial proved particularly encouraging despite collaboration with local authorities and age-related charities. The idea was eventually shelved with Sparrow concluding, as rivals had concluded earlier, that there were fundamental differences between consumer purchasing patterns and preferences in the UK and North America.

Conclusion

Despite the successful introduction of its turnaround strategy and considerably increased turnover in food retailing, the Sparrow Group has not been able to match the profit margins of its more successful rivals. This was thought, in part, to be because of Sparrow's continuing involvement in non-food retailing and the capital cost of acquiring stores in Sparrow's ambitious growth programme. Concern has also been expressed that Sparrow may be more vulnerable than its more profitable rivals to pressure from the emerging discount retailers, as Sparrow has never really been able to match the appeal of Parrot and Robin to more affluent middle-class consumers.

Shortly after the date of this case several of Sparrow's more elderly directors retired from the Board, together with the more youthful IT Director. A fresh management team under a widely respected CEO has now launched a broadly successful revival strategy based on tighter management control, lower staffing costs, higher quality and a more focused range of offerings – all supported by extensive reinvestment in CBS. This strategy has enabled Sparrow to rebrand some superstores to compete more directly with the new discount rivals, liberating Sparrow superstores to be repositioned somewhat further up-market as a relatively low-cost wide-range alternative to the market leaders.

C   A BRIEF NOTE ON THE ROBIN GROUP AND THE PARROT GROUP

In the case of the Robin Group (the third leading retailer) the choice of CBS supplier was based not only on the technical reliability and capability of the supplier's systems but also on the supplier's understanding of Robin's operational circumstances and the potential strength of the relationship between Robin and the supplier. This resulted in major contracts with three different CBS suppliers for different CBS requirements in inventory and logistics systems, checkout systems, and data processing and database management systems. Because of this multiple sourcing strategy, Robin has faced additional problems of system integration and has not been able to take full advantage of the scale economies available through a single source strategy. On the other hand, Robin is less dependent on its CBS suppliers than some of its main rivals and the greater sophistication of more specialized applications has allowed Robin to develop innovative customer offerings such as financial services based on EFTPOS technology and elaborate loyalty schemes.

The Parrot Group (the fourth leading retailer) has followed a dual sourcing strategy, though perhaps somewhat reluctantly. Parrot's experience with CBS persuaded it to follow its own conclusions (as opposed to the advice of suppliers or consultants) with respect to what systems, suppliers and technologies were best suited to its needs. Parrot's established supplier of back-office systems (PES) had at first seemed complacent, unresponsive and uninterested in Parrot's situation, 'never really facing up to the hard commercial world'. But after PES failed to secure contracts for upgrading Parrot's systems it proved much more cooperative and collaborated very closely with Parrot in the subsequent phase of systems development focusing on EFTPOS systems. Parrot now accepts that PES has developed 'reasonably well' a unique level of understanding which constitutes a proprietary competitive advantage in EPOS/EFTPOS systems – 'they know what makes us tick and what will cause us problems but can't interpret our future system needs as well as we do for ourselves'. PES sees its role in broadly similar terms: 'We have achieved our pre-eminence in the retail industry by learning to think like retailers, by putting ourselves in their place and then applying our information management skills.' Nevertheless, in terms of mainframe retail applications, as opposed to smaller-scale systems for back offices and checkouts, Parrot concluded, albeit reluctantly, that PES was 'no longer capable of competing with the major suppliers'.

CONCLUSION

Retail CBS are now accepted as vital to the competitive prospects of superstore operations. This is a continuously evolving area of applications with most leading competitors now experimenting with the latest developments in retailing technology such as electronic shelf pricing, trolley-based scanning systems, interactive video systems for consumer information, and an expanding range of financial service offerings.

The illustrations above of superstore retailers and their relationships with CBS suppliers show that in order to win these large and strategically important contracts it is necessary for CBS suppliers to comply not only with explicit technical criteria but also with implicit criteria of understanding the competitive context of the retailer. Several suppliers found that they failed to win contracts, not because of their technology but because there was doubt over their willingness or ability to devote full attention to the retailer's needs. While there was an excess of CBS demand over supply – which may have been the case for much of the 1980s, as all leading retailers sought to invest in CBS – there seems to have been little need for CBS suppliers to invest in positive marketing strategies aimed at customer interests. But as competitive pressures increased into the 1990s, and CBS suppliers saw profits collapsing, suppliers found that to be successful in winning contracts it became increasingly important to be able to demonstrate a clear and credible commitment to customers, based on a comprehensive understanding not only of the technology but also of the customers' competitive context and operations. Once established, these relationships seemed to offer competitive gains for both sides as each learned about the application and development of retail CBS technology in the customer's context.

There can sometimes also be a noticeable difference of expectation and experience between the CBS suppliers and the leading superstore retailers with respect to the benefits delivered by retail CBS. The CBS suppliers anticipated many benefits based on the potential of the technology and supported by extensive practical trials. But there may be something of the 'Hawthorne effect' in such trials with those involved being perhaps more committed to the introduction of CBS than might be the case more broadly. Retailers such as Sparrow decided, for example, that it was neither necessary nor realistic to invest in full data capture systems; others like Hawk found that pilfering and wastage (usually referred to as 'shrinkage') was reduced only for a short time as human nature found new ways of circumventing systems; and others like Parrot found that staff (and even some managers) do not necessarily welcome the greater pressures and controls, the improved efficiency and the higher productivity expectations brought by successive CBS investments.

There were also a number of significant costs associated with the introduction of CBS, apart from purchase and maintenance costs, which suppliers either chose not to emphasize or were not aware of, yet which became increasingly apparent to retailers and their customers: for example, the costs of staff training, increased salaries for added responsibility, superseded facilities (some of which could not easily be disposed of, such as extra storage space in stores), disruption to procedures, reduced customer contact, the disturbing feeling of being part of an 'automated' process, the chaos caused by occasional system failures, and so on. Similarly, retailers also found that there were important long-term competitive benefits in adopting CBS of which suppliers had not initially seemed to be aware, such as the degree of experimentation which became possible in store design, product development, pricing and packaging; or the enhanced customer services which became possible (e.g. financial services and loyalty incentives); or the flexibility of being able to use local suppliers (CBS suppliers seemed to assume that scale economies were always the objective); or that CBS compatibility could become a crucial issue in mergers and acquisitions.

While such differences of expectation and experience would not normally perhaps be surprising between suppliers and customers, they are not consistent with the unanimous claims of CBS suppliers at the time to be offering 'total solutions' based on a full understanding of customers' requirements built up through ongoing customer relationships. Doubtless, part of this difference can be attributed to the exaggerating effect of marketing promotions and salesmanship but discussions with CBS suppliers (who were used to distinguishing what one source described as 'bullshit from brass tacks') made it clear that they too perceived there was often a considerable and unnecessary gap between the benefits promised by CBS suppliers and the reality of installed CBS. Significantly, most of these suppliers also claimed that many CBS installations were not operated efficiently and that potential benefits were being lost.

With both sides clearly having much to gain from closer collaborative relationships it is perhaps surprising that such relationships have not been more frequent, or more long-lasting where they did exist. It seems that, once established, some suppliers have tended to become less interested in collaboration and sometimes increasingly complacent, seeming to assume that switching costs would protect them from potential rival suppliers, whereas many retailers have become uncomfortable about CBS suppliers (who also supplied their rivals) knowing too much about an increasingly vital aspect of their competitiveness. The scope for learning in such awkward relationships is inevitably limited.

NOTES

1   HDT ties a user's data closely to the software programs and operational architecture of the database management system. It assumes that users know what they want to do with the data, that full and exact data are available and that the characteristics of the data will not change. Within these limitations HDT works reliably and swiftly. RDT (probably invented by two QED researchers) divorces the data from the software program, referring instead to data locations which can contain a wide variety of data types and volumes.

This also means that RDT systems are more easily and quickly installed than HDT. Thus RDT is more flexible, adaptable and manipulable than HDT; for example, this makes RDT well suited to telephone directory enquiry systems which would be impracticable using HDT. The choice between HDT and RDT therefore depends on the nature of the data being managed – the two are not direct alternatives.

2 Oddly, this benefit was not mentioned by any other source interviewed for the research on which this case is based, indeed the reverse was a not infrequent complaint levelled against MTB.

2 *Product development in reality*

This case is a compendium of pieces drawn from published material and research data, all concerned with product development in technology-intensive contexts. The aim of the case is to illustrate something of the practical reality of the product development processes and the problems of managing individuals in these contexts.

The case is in two parts. First, readers should consider the three illustrations below of product development in the computer industry (*Tales of the Tin Hut*; *Microprocessor Pioneers Reminisce*; *Developing the Laptop*), in which those closely involved in product development reflect on their experience, what they were really trying to do, what the environment and experience were like, and the relative roles of technological fascination and managerial control. Readers might also consider the possible role of personal and collective cultural characteristics in explaining some of the differences between these accounts. And, taking the discussion a step further, what evidence is there that relationship management – perhaps the key to successful interorganizational marketing – might also offer useful lessons for the many intraorganizational exchanges inherent in product development processes?

The second part of this case briefly describes the development of two innovative technology-intensive products, *CAFS* and *DAP*, focusing on product features and capabilities. In this case there was a noticeable lack of early attention to potential applications and market demand, with the result that the products failed. When demand did eventually emerge, largely unprompted by the manufacturer, the technology was no longer as innovative and much of the commercial promise initially offered by these products had dissipated.

Readers should study Reading 3 (Cooper, 1996) alongside this case. Cooper's suggested approach to the management of product development would surely have greatly helped the successful development and commercialization of *CAFS* and *DAP* – but to what extent can his recommendations accommodate the very personal motivations and idiosyncratic characters reflected in the first part of the case? These characteristics might be more in evidence in the context of radical or 'revolutionary' technology developments such as early microprocessors, but are they less significant, or more manageable, in more incremental, 'evolutionary' or lower profile developments?

Subsequent discussion could focus on the points below, among others.

Possible questions for discussion

1   To what extent do these illustrations seem to be adequately explained through the models of product development presented in the literature?

2   What additional areas of management theory (e.g. HRM, leadership, social exchange theory, resource competition) might be appropriate to a fuller explanation of what was going on in these illustrations?

3   How realistic do you think these accounts of product development are? Why do you think those involved might perhaps have remembered things differently over the years and what additional insight might this offer to the motivations, organizational objectives and management issues involved?

4   Do you think that product development is likely to be significantly different nowadays? And, if so, why – what might have changed, and what has probably not changed?

5   How might product development processes be different, from the perspective of the individuals involved, in less technologically intensive sectors? Do you think that the processes and experiences described are symptomatic of the technological context, or of the radical nature of the developments in question, or of the character of the individuals, or are they a mix of these and other factors?

6   What was the role of marketing (both formal and informal, external and internal) in such product development, and what might be the role of marketing nowadays? What are the problems of radical product development in technology-intensive sectors? How does marketing address these problems? What other functions might be involved?

7   Consider some current radical technology-intensive products which might be under development and discuss the problems for marketing management involved. Virtual reality technology might be a good starting point for this exercise, or environmentally friendly transport systems, or a depilatory cream for men, or organ farming for transplant markets using cloning technology, or thought-activated interfaces for communicating with computers (under development for military applications), or genetically modified foods.

8   The product development process is largely a process concerned with changes in product design. Can such a process be usefully adapted to manage the development of other marketing aspects of the product, such as its price and packaging? How might this work in practice?

9   To what extent, if at all, can the lessons of product development be applied to service development? For example, how might you go

about developing a product development consultancy service designed for technology-intensive manufacturing clients; or a training service aimed at developing mutual awareness and respect between technologists and marketers in technology-intensive sectors?

10 Bearing in mind that radical product development forms only a small proportion of all product development, even in technology-intensive sectors and amongst especially innovative organizations, how should the processes of *non-radical* and *incremental* product development be managed?

TALES OF THE TIN HUT

[Source: Adapted from an article by Paul Fisher, 'Tales of the Tin Hut: Forty years on a unique group of computer pioneers are reunited', *The Guardian*, 24 April 1993]

In 1952 Ferranti of Manchester hired a team of mathematicians, installed them in a building popularly referred to as the 'Tin Hut' and set them to work as programmers on a prototype computer which was, eventually, to became the 'Ferranti Mark One'. This was perhaps the first commercial computer and the first unit to be sold went to Amsterdam where it coordinated movements of Shell's tanker fleet – a £300,000 export in an era when Britain led the world, and patriotic-voiced newsreel announcers marvelled at how electronic brains could do in 20 minutes what humans laboured over for six months.

Last week, 40 years later, the Old Ferrantians – Britain's first commercial programmers – met in Olaf Chedzoy's house in Somerset. They'd travelled from America, Australia and all over Britain, and their reunion chat was of grandchildren, valves, gardening, random number generation, and how exciting it all was. Such good fun when hardware was engineering and software was programmes rather than programs.

The engineering of the 'Ferranti Mark One' sprawled through a pair of 12-foot-long cabinets stuffed with wires linking racks containing 20 000 [thermionic diode] valves. The machine had 180kb of main memory and was a moody monster: they didn't switch it off for fear of valves blowing [through sudden temperature changes]. Memory decayed for no apparent reason, or accumulated extra digits when the room lights were switched on. On good days the computer would be closed down for three hours of maintenance when the engineers would deliberately alter voltages to encourage dodgy components to blow. Back then, programmers laboured over six-inch-wide screens. These held the equivalent of 3kb of RAM stored as magnetized charges on a cathode ray tube (CRT). Lights twinkled on displays showing 32 lines of 40 digits. 'Ones were brighter than noughts,' Chedzoy remembers. 'We thought in binary and there was a huge satisfaction in watching our patterns highlighted as programmes ran.' Speakers pulsed low for slow programming loops and high for short ones. 'We made it play the national anthem for customers,' Chedzoy says. 'They didn't know whether to stand to attention or not.'

The system was developed from Manchester University's 'Manchester Mark One'. That was where Alan Turing went after his work on code-breaking systems in Bletchley during the Second World War. These computer pioneers didn't say much about him, maybe because they're of that generation which was embarrassed by Turing's homosexuality. And anyway, he was up at the university and they were down in the Tin Hut.

Turing had gone to Manchester posing the question: *Can machines think?* Tony Baker went there to discover if they would sell. He'd trained as an actuary and was seconded from Royal Liverpool Insurance to investigate 'how to make something of computers in commerce – nobody believed us, and IBM was saying it wouldn't work'. Baker's specification for an insurance system may mark him as the world's first commercial systems analyst.

The core of the team, led by John Bennett (to whom everybody still deferred), went to offices in London. Reliability became the new order, CRT storage was abandoned and, in an early example of computing's exponential progress, the resulting 'Perseus' system cost about £50,000. The first sale was to South African Mutual Insurance. 'At that time', Bennett says, 'black South Africans were buying life insurance and apartheid prevented the employment of non-whites to process the paperwork; not enough young white women, the main source of clerical work, could be recruited'.

'We knew we were going somewhere but we didn't know where', says Hugh Ross, perhaps the first computer salesman. 'We had no precedents and you have no idea how hit and miss it all was. None of us imagined computers would become so simple that children would use them. Who'd have known how word processing would spread? Mind you, we anticipated handwriting recognition, computerized chess, and language translation.'

In Manchester, nearly half the programmers were women. Conway Berners-Lee, who married one of them, said 'Ferranti hired intelligent girls very cheaply but this gave them a big cultural problem because, prior to that, the company had only employed women as typists or factory hands.' 'Men got more than women', Mary Lee added. 'It was grossly unfair and there was a rebellion. The personnel officer was shocked we'd even discussed our wages.' She was on £400 a year.

'The Tin Hut marriage rate was high', her husband said. 'The Robinsons . . . the Bennets . . . the Clarkes . . . us.' And all bar one of the marriages have lasted a lifetime. Many of these pioneers had moved on to professorships, or stock options and top executive jobs. They'd been the culmination of a measured progress from military radar work to academia to commerce, and the heroically named 'Pegasus' computers had made Ferranti a lot of money.

'Why hasn't the British computer industry done as well as the American?', someone asked. 'We fell down in access to markets', Berners-Lee said. 'That was the key because IBM moved in and exploited its vast accounting machine base.' He betrayed some bitterness as the government [forced through] arranged mergers whereby Ferranti, British Tabulating Machines, Power Samas, English Electric and several other pioneering British computer companies became absorbed together as ICL, with ICL now becoming [80 per cent] owned by the Japanese company Fujitsu.

MICROPROCESSOR PIONEERS REMINISCE

[Source: Adapted from an unattributed article 'Microprocessor Pioneers Reminisce: Looking Back on the World of 16-Pin, 2000-Transistor Microprocessors', *Microprocessor Report*, 5(24), 26 December 1991, pp.13–18]

Introduction

The Autumn of 1991 marks the twentieth anniversary of the microprocessor as a commercial product. *Microprocessor Report* invited ten pioneers to reminisce about the early days of the microprocessor, and how much things have changed since then.

The question of 'who invented the microprocessor?' is, in fact, a meaningless one in any non-legal sense. The microprocessor is not really an invention at all; it is an evolutionary development, combining functions previously implemented on separate devices into one chip. Furthermore, no single individual was responsible for coming up with this idea or making it practical. There were multiple, concurrent efforts at several companies, and each was a team effort that relied on the contributions of several people.

Regardless of whose patent is ultimately deemed the winner, all the people who built the first microprocessors deserve recognition for creating the products that led to a radical reshaping of not only computers, but everything electronic. Here, in their own words, are excerpts from comments made by these industry pioneers.

Lee Boysel

In the late 1960s I worked at Fairchild. Fairchild had two operations going with MOS. One was the R&D group, the superstars of processing who came up with all the great processes, the group that broke off and started Intel. And I ran a sort of blue-collar LSI [Large Scale Integration] design operation in Mountain View. You know, we were the people who did the actual circuit design and the like. Of course, a natural rivalry exists between these two groups.

As it turns out, after a while we began to get a little of the glory. We started designing some of the first ROMs [Read Only Memory], RAMs [Random Access Memory] and the like. It was pretty neat. But unfortunately, when our volume went up our fab [fabrication] line failed us because we had contamination and all kinds of problems. The R&D folks shut our line down. They weren't allowed to do that, but they just shut down our MOS fab line and insisted that we go up to R&D and take a course in process physics by Andy Grove. Now, let me tell you, if there's one person you don't want to take a physics course from, it's Andy Grove.

At any rate, we took the class. It was brutal. There were final exams and everything. They really put it to us. After our last final exam they were going to give us a letter grade. A couple of days went by, and we all received our letter grade. They flunked us all! They gave us all Ds and Fs. Well, that meant war between the two groups.

So we went to war. It turns out that the folks from R&D, every time they would bring us a new process (in those days, like silicon-gate), we said, Buzz off, we don't want that stuff. And every time we went to them with very large packages with lots of pins because we needed those to put our LSI devices in, they told us to buzz off. So it was mutual. Anyway, the war raged on.

We all went our separate ways when Fairchild split up. The R&D folks went to Intel and I pulled my group out and we started Four-Phase. It's interesting how difficult it is to change old mindsets. It was years before Four-Phase upgraded our process and it was years before Intel let the designers use big packages with lots of pins. This is okay if you are making memory devices, but when it comes to putting a microprocessor in a 16-pin package, you talk about tough! You don't know how tough it is.

Federico Faggin

Around Christmas 1970, I got in my hands – they were sweaty hands – a box of 2 inch wafers [on which microprocessors are imprinted in the fabrication process]. They had inside the first run of the [new Intel] 4004. Everything was set up to test the device. I loaded the first wafer in the prober station, went down with the probes and looked at the meter to see if there was a short [circuit]. There wasn't any, so I breathed a big sigh of relief. There was current flowing. It wasn't as much as I expected, but there was current. I then started applying signals to the inputs, trying to figure out what was coming out at the output. Well, what was coming out was not what I expected. In fact, it was so different from what I was expecting I was scared. A knot began to start in my stomach. I decided that it must have been a bad die [the metal 'stamp' used to imprint microprocessor circuits onto wafers]. So I went to the next one and found the same problem, the same symptoms.

If you are in this business you know that if you have seen two dies alike, you've got a problem. I went down to a third one just in case, and it still was as bad as the others. By that time I was white in my face. Fortunately my boss wasn't around. I picked up the wafer and looked under the microscope to find out if there was anything that was visibly wrong. And, lo and behold, there was something wrong! One masking step was missing. The buried-contact layer that would normally connect polysilicon to the junctions was missing. As a result, most of the gates were floating. That was the reason why the current was so low.

At that point, I was both relieved and mad at the same time, which is a funny feeling, I'll tell you. Three weeks later the next run of the 4004 came out. By that then it was mid-January 1971. This time all five layers were in. It came out at about night time when people were leaving, and I felt the same as the first time, same nervousness, same knot in my chest. I started probing the device and things were working. I got very excited and continued to test the device until four o'clock in the morning. By that time, working alone in the lab, it was kind of fun. There was nobody around. By four o'clock I had tested pretty much all of the device. There were some things I didn't understand which later were found to be minor problems and were fixed, but pretty much the part worked completely. That was the night when the 4004 was born.

Gary Boone

In the spring of 1971 at Texas Instruments (TI), the good news was we had a functioning 8-bit processor on a single MOS chip. The bad news was our customer decided not to use it. So I was sent to explain our new 8-bit CPU [Central Processing Unit] on a chip, as it was termed, to the oracle of computing at TI in charge of a large scientific computing project. I will never forget what he said: 'You know, computers are getting bigger, not smaller'. But it got better. After some more lessons in which way computers were going, he said, 'Why don't you go home and do something useful?'

There are some interesting lessons in this story. One is, when you are explaining a radical idea it often happens that the idea will be evaluated in terms of the evaluator's experience rather than in terms of developing markets. There is a more subtle point, however. Put yourself in the place of the oracle. How many of us would have predicted a thousandfold or ten-thousandfold increase in the installed base of anything? I suspect not many.

Ted Hoff

Our first products were developed for specific customers. We negotiated the rights to sell the MCS-4 family to other people early in 1971. A number of us, including myself, went to the marketing people and said,

'Now we should offer this as a regular product'. One of the more experienced fellows took me aside, patted me on the back, and said 'Now look, they do 20 000 minicomputers a year. We are late to this game. If we're lucky, we will get 10 per cent of the market. It is not worth the trouble for 2000 chips a year'. He also made the comment, 'Look, we've got diode salesmen out there doing their best to sell memories, and now you expect them to go out and sell computers?' Fortunately, the product was eventually released.

We discovered another problem – which Gary mentioned too – the idea of computers getting bigger. We found we had a problem in supporting these small microprocessor devices. So what do you do? You want to hire people to help support the product, to develop code and the like for these new machines. But all the prestige was associated with the big mainframe computers. In fact, one fellow just out of college came into interview about developing software for the MCS-4 and MCS-8 families. His first question was: 'What size 360 [a mainframe system] am I going to get to work on?' I replied, 'No, we're thinking of a much smaller computer than that'. He said, 'Well, I'm not interested' – and he walked out. Fortunately, it took a few years, but the media discovered the microprocessor, and after that the college kids started sending us their resumés, trying to get in on the game. That really shows what a difference publicity makes.

People had a very hard time even thinking about a computer being inexpensive. For so many years the computer stood as the prototype of the most expensive thing you could think of. At one workshop where we were talking about the early microprocessors, someone in the audience got up and said, 'I could see putting several microprocessors together in one system'. Someone else got up and said, 'That's nonsense. How would you keep them all busy?'

Hal Feeney

The 4004 microprocessor was done as a custom calculator product for a single customer. The 8008 was done as a custom product for a terminal manufacturer. Both of these devices had computer basics in their design. The customer for the 8008 went away. So here we were with a working product [in effect, a computer]. What do you do with a computer? You reprogram it and do something else with it. At the time we were scratching our heads saying, 'What can be done with these things?' But, in mid-1971, there was a big question over whether or not Intel would take the microprocessor to market at all. Until then, Intel had been very successful in memories. We had these things that needed all this programming and most semiconductor devices at that time were developed and brought to market with just a two-page data sheet. I think that if anybody had told Intel they would need huge users' manuals, training classes, far more than even some of the very crude development systems we made at the time, and hundreds of application engineers out in the field, it may have delayed the birth of the microprocessor by some period of time.

Gary Daniels [at Motorola for over 20 years]

In 1974, the Motorola 6800 microprocessor was introduced. I want to compare that product with today's products [such as Intel's 88110 microprocessor]. The 6800 used the new 5-V minimum silicon gate NMOS process, and the transistors were 8.0 microns in dimension; today we are doing 0.8–micron devices in CMOS. The 6800 had 5000 transistors; the 88110 has over one million. We had a tough time getting the 6800 to run at 1 MHz; the 88110 runs at 50 Mhz. In the design area, where I was a design manager when we first started up in Austin, the design tools were basically paper and pencil. We had check plots that we checked by hand that we would wrap around a wall. They were 20 feet long and we would trace with colored pencils – we used crates of colored pencils.

To put the volume in perspective: Motorola shipped 10 000 micro-processors in 1975, mostly to US customers. We will ship 200 million microprocessors in 1991, and at least half of those will go to inter-national customers. We built all of those microprocessors [in 1975] in about one-third of one 3 inch wafer fab in Austin; today we build micro-processors in nine wafer fabs around the world, all 4 inch or bigger, most of them 6 inch, not counting the MOS11 pizza-size wafer fab we will open up next week.

In terms of applications, I used to stand up at business meetings and try to explain what we were going to do with these things. The truth was – I can finally confess – we simply did not know what the application was. We billed this as a replacement for random logic, but the truth is we really didn't know the applications.

According to the analysts, this year [1991] the computer industry will consume some tens of millions of microprocessors. In this same year there will be 50 million automobiles built, each of which will have an average of 10 microprocessors. That number may surprise you, but there are about 500 million micros in automobiles. In the consumer industry, there will be 100 million color TV sets built, each of which will have 2 to 3 microprocessors, if you include the little remote control beeper. There will be 30 million VCRs built, and another 10 million camcorders, all of which have 2 or 3 microprocessors.

Masatoshi Shima

While I cannot claim that I was the first microprocessor inventor, might I say that I was the first microprocessor customer for volume? I used more than 50 000 units of the 4004 CPU.

In 1968, 23 years ago, I worked on desktop calculators. Many people were getting tired of utilizing hard-wired logic for desktop calculator's OEM business, changing the specifications. I was told by my manager to find a better way. I introduced stored-programming technology to make a desktop calculator machine with read-only memory.

In late 1968, after I had developed that desktop calculator, I wanted to make it with LSI. I found two good companies had high-integration MOS process technologies, Mostek and Intel. Busicom's Osaka factory chose Intel to make one-chip calculators using LSI. I came to the US in June 1969 to develop the decimal computing LSI general-purpose chipset. When I came here, I found that Intel had no logic engineers at all. I was quite surprised. In the next few months I discussed this with Ted Hoff and Stan Mazor, with lots of arguments.

The logic schematic which I had brought over here seemed quite simple to me. But the Intel people said, 'No, it is impossible to integrate'. Also at that time, I expected it to utilize a 40-pin package, but only a 16–pin package was available at Intel. As a result, I had to change the logic schematic quite a lot. Finally, sometime in August 1969, Ted Hoff came up with a great idea. But there was one big problem with his idea: the instruction set was too simple. I judged it was too risky to utilize Ted Hoff's idea for a real-time application. But the idea was so nice.

Then I decided to utilize my own good technology from Japan. The name is improvement technology. I accepted Ted Hoff's idea with my original improvement, adding instructions and functions with the LSI family chipset. Finally I agreed completely with Ted Hoff's idea. I then returned to Japan in December 1969. After the final agreement with Intel, I came back here once again in April 1970. Federico had joined Intel just one week before I returned. I thought I had come back here to check the logic and the status of the product development. They told me, 'We have no logic engineers and nothing has been done yet'. So I made a call to Japan, 'What should I do?' My company said, 'Do it yourself'. Then, finally, I became a semiconductor engineer and designed the 4004 CPU logic. After the 4004 logic design was completed, I went back to Japan and developed the desktop calculator using the 4004 chipset. But many times I was asked by Dr Noyce, 'Are you sure you want to buy 50 000 kits of 4004 systems?' I said, 'Yes, it's very small volume'. But at that time nobody believed the microprocessor would be such a nice business.

In 1972, I once again came here and joined with Intel to develop the 8080 chip set. I found a very good manager there, Federico Faggin. I came here on November 8, 1972. Next week, he said 'Let us start the job'. Hal Feeney, Ted Hoff, Federico Faggin and Stan Mazor sat down in a room just talking about what was to become the 8080. After the meeting, they said, 'Shima, you should do it'. Finally, Federico told me, 'I assigned one mask designer to you. You can use him beginning January 2nd'. I had to fix the spec and write the manual, everything. But finally, I got the 8080 done because I had a very good manager.

Bill Mensch

I remember all the simulation tools that we had at Motorola. Motorola had a budget that would allow us to get any tool we needed when we needed it, and supported us very well as engineers. We later went to a company called MOS Technology in Valley Forge Corporate Center where we had no simulation tools. I had to write the model for the MOS transistor and a little FORTRAN simulator of the correct decimal logic so that I could simulate NMOS transistors.

The most touching moment was when Chuck was using thumb-wheels on this black box to test out the first chip. Rod and I, with all the nervousness inside, couldn't even look at the chips – and if anybody has designed a chip and it comes out, you are just so nervous, it's like having your wife give birth. Anyhow, there Chuck was saying, Load A works! Rod and I were over at the other bench going, Hurrah! It was great. But we had no automated testers, so we couldn't figure out the opcodes. It was painful. Were there 75 or 76 opcodes? Each one was five minutes apart. This dragged on for hours and Rod and I were going, Uggghh. It was good stuff.

Chuck Peddle

Almost everybody that worked on the early microprocessors came out of the calculator industry. Nearly all of the applications were calculator based. Today, all of you think that what we have done, getting better and better and better, is the right way to go. Guys like Hal, Pujab, the two Steve's and so forth, said, 'We don't need another calculator. We are going to do something new and wonderful and great'. I'm afraid that almost everybody in this room is in the same trap as the linear guys that we have already talked about here. One of the reasons we left Motorola is that, like any other big company, Motorola has a creation-inhibiting team, and they inhibited us doing our thing. Federico [who was at Intel] also had to go off and do his own thing.

Somewhere out there are a bunch of guys in a garage, or a bunch of guys with real fire in their bellies – a couple of them are up here – and I think they've still got the fire, and I hope it works for them. But all of you should be looking also for the customers with a fire in their bellies, guys who believe that having something on your TV set that you could play with is an interesting idea; guys who believe that in their garage they can make the computer industry happen. Six of us decided Motorola wasn't going to let us do it, so we packed up and went to Pennsylvania to make it happen. Federico had the guts to leave the leading company in the business to go off and do something else.

I hope that each of you will take the time to listen to the guys in the garage and pay attention to the guys who aren't thinking linearly, who will turn personal computers into something new and wonderful and nothing that any of you can think of today.

DEVELOPING THE LAPTOP

[Source: Edward Huggins, Head of Communications, Epson Computer (UK), quoted in Cobb, R. (1991), 'Success at your finger tips', *Marketing*, 26 September, pp. 24/26]

'At the time we launched the first portable in 1982 we saw a global market. There were visions of top executives, sitting in first class cabins of aircraft, busily entering reports into their laptops, doing spreadsheets and calculations, and treating it as an extension of their office. In fact, there was no such market. Business people do not work like that. It was a dream. . . . Instead the portable has found applications for more specific functions, such as field sales. It is also doubling as a desktop for managers, with the advantage that it can be put away when not in use. And it is used from home. . . . Some [portable computers] are more a fashion accessory than a serious business tool. . . . We are very keen on the portable market and are bringing out new products. But we have to accept it is growing more slowly than everybody expected.'

CAFS AND DAP: TWO PRODUCTS IN SEARCH OF A MARKET – A CASE IN PRODUCT DEVELOPMENT AND MARKET ANALYSIS

Below are accounts of two products developed initially by a leading UK computer company (thinly disguised here as 'Sky Computers') and of how their technological promise was not matched to early commercial success. The case is drawn from research data by the author (Wilson, 1994).

CAFS-ISP (Content Addressable File Store – Information Search Processor)

CAFS-ISP is an award-winning Sky proprietary product which allows high speed searches of large databases by many simultaneous users. CAFS was developed for the BT Directory Enquiry System in the late 1970s but it was hampered by the low capacity of the data storage disks which Sky used and by the fact that it ran under one of Sky's more obscure proprietary operating systems. So BT chose not to buy the system and few others did either.

In 1984 Sky brought out a revised version of CAFS using standard disks and running under Sky's highly respected VME (virtual machine environment) mainframe operating system. The revised product sold strongly. The MoD (Ministry of Defence), amongst other users, found CAFS very useful for a variety of different tasks and asked Sky to develop a version specifically for investigating the MoD's own extensive databases. This MoD version of CAFS was later developed specifically for police force applications in the UK, under the name of INDEPOL, and subsequently sold to many police forces around the world. Other users have also seen the potential of CAFS and INDEPOL for their own operations, adapting the technology in collaboration with Sky to produce many different applications, often with wider commercial prospects for the individual applications – for example, the detection of fraudulent multiple share applications (Touche Ross), fraudulent insurance claims (Australian Public Service), patterns in aircraft incidents (Civil Aviation Authority), patterns in movements through customs to detect contraband (New Zealand Customs), and coordinating complex schedules of repairs (Hull Telephone Company).

DAP (Distributed Array Processor)

DAP is a general architecture (or set of integrated microprocessors) for computers using parallel processing – a design configuration which enables far more rapid data processing than is possible with conventional serial processing configurations. The first DAP was released in 1979 as a 64×64 array, running on Sky's 2900 P Series mainframe and using bulky MECL 10000 microprocessors which made the product very large. When the P Series mainframe was upgraded through the issue of the S Series, the DAP product itself was not upgraded in line with the mainframe series and so only five of the increasingly outmoded DAP products were sold. In 1982 the MoD contracted Sky to produce a version of DAP called MILDAP, a 32×32 array with much smaller and more efficient microprocessors, so that the whole product could be run on one of Sky's PERQ desktop workstations. MILDAP was eventually delivered to the MoD in 1985. Using this military version of DAP as a foundation, Sky then went on to develop further commercial versions of DAP intended for organizations needing a 'supercomputer' at a reasonable price.

Eventually in 1986, convinced that DAP had little commercial attraction as a Sky product after only 17 sales and over £30 million of investment, all rights to DAP and associated software were transferred to a new company named Blue. Blue was a joint venture formed largely by the management and staff from Sky's DAP Division (who raised £4 million between them) and Sky itself (which retained 25 per cent of the equity) with the balance being provided by various UK venture capitalists. Blue continued to develop DAP and started to provide products in

1988 on an OEM (original equipment manufacturer) basis for Sky and other computer manufacturers to exploit in selected markets. Most notably, US military markets provided strong demand for DAP-based products and Blue soon moved its headquarters to California. Major US customers included the Department of Defense (DoD), Lockheed, the US Army Corps of Engineers, and NASA. For example, Blue's DAP technology convincingly won a US technical trial to identify the most suitable controlling system for the Brilliant Pebbles element of the SDI ('Star Wars') programme in which thousands of metre-long computer-guided projectiles would intercept incoming missiles, battering them into destruction.

In collaboration with a Texas company, Blue later developed minia-turized radiation-hardened versions of DAP-based supercomputers using the more resilient but expensive gallium arsenide instead of sili-con as the base material for the microprocessors. These versions were intended for application in markets such as space systems where size, weight and resistance to radiation were at a premium.

Blue's principal rivals for DAP contracts were Thinking Machines of Massachusetts with an offering which was more expensive, larger and less robust than DAP; and Maspar of California (a spin-off from Digital Equipment Corporation) also offering more expensive though increas-ingly rugged supercomputers which were more comparable in per-formance terms to DAP.

By early 1990 Blue had sold 75 DAP systems, including sales in such markets as speech recognition (Apple Computers), helicopter detection of minefields using laser reflection (US Army), searching large text databases (Reuters), DNA research (genetic laboratories), image pro-cessing, radar analysis, neural computer networking, fluid mechanics modelling, and medical graphics imaging.

Comment

The history of CAFS and DAP provides one illustration of the changing strengths and weaknesses of Sky over the 1980s as it has evolved from a technology-driven manufacturer of computers to a market-driven sup-plier of integrated total solutions to IT needs. CAFS and DAP were developed initially as technologies which were interesting *per se* to a technologically oriented company, rather than with any specific market in mind. The emerging products were technically extraordinary but too cumbersome, complex, expensive and underpowered for practical com-mercial applications. At which point the technologically minded orga-nization appeared to lose interest, believing, perhaps too readily, that there was no demand for the product. Nevertheless, outside parties (e.g. MoD, DoD) and more determined groups within Sky perceived the potential of the technologies in a different configuration and went about developing the technology in more useful forms. Sky then seemed to recognize at least something of the commercial potential of the technology while concluding that these markets were not in the first rank of Sky's pressing strategic priorities. So collaboration with third parties was used to develop the systems, thus preserving Sky's access to the technology while allowing investment priorities to be diverted elsewhere.

3 Mini-cases

MINI-CASE 1: PROFESSIONALISM IN PURCHASING: TWO EXAMPLES

An example of an organization with a low degree of purchasing professionalism is provided by a UK development authority (UKDA) in the 1980s charged with managing the development of a major industrial and urban 'new town' based on a scattered conurbation of largely unprosperous small towns. Here there were few direct competitors as such to UKDA once it had won the contract for the development, and the strategic priority was to generate urban and industrial facilities according to an agreed timescale and within a broadly defined budget. UKDA's purchasing was handled by a small clerical staff in a temporary office, supporting two purchasing officers who reported to a senior manager with many other responsibilities. One of these two purchasing officers dealt with building materials and services while the other covered everything else from ballpoint pens and staples to vehicles and premises. Inevitably, the lower profile items (such as sand for one officer, or stationery for the other) were given far less attention than the more expensive items even though, given the scale of the orders, it was often the low-cost commodity purchases which formed the bulk of the purchasing bills and where considerable savings could have been made. With little purchasing attention given to reorders of low-cost items, the apparent consumption of things like paper, pens, sand, constructional timber and nails increased rapidly, not least because there were few significant checks on the management of such purchases. Perhaps inevitably, given the lack of professionalism and strategic priority given to purchasing, there was a great deal of wastage and unexplained loss (including pilferage).

In contrast, an example of a more professional approach to purchasing is provided by the car manufacturing factory located a few miles away from the UKDA offices. Here, one of a team of specialist senior purchasing officers (SPOs) would negotiate with a range of suppliers to fix on the optimal price structure for commodity items such as industrial gases, petrol, electricity, steel pressings, and welding materials. The

SPO would also send junior purchasing staff (JPOs) to examine how the subsequent purchases were used and consumed within the production processes, and whether consumption experience should lead to any changes in the technical specifications for the next set of purchases. Thus, for example, in price negotiations with the electricity supplier, the CPO agreed to punitive charges for electricity consumption during times when the production process was suspended (e.g. at night – a 16-hour, two-shift system was in operation) in exchange for a further discount to the rate at other times. And the CPO circulated warnings to everyone not to use unnecessary electricity during high-tariff periods. Equally, factory-floor observations by a JPO showed that a recently introduced cheaper form of wipe (hundreds of which were routinely used every day in the manufacturing, maintenance and housekeeping functions) was proving too fragile for the industrial environment in which they were being used resulting not only in rapidly increased consumption and excess litter (as half-used, torn wipes were discarded) but also in staff irritation and consequent quality errors. The JPO quickly reinstated the previous supply of wipes, returned the fragile wipes to their supplier with an invoice for compensation, changed the sample testing procedures to reflect factory usage more closely, and entered discussions with several wipes suppliers for the possible development and purchase of a range of specialist wipes for different purposes around the factory.

[Source: the author's personal experience and empirical research]

MINI-CASE 2: JUST SOME OF THE ISSUES IN NEW-TASK BUYING FACED BY A CAR MANUFACTURER

Piece price is the most obviously important factor but the cheapest is not necessarily the best. Even if the quality is acceptable, questions have to be asked about the supplier's motivation to quote a low price. Was the bid designed to eliminate competition? Does the supplier have a history of frequent price rises? Has the supplier understood the specification? Is the supplier recovering the low piece price by quoting high vendor tooling? The cost of vendor tooling (required by the supplier for manufacture of the part but often paid for by the customer) can vary substantially. Some of this cost may be caused by compensating for low piece prices but much is often attributable to the level of sophistication of the tooling. Is it too sophisticated or not sophisticated enough? Are the volume forecasts accurate and is the anticipated length of time over which the tooling will be required sufficient to justify major capital investment? Is the tooling easily modified? Will the customer's investment in facilities at the supplier be used for purposes unrelated to the customer's needs and, if so, how is this reflected in the costings? In addition to the financial costs, the factors of quality and quantity are extremely important. Will the part meet the required inspection standards which are especially important if the part is associated with high warranty claims (e.g. windscreens, tyres, paintwork) or compliance with legislative regulations (e.g. seat belt fittings, emission controls) or high-profile branding aspects (e.g. badges and styling) or safety aspects (e.g. brakes, crumpling rate) or customer 'pet hates' such as rattles and odours? Will the part be supplied in sufficient volume to meet production programmes (especially important if the part could cause a track (production line) stoppage or is expensive to retro-fit)? Can the supplier comply with the customer's IT requirements (e.g. EDI,[1] CAM, CIM, CAD, SPS, policy towards technology standards)? There are also political factors, for example, is the supplier UK based? Will the part count towards minimum UK content agreements? Does the supplier use the customer's vehicles in its own operations? Are there other parts sourced, or potentially sourced from this supplier which could be involved (or become involved) in the negotiation? Is the supplier used by any of the customer's subsidiaries or associated companies, and, if so, what is the supplier's record of performance? Finally will the anticipated supply flow meet scheduling requirements (especially important for the introduction of upgraded and new models)? If not, can commercial pressure or specialist advice or additional money improve delivery performance?

> [Source: the author's personal experience, company documentation, and empirical research]

MINI-CASE 3: ENERGY PURCHASING AT THE BIG BUILDING SOCIETY (BBS) (NAMES CHANGED)

Combined expenditures on gas and electricity topped £5.1 million last year for the BBS's 682 branches and 11 corporate centres. In recent years only ten of the BBS's sites have been involved in the early trials for a competitive electricity market and a further 50 locations have been involved in the trial competitive gas market. Until now this has proved a manageable number for BBS's energy manager, Ben Davis to deal with. But with full competition on the horizon, he needs help. His new tactic is to find someone else to handle the company's complex energy purchasing requirements. Davis has a smaller energy bill than that of, say, Boots (£30 million) and more modest aspirations for becoming directly involved in the market. 'We shall use external consultants to handle our energy requirements,' he explains. To that end Davis interviewed 16 power brokers in 1997. Once selected, the winning broker will handle BBS's energy database, tender for both gas and electricity, deal with bids from all suppliers, check the bills and monitor usage.

To assist the winning broker, Davis is preparing a mountain of energy-related information. This centralized database should prove a boon when the broker begins negotiations with potential suppliers. Many organizations lack such information because they delegate control of energy budgets to individual cost centres and utility bills are dealt with purely at site level. For companies like these, the advent of negotiating all accounts *en masse* could prove tricky.

Davis is in no rush to have everything in order by the 1 April 1998 deadline (when preliminary deregulation stages begin – full deregulation follows next year). Only 150 of Davis' sites will be eligible to join the competitive market at that point. 'I think it will be a fracas so I will probably hold back and wait for a little while,' he says. Holding back without commitment will mean Davis misses the price cuts likely to be offered as an incentive both by suppliers seeking to persuade customers to switch, and by those encouraging loyalty. However, the loss of savings in the short term will be offset by a greatly reduced 'hassle factor'. So far Davis has opted against making any hasty decisions. 'I honestly expect to get a better deal by waiting until later,' Davis says. Indeed some of the offers he has received so far fail to match even the price cuts for all tariff customers which will be imposed next year by the regulator. He has also not switched any of his gas suppliers, even at some of the smaller sites where the opportunity to do so already exists [the gas market is being deregulated earlier than that for electricity]. Moreover, taking one of the early deals would have meant remaining with 14 different suppliers, which is not Davis' plan. 'I really want to go for a single electricity supplier – one which can handle electronic billing.' Nor is Davis looking for a joint electricity and gas supplier. 'My choice is to go for open tender on both. Historically, the expertise needed to supply gas and electricity differs greatly and I would be cautious about the ability of a single supplier to provide both.'

Nevertheless, despite this cautious approach, Davis expects to shave £180,000 from BBS's electricity bill this year and half as much again in 1999. The company spends less on gas but still expects to see savings of £40,000.

[Source: edited from an original article (Moore, K. 'Power Struggle'), in the February 1998 issue of *Management Today*, pp. 62–66, with the permission of the copyright owner, Haymarket Management Publications Ltd]

MINI-CASE 4: ADAPTING AND COMPROMISING OVER PRODUCT SPECIFICATION: WHEN TO CHANGE, AND WHEN NOT TO CHANGE

When to change (for customers) . . .

A manufacturer of furniture planned to use Dutch elm as the principal timber for a new range of reception and foyer furniture for the luxury hotel sector. Elm was preferred for its durability, light colour and deep lustre when polished. If successful, the manufacturer planned to expand

and develop the range into the market for prestige corporate office furniture. However, the manufacturer's timber supplier suggested that European oak be used instead of Dutch elm because of oak's lower price and greater availability – Dutch elm disease had greatly reduced the stocks of mature elm. On the other hand, using oak would also result in increased tooling costs and would require some rethinking of the fixing methods and fittings to be used because of oak's relatively high acidity which wears tool edges and corrodes brass fittings over time. Establishing first that major potential customers had no significant preference for elm over oak given the cost implications, the manufacturer decided to specify oak. The new oak range later proved especially successful in the 'home-office' market for householders wanting executive office facilities in their homes (e.g. for teleworking). The manufacturer's marketing department were able to make effective use of the popular association of oak with consumer values such as heritage, affluence and 'Englishness' – all of which appealed both to companies building executive homes and to the potential purchasers of such homes.

. . . and when not to change?

Two years later the manufacturer's marketing director was considering the possibility of entering the flat-pack market for self-assembly oak furniture for home-offices, prompted by an approach from a mail order company specializing in quality furniture and household effects. The flat-pack specification would, of course, require extensive technical redesign of the furniture and this would inevitably result in a somewhat less durable and reliable product. She concluded that this development might be profitable using a different branding strategy, and that this contract could open up all sorts of potentially lucrative opportunities in a growth market as yet untapped by the company. She also concluded that this would take the company much closer towards consumer markets where she felt the company lacked the necessary experience, competences and customer credibility. She declined the approach. The mail order company then sourced the furniture from an overseas rival which had been looking for a low-cost entry to UK markets for some time.

When to change (for suppliers) . . .

Abbey National (now a bank) was one of the first building societies to develop an automatic teller machine (ATM) network in the UK and its sourcing decision for its first batch of ATM terminals was therefore important not only for Abbey National but also for the ATM consortium (known as Link) in which Abbey National was a leading member. Abbey National short-listed five ATM terminal suppliers for the contract. Two suppliers offered OEM systems sourced from elsewhere and were ruled out because Abbey National was not convinced that the systems would be supported in the long term. The IBM system was discarded also, despite intense salesmanship, because IBM was not prepared to enlarge the one-line display screen (according to Abbey National's specification) for such a small order. This left the NCR and Burroughs offerings which were comparable with respect to reliability, ergonomic design, ease of maintenance, and supplier support. The deciding factor related to the built-in printer which, in both cases, simply printed a numerical sequence on deposit envelopes and debit slips, matched to an internal ledger record which was manually logged by staff into the main computer system at a later stage when they came to clear deposits from the ATM. Abbey National wanted ATM terminals to print full transaction details on envelopes and slips, enabling swift automatic calculations of credit, debit and interest, and avoiding potential customer disputes. Unlike Burroughs, NCR agreed to redesign its printer and so won the contract, despite being more expensive than the Burroughs alternative. This Abbey National contract was only for 200 terminals, but NCR recognized the strategic importance of the Abbey National decision for the other members of the Link consortium. NCR later sold over 900 ATM terminals to Abbey National and thousands more to members of the Link and Matrix ATM networks, emerging as the market leader for ATM terminals in the UK and Europe.

[Source: the author's personal experience and empirical research]

MINI-CASE 5: GOODS RECEIVING AND PAYMENT SYSTEMS IN A UK CAR MANUFACTURER

In 1984 a leading UK car manufacturer was considering how to coordinate the goods receiving system at its main factory under a single integrated computer system which would link to automated payments, inventory and reorder systems. The existing system linked to supplier payment systems and embraced inspection, rectification and inventory management functions including a large automated storage and retrieval system based on barcodes, as well as extensive conventional warehouse systems. An internal finance analyst was asked to prepare an illustrative flow-diagram of the existing systems as a starting point for the design of the computerized system. The analyst discussed the systems and how they operated with all the managers involved and drafted a diagram. He then went from one manager to another adjusting the diagram in line with their comments until they all agreed that the diagram was as close to reality as was likely to be achieved, even though it still did not reflect what actually happened. The system was extensively documented with seven copies of the main documents, and involved several different departmental computer systems. Nevertheless, every manager had a subtly different opinion as to what the 'system' did, what it was intended to do, and how useful it was – just as they all had their own ways of short-cutting and circumventing the system when they felt it

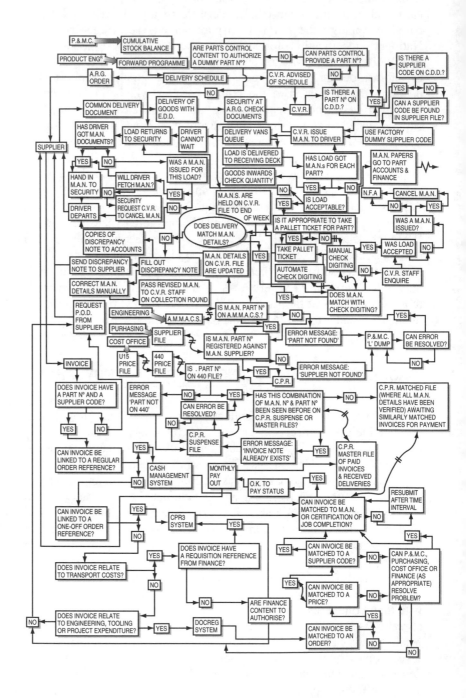

was appropriate to do so. So managers found little difficulty in 'managing' the system to their own ends. Eventually, senior management concluded that it was necessary to design the new computer system from scratch. To show something of the complexity of the previous system, and the scope for multiple interpretation and divergent development, the analyst's handwritten diagram is reproduced above.

[Source: the author's personal experience and empirical research]

MINI-CASE 6: A REPORT ON WINDSCREEN PROBLEMS BY A QUALITY INSPECTOR

This illustration is adapted from a real report by a finance analyst at a major UK car manufacturer. Details have been adjusted to disguise sensitive aspects. Bear in mind that windscreens are expensive items and that breakages in the fitting process cause hazards both to staff and to delicate production equipment, and can ruin paintwork with scratches. What was the role of purchasing in the lead-up to the problem; how might purchasing participate in its resolution; and what lessons are there for avoiding this sort of problem in the future?

The problem

Recently there has been a spate of breakages of bronze-tinted windscreens from *Jointex* which are shattering in the process of fitting them to vehicles. Bronze screens are fitted to high-specification models. Similar but less severe problems have been found with standard screens from *Jointex*. On changing to *Glacier* (the second approved screen supplier, providing 25 per cent of screens in a dual sourcing arrangement) breakages were greatly reduced and were within normal expectations. These problems were reported to Materials Control, Production, Plant Finance and the *Jointex* representative. All dimensions were checked and found to be within the allowed tolerances but it was noted that the outside layer of the screens is thicker than the inside layer. On most of the damaged screens the outside layer is unbroken with damage only to the inside layer. Most of the broken bronze screens seem to have broken in about the same place on the screen. The bronze screens are fitted with a special insert in the rubber surround seal, making a better fit. Standard screens do not use the extra insert.

Jointex glass

The screens are received from *Jointex* in metal pallets that vary in the amount of protection they give to the glass. Some pallets have strips of serrated or slotted rubber where each screen fits into a slot. In some pallets the strips are missing and the screens rest on the metal frame of the pallet. Some pallets have a wooden strip taped over the rubber strips so that pallets designed to hold 50 screens do in fact contain 70 screens. When damaged glass is found in pallets it is removed but the remaining screens in these pallets, though seemingly OK, often break when fitted to vehicles. *Jointex* seem to dispatch the majority of their screens in these pallets of 70 (designed for 50). The screens are packed, inclined, to rest on wood or polystyrene inserts. Thus approximately one tonne of glass is packed in each pallet with no individual support for each screen. Consequently, even if the screens are not broken or damaged they are susceptible to pressure during transit. Securing straps around the glass have been found to be slack on arrival thereby allowing to-and-fro movement, or side packings omitted allowing glass to slide. All these facts have been shown to the *Jointex* representative. Because of our JIT stock policy screens are often delivered direct from the delivery vehicle to the sub-assembly location. In winter months the temperature of the glass on delivery can be very low, well beneath the 17–18 °C recommended for assembly. This again causes more breakages than usual.

Glacier glass

The quality of *Glacier* packaging and transporting is far superior to that of *Jointex* with corrugated cardboard cushioning between each screen in pallets holding 45 screens only. The only problem experienced with *Glacier* screens is that the design of the securing straps is such that they can get caught by the forks of the forklift trucks and pushed into the glass, occasionally shattering the first few layers of glass.

Recommendation

Jointex screen scrap is far in excess of *Glacier* screen scrap and as the sub-assembly processes are the same for both screens, we feel that the difference must lie in *Jointex*'s methods of transportation, packaging and quality. (NB. *Jointex* disputed this analysis angrily, saying that there had been no complaints about screen deliveries for many months, that other customers were content with such arrangements, and that these sensible adaptations to packaging and delivery arrangements enabled them to hold the unit price of screens down below that offered by rivals which was why *Jointex* had been selected as the prime screen source in the first place.)

MINI-CASE 7A: THE PROBLEMS OF COST-BASED PRICING . . .

In 1959 a car manufacturer launched a radically different car, unlike anything available from rivals. The new car was priced at £500, far below the price of any other car at that time. The market leader bought five of these cars for tests and 'vehicle stripping' in order to ascertain their performance and how they were assembled, what components and techniques were used, what production engineering and design methods were used and how the car could be profitably marketed at such a low price. For the purposes of the vehicle strip process the new car was placed at the centre of a huge tarpaulin in a large warehouse – and taken apart. Everything was disassembled: the wiring harnesses, the seats, the engine cylinders, the battery, the wheel assemblies . . . Even the box-section steel carcass was dissected to check for injection waxing and rust-proofing, and the paintwork was finely sliced to expose the number of layers and composition of the paint. At the end there was a series of tidy piles of bits all over the tarpaulin. But all the costs revealed in the strip (including labour and tooling etc.) seemed to add up to more than £500. The next car was stripped to check the estimates. And the next. With two cars tested to destruction on the proving ground and three cars piled on three tarpaulins in the warehouse, the puzzled rival abandoned the exercise and set about developing their own version to capture a share of what was proving to be a booming market.

Much later it became apparent that the car's price of £500 was not based primarily on costs, since the manufacturer had no real idea of what the costs were likely to be; nor on market research – there were no comparable products and many of the customers were 'new' in that they would not otherwise have been able to afford a new car. The price tag was chosen because it was thought to be in the right ball park and it had a nice ring to it so the advertising people would be able to do a lot with it. And they did. Despite its huge popularity, the car lost money for a long time because the costs were very much greater than had been estimated. But eventually the car proved commercially successful, especially in Japan, making substantial profits but, more importantly, endearing itself to drivers (a thriving 'fan' club developed) who then graduated to larger cars in the same manufacturer's range. After a few years rivals launched their own versions but none ever seemed to catch the popular imagination in the same way as the life-style trends of the 1960s evolved into those of the 1970s. The pricing decision proved to be inspired and the car is still in production.

[Source: the author's personal experience and empirical research]

MINI-CASE 7B: . . . AND OF MARKET-BASED PRICING

A small UK pharmaceutical company produced a new drug – *Star* – which alleviated various gastric problems. There was only one other drug available at the time which would rival the new product – *Gastroban* – but this drug was well established, popular and widely used. The market for gastric therapies of this sort was (and still is) global and growing fast, especially in western economies, driven by the stress of contemporary working patterns, unhealthy diets and limited recreation. *Star* offered slight advantages over *Gastroban* to patients: it could be taken as a pill (*Gastroban* was taken by injection) and so was more appealing to patients; it could be taken more often and in varying dosages and so could be prescribed for a wider range of cases and at an earlier stage; it had fewer and rarer side effects. Even taken as a package, these slight advantages were not considered by the US licensing authorities as sufficient to merit more than a class C licence, denoting *Star* as basically an imitative 'me-too' product. *Star* had some non-clinical advantages also. As a pill it was cheaper to manufacture, distribute and store and so the price could be lower than *Gastroban* while still profitable. As it did not need injection, doctors could prescribe it with less need for patient training and fewer surgery appointments. On the other hand, *Gastroban* was marketed by a major international company with a wide range of successful products and excellent long-standing relationships with the doctors who decided which therapy to prescribe – and much to lose if *Gastroban* stopped generating profits for new product research.

The Board gathered to decide on the marketing strategy for *Star* and, crucially, the pricing strategy for the new drug. The marketing analysts made an impressively researched presentation outlining the competitive situation and stressing the competitive advantages and financial resources of *Gastroban*, the established market leader. They recommended a price set at 10–15 per cent lower than *Gastroban* which, they forecasted, would generate very substantial profits. The CEO deliberated and then announced, with no further discussion, that the price for *Star* would be 40 per cent *above* that of *Gastroban*.

The decision proved astoundingly successful. Ten years later the manufacturer was one of the largest pharmaceutical companies in the world (with the benefit of a few careful acquisitions) and half the company's profits were flowing from *Star*. But it could have been different. *Gastroban* still retained enough support to discourage panic reaction from its manufacturer and it was later adapted into pill form and achieved some growth in a very buoyant market. Other products and problems soon diverted competitive attention. *Star*'s market analysts soon got over their feeling of being ignored, though some did leave, and the CEO's reputation for visionary leadership proved useful in attracting investors when the company became listed in exchanges around the world. But how much of this did the CEO know, or guess, at the time? How much was intuitively picked up from the many previous briefings by the analysts and technologists and doctors? Was this a visionary decision – or the outcome of a long cumulative pattern of subtle and invisible influences? And how much of the success of the decision was really attributable to the success of the implementation of the decision, by *Star*'s sales representatives and marketing staff and the medical staff who supported *Star* and spread the word?

[Source: the author's empirical research]

MINI-CASE 8: UNCOOPERATIVE SUPPLIER–CUSTOMER RELATIONSHIPS IN THE US AUTOMOBILE INDUSTRY

The following sequence of events shows how such relationships can affect every stage of the development of new models:

1   A long internal design process results eventually in 'finalized' versions of parts from R&D engineers (despite no discussion of production practicalities with prospective suppliers).
2   The designs are sent to current suppliers for quotes at specified volumes and quality tolerances, based on short-term contracts (to avoid being locked in to particular suppliers).
3   Suppliers give low quotes to secure the contracts despite the initial costs of tooling and capital investment, confident that they can subsequently recoup profits through spares, inflation increases, upstream price increases and follow-on contract renewals.
4   Buyers recognize what suppliers are doing and form independent estimates of costs – hampered by suppliers withholding confidential data.
5   At prototype and production engineering stages many problems emerge due to lack of prior collaboration with and amongst suppliers (and even between internal departments) generating further irritation between suppliers and buyers.
6   As manufacturing gets under way, pressure to reduce costs encourages buyers to seek further quotations from new suppliers, generating suspicion and uncertainty amongst existing suppliers who warn of the need to recoup their initial set-up costs, if necessary through increased prices of their other products purchased by buyers.
7   Routine engineering changes from head office staff are designed in ignorance of the manufacturing realities and imposed on production staff who take their frustration out on purchasing staff who reflect this in discussions with suppliers.
8   Quality problems arise as suppliers attempt to minimize costs and re-engineered components do not fully integrate with the evolving design, but buyers are barred from intervening in supplier operations; disputed liability for rectification and scrap generates further friction.
9   Increasing demand for the model and incremental launch in new geographic markets generates fluctuating production volume but cost pressures do not allow for stockpiling – so suppliers are subjected to unscheduled variation in order levels and extra transport costs, putting further strain on quality standards. . . .

[Source: Based on material from Womack *et al.*, 1990]

MINI-CASE 9: *MIELBON VITE* – TELESALES STAFF REPLACE FIELD SALES REPRESENTATIVES

Mielbon is the French arm of an international supplier of computer systems for organizational customers. In 1990 Mielbon set up a temporary telesales operation called *Mielbon Vite* to provide organizational customers with a swift (same-day delivery) reordering service for the more common computer spares and consumables. The new service was initially designed as a stop-gap service to ease what was thought to be a short-term backlog of orders which the sales force could not clear fast enough. The service was made available as an extra facility for existing customers who did not want to wait for a sales visit. *Mielbon Vite* proved hugely successful and soon extended its scope to a wide variety of basic hardware, software, consumables, cables, manuals and so forth. Within months Mielbon found that many new organizational customers were using *Mielbon Vite* to place orders for purchases that would normally have been processed through sales staff visits. By the end of the year *Mielbon Vite* was the most profitable, productive and fastest growing department in the national operation. Clearly, customers did not share Mielbon's assumption that personal selling and technical explanations were necessary to market the complex computer systems in question. Despite the reservations of the marketing director (once a sales representative), Mielbon had little choice but to establish the temporary *Mielbon Vite* service on a permanent basis, redirecting resources from a reduced field sales force to the hiring and training of telesales specialists, setting up systems to capture customer information data from telesales transactions, and adjusting the Mielbon marketing strategy to reflect the dynamic new service which was attracting new customers away from rivals. Most rivals were already setting up similar operations.

[Source: the author's empirical research]

MINI-CASE 10: THE MCI CASE: SALES FORCE MANAGEMENT

The problem

In 1983 it became clear to Jack Bloom, Chairman of Mainframe Computers Inc. (MCI), that MCI would have to change from selling 'technology boxes' to anyone who was interested, to a more market-oriented strategy based on selling integrated computing systems designed around specific customer needs (known as 'total systems solutions') into vertical markets (e.g. banking, retailing, government agencies). The principal restraint in doing so was perceived to be MCI's two field sales forces.

The major accounts sales force (MASF) was organized nationally to deal with key accounts on a personalized client basis in long-standing relationships where MCI had developed an intimate understanding of the client's business operations and needs. The MASF already had what amounted to a vertical market orientation, being focused so closely on the needs of their long-established specific clients. However, the general sales force (GSF) activity was characterized by quick sales of relatively cheap systems to smaller accounts and with low levels of after-sales support. The GSF was organized regionally in Commercial Business Centres which acted as showrooms, warehouses and sales venues. Though very good at its job, the GSF was product oriented, prided itself on 'shifting boxes' and had no real interest in total solutions or in exploring customers' underlying problems. The GSF was paid largely on commission and aimed to make as many sales as possible on an opportunity basis and regardless of the market or niche in which the customer operated.

Bloom decided it would be too difficult to retrain and re-orientate the GSF to an exclusive focus on vertical markets, because this would be opposed to everything they believed in and understood about their function in MCI. GSF staff would have to spend valuable selling time persuading one client, probably with a relatively small budget, to consider a total system solution when, in the same time, they could have sold several 'boxes' to several different customers. Even more against the culture of the general sales force would be the requirement to ignore prospects, no matter how attractive, in non-targeted vertical markets.

The problem for MCI was how to move to a vertical market orientation with a comprehensive systems offering without:

- alienating the GSF
- expensive and lengthy retraining
- avoidable disruption to turnover
- blurring the new image of MCI with low-margin, commodity products (although these did provide a welcome, if modest, contribution to turnover and did seem to be a growth market).

Bloom also wanted to recruit a pristine sales force to be trained in the context of the fresh MCI approach with a different culture appropriate to the future strategic orientation of the company.

MCI's approach to the problem

The solution that MCI adopted was to sell off the Commercial Business Centres to the GSF in a series of regional management buy-outs. This kept the GSF content, provided MCI with a low visibility outlet for commodity sales minimizing disruption to turnover, and cleared the way for developing a new sales force. MCI's concern for the quality and priorities of its new sales force was reflected in the care taken in training: 5–6 weeks full-time per person per year, plus on-the-job training.

Nevertheless, it took MCI almost five years to thoroughly internalize the strategic 'vertical market' reorientation into its organizational culture.

[Source: the author's empirical research]

MINI-CASE 11: HOW IBM WON A MAJOR HOSPITAL CONTRACT . . .

'Many of the others were ahead of IBM in technology wizardry and heaven knows their software is easier to use. But IBM alone took the trouble to get to know us. They interviewed extensively up and down the line. They talked our language, no mumbo jumbo on computer innards. Their price was fully 25% higher. But they provided unparalleled guarantees of reliability and service. They even went so far as to arrange a back-up connection with a local steel company in case our system crashed. Their presentations were to the point. Everything about them smacked of assurance and success. Our decision, even with severe budget pressure, was really easy.'

[Source: cited in Peters and Waterman, 1982]

. . . AND HOW DOVE COMPUTERS WON A SIMILAR HOSPITAL CONTRACT

The purchase of a HISS (Hospital Integrated Support System) mainframe system for the Wellington Area Health Authority in 1990/91 has been described as arguably the most exhaustive purchasing process ever witnessed in the market for health computer systems. The outcome was summarized by the Project Director: 'What we had set out to do was [to] find a true patient-based system as patients are our central focus. Unfortunately, the only thing we could find was hospital-oriented systems . . . However, Dove came up with a collection of software products which – with their help – we can build into Wellington's requirements . . . We chose Dove's healthcare system because it had the required functionality and the best systems architecture for our longer term purchaser/provider requirements . . . Another significant influence was that we felt confident that the partnership potential between Dove and ourselves was good and positive.'

[Source: author]

MINI-CASE 12: INTERNAL MARKETING: TOP-DOWN OR BOTTOM-UP?

A large UK manufacturer of automobile components suffered in the early 1980s from a reputation for poor quality which it had probably deserved in the 1970s though the reputation lingered long after corrective action had been taken. The effects of this reputation extended even to the workforce for whom a certain casualness in production practices and a dismissive attitude to the latest management 'fad' about quality had become part of the culture. Workers on the factory floor seemed more concerned about getting good reception for Radio One and furnishing their rest areas with comfy bench seats purloined from vehicles than with finding ways to improve production standards and effectiveness. Production managers seemed more concerned about preventing radio theft and catching workers smoking on the production line or skiving, and protecting their own bonus payments by manipulating production schedules. You can imagine the effect on potential customers of some of the stories that the production line workers used to tell in the local pubs.

A long legacy of industrial disputes in the 1970s did not help to endear senior management initiatives to the workers, or even to middle managers. The culture and history also encouraged managers to view the quality issue as a problem of poor workers rather than as anything to do with management systems and standards.

Eventually, following advice from consultants, a huge investment was made in an internal marketing programme aimed at persuading everyone – managers and production workers alike – that quality was a matter both of systems and of mentality. The 'road show' as it was called was set up successively in each factory and the show was presented to everyone in turn (including special shows for suppliers and distributors), even though this involved shutting down the production tracks for a time. The show involved special lighting and sound effects, dancing girls, the chief executive and others making personal contributions, refreshments, handouts and inscribed pens, etc.

Many of the workers were stunned at the 'Las Vegas' style and dismissive of the whole effort as clearly unconnected with the reality of their work – as the feedback questionnaires made clear. Discarded leaflets, questionnaire forms, party hats, whistles and pens littered the site long after the event closed and moved on to the next factory.

It took many months of persistent, low-key, low-level, interactive consultation and mutual problem analysis before the entire workforce began to accept that quality was everyone's problem and everyone's responsibility, that the company did indeed have high-quality products, and that it should be proud of what it achieved every day. So this particular example of internal marketing proved an expensive and counterproductive mistake until it was done collaboratively and treated as a relationship management problem. Now the company enjoys an excellent quality record and a high public perception for quality.

[Source: the author's personal experience and empirical research]

MINI-CASE 13: PURCHASING AND INVENTORY MANAGEMENT AT JIMMY'S

St James' University Hospital in Leeds, widely known as *Jimmy's*, is one of Europe's largest teaching hospitals. At the time of this case it employed around 4500 people to support the 90 000 in-patient treatments per year and over 450 000 total admissions. Under increasing pressure to reduce costs, to contain inventory and to improve service, the Supplies Department had recently undertaken a major analysis of its activities, helped by the consultancy division of Lucas Industries, the UK-based manufacturing company, which was able to make benchmark comparisons with private sector strategies and practices with respect to purchasing and just-in-time (JIT) inventory management systems.

The initial review highlighted that Jimmy's had approximately 1500 suppliers of 15 000 different products at a total annual purchasing cost of around £15m. Traditionally, the Supplies Department ordered what the doctors asked for, with many cases of similar items being supplied by six or more firms. Under a cross-functional task force comprising medical and supply staff, a major programme of supplier and product rationalization was undertaken which also revealed many sources of waste and inefficiency. For example, the team found that wards used as many as 20 different types of gloves, including surgeons' gloves at £1 per pair, yet in almost all cases these could be replaced by fewer and cheaper general purpose gloves at around 20p per pair. Similarly, anaesthetic items were reorganized from multiple sourcing involving six suppliers to a single source.

The savings in purchasing costs, inventory costs and general administration were enormous in themselves, but the higher order volumes also helped Jimmy's to negotiate lower unit prices. Successful sole suppliers were also willing to deliver more frequently and in smaller quantities. Peter Beeston, the Supplies Manager, said: 'We've been driven by suppliers for years . . . they would insist that we could only purchase in thousands, that we would have to wait for weeks, or that they would only deliver on Wednesdays! Now, our selected suppliers know that if they perform well, we will assure them of a long-term commitment. I prefer to buy 80 per cent of our requirements from 20 or 30 suppliers, whereas previously it involved over a hundred.'

Jimmy's also introduced a simple kanban system for some of its local inventory. In Ward 9 storeroom, for example, there are now just two boxes of 10mm syringes on the shelf. When the first is empty, the other is moved forward and a replacement is then ordered by placing the empty box outside the Storeroom where codes are periodically read by patrolling Supplies staff using a mobile data recorder and barcode reader.

Jimmy's managers described some of the benefits of the changes: 'Value for money, not cost cutting, is what this is all about. We are standardizing on buying quality products and now also have more influence on the buying decision . . . from being previously functionally oriented with a number of buyers, we now concentrate on materials management for complete product ranges. The project has been an unmitigated success and although we are only just starting to see the benefits, I would expect savings in cost and in excess inventory to spiral! The report on Sterile Wound Care Packs shows the potential that our team has identified. The 'old' pack cost 60p and comprised four pairs of plastic forceps, assorted cotton wool balls and a plastic pot. The price did not include gloves which were sometimes necessary in addition to the forceps. The 'new' pack at 33p comprised a pair of latex gloves (replacing the forceps), assorted swabs and the plastic pot. The new pack delivered overall purchase cost savings of around £20,000 in the first year.'

[Source: Slack, N. (1995) *Operations Management*, Pitman Publishing, London, pp. 628–629]

NOTE

1 EDI = electronic data interchange; CAM = computer aided manufacturing; CIM = computer integrated manufacturing; CAD = computer aided design; SPS = statistical process control (all these are particularly important for motor manufacturing).

—Index